Soft
Architecture
Machines

Soft
Architecture
Machines

Nicholas Negroponte

The MIT Press
Cambridge,
Massachusetts,
and London,
England

Library of Congress
Cataloging in Publication
Data
Negroponte, Nicholas.
   Soft architecture machines.
   Bibliography: p.
   1. Electronic data
processing—Architecture.
1. Title.
NA2540.N375
729'.028'54
73-8720
ISBN 0-262-14018-7

This book was input and
edited by the author on an
IMLAC PDS-1 at the Architecture Machine Laboratory.

Further editing was done on
the IMLAC at The MIT Press,
with composition in Helvetica
on a Linotron 505 by Radnor
Graphic Arts.

Printed and bound by Halliday
Lithograph Corporation in the
United States of America.

To members of the Architecture Machine Group who have spent half a decade helping to pass from fancies to facts.

Contents

Preface

The position that computer-aided architecture is an issue of machine intelligence is an uncomfortable one. While I sincerely believe that the case is strong, the paradoxes and setbacks are overwhelming to the point of making this position quite self-defeating for the researcher. Nevertheless, the fruits of continuing and the consequences of capitulating are so great that one can easily find incentives to try earnestly to understand the makings of intelligence and the makings of architecture. Without this understanding, I believe, the future of architecture, as aided, augmented, or replicated by computers, will be very gloomy in the technical hands of one-track-minded autocrats.

In contrast, I believe that computers have the potential for assuring a responsiveness, individuality, and excitement in all aspects of living, to a degree hitherto unseen. For the first time in history, for example, we can see the possibility of everybody having the opportunity to live in a man-made environment that responds to and is "meaningful" for him or her. Ironically, the computer sciences, generally associated with elite and often oppressive authorities, can provide to everyone a quality of architecture most closely approximated in indigenous architecture (architecture without architects). There is no doubt that computers can help in the humdrum activities of making architecture tick: smooth circulation, sound structures, viable financing. But I am not interested in that—I am interested in the rather singular goal of making the built environment responsive to me and to you, individually, a right I consider as important as the right to good education.

It is curious that although the United States government has launched major programs in building technology, particularly in housing, it has had almost no interest in the "design technologies." As a consequence we are on the way to achieving efficient, financially secure, and structurally sound ways of building the same junk cheaper and faster, without devoting an equal measure of time to scrutinizing the design process itself. In this volume I examine the design process in terms of its being conducted (not necessarily by professionals) in concert with computers —in particular, with a class of computers that someday may exhibit intelligent behavior. I consider three potentials of the computer: (1) the computer as a designer, (2) the computer as a partner to the novice with a self-interest, and (3) the computer as a physical environment that knows me.

Each of these themes stems from both specific experimentation and specific acquaintances over the past eight years, most recently during the period of building an "architecture machine." The following chapters will enumerate specific experiments. At this point I would like to acknowledge some important friendships, particularly because I have witnessed and not resolved some deep philosophical schisms between two major, perhaps personal, influences. On the one hand, I listen carefully to Marvin Minsky and Seymour Papert, share their interest in understanding intelligence and learning, but seriously wonder about their emphasis on problem solving, symbol manipulation, and descriptive systems. On the other hand, I listen to Warren Brodey and Avery Johnson, share their interest in soft robots, but see no evidence of progress or even potential. To help soften the dichotomy, I am very grateful to have as friends and colleagues Steve Coons, Aaron Fleisher, Joseph Licklider, Gordon Pask, and Oliver Selfridge, each of whom has provided many instances of well-seasoned wisdom that can turn contradictory arguments into complementary approaches.

From the "architectural" point of view, Yona Friedman and William Porter are the only two architects with whom I have shared a continuing interest in computer-aided architecture. Otherwise, there is general aloofness and skepticism as to whether any of this really has to do with Architecture. Or are we just playing with expensive toys?

Interesting, though hardly justifying, is the fact that they are not expensive. The Architecture Machine Group has built a multiprocessor minicomputer configuration composed of a family of inexpensive devices, some homemade. This has been achieved through the technical assistance of electrical engineering students and staff at MIT, in particular Randy Rettberg, Mike Titelbaum, and Andrew Lippman, each of whom has borne the burden of being depended upon one hundred and sixty-eight hours a week.

James Taggart and Steven Gregory have been responsible for making things work, developing, respectively, applications and systems software. More recently Mike Miller and Chris Herot have nursed the graphical systems with relentless perseverance. Each of these four gentlemen represents a rare kind of student, one who passes from student to colleague in a matter of months. They deserve special acknowledgment as it is with them that I spend most of my time on a day-to-day basis, and their ideas are reflected throughout this volume.

Leon Groisser has been a partner in all my ventures, especially in the early days of URBAN5 and *The Architecture Machine*. More recently he has assumed a desperately needed advisory role, providing unreserved criticism, counterbalancing wild fantasies, and bailing us out of trouble in my absence. If a man-machine relationship is possible to the degree suggested in the following chapters, I will consider the acid test to be: Can I have the same relation with a machine that I have with Leon?

Finally and most importantly, it is necessary to acknowledge the individuals and organizations that have supported our work. Most of our contracts and grants have been small but overlapping. As a consequence of some cases of redundant funding, we have been able to support a wide variety of student experiments and have been able to show each sponsor wide-ranging results.

John Entenza must be acknowledged first, because he was the first person to provide outside support to the Architecture Machine Group, thus assuming the risk of sponsoring a new enterprise. Under his directorship, the Graham Foundation made a substantial donation for the fellowships of Huck Rorick and Sean Wellesley-Miller and for a "scholars' fund" to be used for student projects. Beyond fiscal support, however, John Entenza gave us the recognition and credibility that made further support possible.

The National Science Foundation has supported our sketch recognition work. The Ford Foundation has sponsored the development of a Computer Teaching Laboratory in the School of Architecture and Planning. The Advanced Research Projects Administration has supported experiments in computer graphics through Project MAC and The Cambridge Project, both of which are based at MIT. And, most recently, The Koch Trust has sponsored our studies in computer-aided design, as well as a great deal of the research that went into the making of this book; I thank Bill Koch for this assistance.

Nicholas Negroponte
Patmos, August 1972

Author's Note

The writing of this book was completed in the summer of 1972. By fall it had advanced to a computer-readable format (paper tape). It is appearing only now, in 1975, for a number of reasons related to its production. The author and the publisher share the embarrassment that most of the delays were caused by the use of automation, in particular, computerized typesetting. The only redeeming aspect of this episode is the shared belief of those involved that, while this is a feature of computerization today, it is not an inherent and everlasting property.

Introduction

This book reports on a series of experiments conducted by the Architecture Machine Group at The Massachusetts Institute of Technology from 1968 through 1972. Each chapter moves progressively further and further away from what you might consider to be architecture or might view as the design process used by architects. As the book progresses you will notice that first the process and then the artifact are "assisted," "augmented," and eventually "replicated" by a computer.

The reader will recognize in the following chapters an underlying theme that is antiarchitect. This must not be confused with an antiarchitecture bias. Each chapter removes the architect and his design function more and more from the design process; the limit of this progression is giving the physical environment the ability to design itself, to be knowledgeable, and to have an autogenic existence. The general assumption is that in most cases the architect is an unnecessary and cumbersome (and even detrimental) middleman between individual, constantly changing needs and the continuous incorporation of these needs into the built environment. The architect's primary functions, I propose, will be served well and served best by computers. In this sense the book is about a new kind of architecture without architects (and even without surrogate architects).

How does architecture evolve? How do people design? These are questions that have no answers, because we can never set down the rules of evolution or the rules of design in a context-free manner, as we do in algebra or calculus. It is for this reason that the following chapters search for questions as often as answers, questions that frequently cannot even

promise a better understanding of either intelligence or architecture. All aspects of the themes of *Soft Architecture Machines* that I will treat stem directly from the day-to-day building and application of a rather hard Architecture Machine.

In 1968 *The Architecture Machine* was written as an epilogue to three years of experimentation that yielded both technical achievements and philosophical setbacks. The book was composed much like a child's painting in that the picture came out correctly, but the theoretical self-consciousness was, at best, crude. In some sense, these past four years have been the passing from an idiom to a reality, following (not necessarily consciously) notions set down in *The Architecture Machine* with an uncanny precision. The prognostications of hardware enumerated in wanton fantasy have been achieved and even superseded in the actual Architecture Machine of 1974. Ironically, the joys of having a handsome computing environment in which to conduct experiments are counterbalanced by nagging doubts about what constitutes a good experiment. All too often we spend our time making better operating systems, fancier computer graphics, and more reliable hardware, yet begging the major issues of understanding either the making of architecture or the makings of intelligence.

The first chapter of this book emphasizes polarities in both attitudes toward and techniques of thinking about thinking. Any design activity is characterized by intelligent behavior in that there must exist an understanding of goals, purposes, and meanings, and that this understanding can only follow from a more primitive understanding of the world, based on such concepts as solid, contained, facing, and so forth. We are at such an

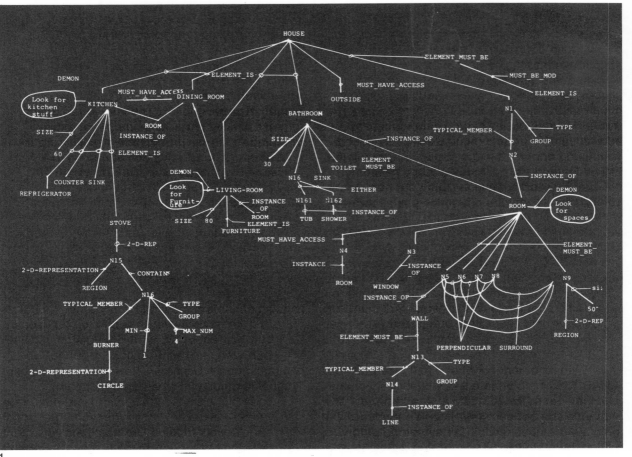

HOUSE

DEMON

ELEMENT_MUST_BE

MUST_BE_MOD

ELEMENT_IS

ELEMENT_IS

MUST_HAVE_ACCESS

Look for
kitchen
stuff

KITCHEN

MUST_HAVE_ACCESS

DINING_ROOM

OUTSIDE

N1

TYPE

SIZE

ROOM

INSTANCE_OF

BATHROOM

TYPICAL_MEMBER

GROUP

60

ELEMENT_IS

SIZE

INSTANCE_OF

N2

COUNTER SINK

30

TOILET

ELEMENT
_MUST_BE

INSTANCE_OF

REFRIGERATOR

DEMON

N16

SINK

DEMON

Look for
Furnit-
ure

LIVING-ROOM

INSTANCE
_OF

EITHER

Look
for
spaces

N161

N162

STOVE

SIZE

80

ROOM

ELEMENT_IS

TUB

SHOWER

INSTANCE_OF

ROOM

FURNITURE

2-D-REP

MUST_HAVE_ACCESS

ELEMENT
MUST_BE

N15

INSTANCE

N4

N3

N9

2-D-REPRESENTATION

CONTAINS

ROOM

INSTANCE
_OF

N5 N6 N7 N8

si;

REGION

N16

TYPICAL_MEMBER

TYPE

WINDOW

INSTANCE_OF

50˚

GROUP

2-D-REP

BURNER

MIN

MAX_NUM

WALL

REGION

2-D-REPRESENTATION

4

ELEMENT_MUST_BE

PERPENDICULAR

SURROUND

CIRCLE

1

N13

TYPICAL_MEMBER

TYPE

N14

GROUP

INSTANCE_OF

LINE

1

2

3

1 Part of a network describing "houseness." This structure is typical of representation schemes used to "instantiate" a house. This diagram is from Christopher Herot, "Using Context in Sketch Recognition" (Cambridge, Mass.: MIT, Thesis for M.S. in Department of Electrical Engineering, 1974).

2 Computervision Corporation's digitizer-plotter used as part of its computer-aided design and drafting system. The mechanism affords the opportunity to enter and plot back graphical data on a large surface, like that to which draftsmen are accustomed. Courtesy of the Computervision Corporation, Burlington, Massachusetts.

3 A close-up of the two-pen plotting head and transducer which controls servomechanisms. The switch to the right of the two white buttons allows for X-Y lockout. This feature enables a sensing of direction of departure in drawing and locks the appropriate motor to simulate a T-square. Courtesy of the Computervision Corporation, Burlington, Massachusetts.

4 A simulated stage of growth of a do-it-yourself building system designed by Carlos Tejeda, Miguel Angel Yanez, and Carlos Barrenechea, Mexico City, June 1972. Illustration courtesy of Iberoamericana University.

1 A view of household machines from the early 1950s.

2 Drawing by Donald Reilly; © 1971 by The New Yorker Magazine, Inc.

"And how are we feeling this morning? Reply when you hear a beep."

early stage of understanding the ingredients and motivations of intelligent behavior that we must of necessity work at this most primitive end of the scale of knowledge. Consequently, much of the actual experimentation appears to have little to do with yielding a better country house for Aunt Fiffy.

The second chapter can be viewed as a more direct analysis of design activities. The goal is to achieve a closer coupling between man and machine and to achieve higher levels of replication of tasks. This is to say, we propose to sidestep the typical partitioning of labor, letting the machine do what it is good at doing and letting the man undertake what he is good at doing. The proposed model for joint venture is most closely approximated by the working relationship enjoyed by two professionals who happen to be good friends. This implies physical interfaces and inference-making procedures more sophisticated than those presently available to computers.

The third chapter moves outside the conventional and professional roles of the architect. It is an application of the machine intelligence posture to an ever-growing concern about who should and who should not control the design of my house, for example. In short, the theory is that I can be the best architect for my needs, and I do not need a paternalistic human or mechanical architect to dictate my decisions. I need an understanding friend (not necessarily a professional architect), preferably one with whom I can share the risks.

The last chapter is my view of the distant future of architecture machines: they won't help us design; instead, we will live in them. The fantasies of an intelligent and responsive physical environment are too easily limited by the gap between the technology of making things and the science of understanding them. While proposing that a room might giggle at a funny gesture or be reluctant to be transformed into something else seems so unserious today, it does expose some of the questions associated with possibly cognitive physical environments of tomorrow. I strongly believe that it is very important to play with these ideas scientifically and explore applications of machine intelligence that totter between being unimaginably oppressive and unbelievably exciting.

The appendixes present a somewhat more pragmatic view of computation as applied to the making of Architecture Machines, outline techniques, and attitudes of computer-aided design, and describe some aspects of teaching computer sciences. Read alone, they represent a more traditional view of design education and design behavior in that the processes are ones that we have encountered during our experimentation, and ones that we perforce understand better than some of the concepts of preceding chapters.

The following essay by Gordon Pask introduces a machine intelligence paradigm with a rigor I often lack. Although I recognize the disconcerting disparity between the cybernetic vernacular of Gordon's preface and the loose jargon of my own text, I leave the disjunction for the reader to enjoy or to ignore, because I believe that this paper is one of the most definitive statements on artificial intelligence since Turing's "Computing Machinery and Intelligence" (1950).

1 Aspects of Machine Intelligence

Introduction by Gordon Pask

The current status of mindlike computer programs is summarized, at a philosophical rather than technical level, in the following short but authoritative papers: Minsky (1968), Simon (1966), Turing (1969). Whoever wishes to delve into this subject in greater depth may read the books where these papers are published in their entirety, augmenting them, to obtain comprehensive background, by Ernst and Newell (1969); Ashby (1960); Cohen (1966); Fogel, Owens, and Walsh (1966); Von Foerster and Zopf (1962); Uttley (1959); Von Foerster et al. (1968); McCulloch (1965); Oestreicher and Moore (1968); Amarel (1969); Rose (1970); Minsky and Papert (1969); Feigenbaum and Feldman (1963); Banerji (1969); and Garvin (1970). It is also worth perusing all volumes of the journal *Artificial Intelligence*.

Henceforward, it is assumed either that the reader knows the *kind* of symbolic operations performed by computer programs and other artifacts, that he will study the matter at leisure, or that he will take these operations for granted. With this supposition in mind I shall give a personal and possibly idiosyncratic view of the conditions under which *artificially intelligent* is a properly used term and offer an interpretation of these conditions with respect to *use* of the *architecture machine*. Apart from the pictograms or ikons developed in the text, the only special symbols used are the special brackets $<$ and $>$ which enclose *ordered* collections of objects; the equality sign $=$; and $\triangleq$, which is read as " *defined as equal to.*"

Overview

The contention is as follows: Intelligence is a property that is ascribed by an *external observer* to a *conversation* between *participants* if, and only if, their dialogue manifests *understanding*. Each italicized word in this sentence requires careful attention. To give the flavor of the argument, *understanding* will be defined both in terms of the processes that give rise to such an interchange; roughly, understanding of a *topic* ≜ (defined as equal to) a *relation* implies the existence of a *concept* ≜ a *procedure* (for bringing about or satisfying the relation) and a *memory* ≜ a *reproduction* of this *procedure*, together with a self-replicating organization, of which topic, concept, and memory are a part.

This point of view emerged in the late 1950s and has been reported, chiefly in conection with experimental data, in a series of publications. (See Pask, 1959, 1960, 1962, 1963, 1965, 1966, 1968, 1969a, 1969b, 1970a, 1970b, 1972a, 1972b; Pask and Feldman, 1966; Pask and Lewis, 1968; Pask and Scott, 1971). It resembles Von Foerster's theory of finite functional systems (1970b; see also Von Foerster, 1970a). It grew concurrently as part of a school of thought encouraged by McCulloch and owing a great deal to his concept "redundancy of potential command" (1965). Various formulations are possible. The present argument is most easily referred to Leofgren's (1968, 1972) mathematical model; an alternative formulation is given in Barralt-Torrijos and Ciaraviglio (1971). In this paper, mathematics is put aside in favor of ikons that *do*, however, have a deep logical connotation and are *not* simply loose visual analogies.

Insofar as *intelligence* is a property adduced by an external observer, the conversation has a great deal in common with the gamelike situation underlying Turing's Test (1963) (for intelligence in a somewhat different sense). But Turing's game and my conversation are not identical, and the interested reader may profitably compare the two and, in some respects, contrast them.

Aphorisms and Arguments in Support of the Definition

1. An external observer speaks in a metalanguage ($L*$) used to discuss theories, describe experiments, and prescribe designs for equipment. The metalanguage is a natural language, very often scientific English.

2. The observer can distinguish stable entities of various kinds. Two kinds are of special importance: "mechanical individuals" or *M Individuals* and psychological individuals" or *P Individuals*. In both cases, the stability is due to the same root cause—self-replication. But this fact is frequently suppressed in the case of M Individuals, since the replication process (being biological or due to the operation of natural laws) does not intrude into the phenomena under scrutiny.[1]

2.1. An *M Individual* is distinguished by the familiar methods of classical physics and behaviorism. For example, a man is such a thing; so is an animal; so is a unique machine. It has a spatio-temporal location and is usually juxtaposed with another *M Individual* called its *environment*.

2.1.1. The term *environment* is specifically reserved for entities that can be described or prescribed in the manner of *M Individuals*: that is, in terms of *states* and *state* transitions (whether in the sense of automation theory or the very different sense of physical states) where *state* $\triangleq$ the conjoint values of all descriptive attributes, and *state transition* $\triangleq$ an operator carrying one class of states into another.

2.1.2. In the $L*$ description of a typical experiment, pairs of *M Individuals A* and *B*—one, perhaps, an environment—are coupled (Figure 1) via an *interface*. Apart from this interaction, they are isolated.

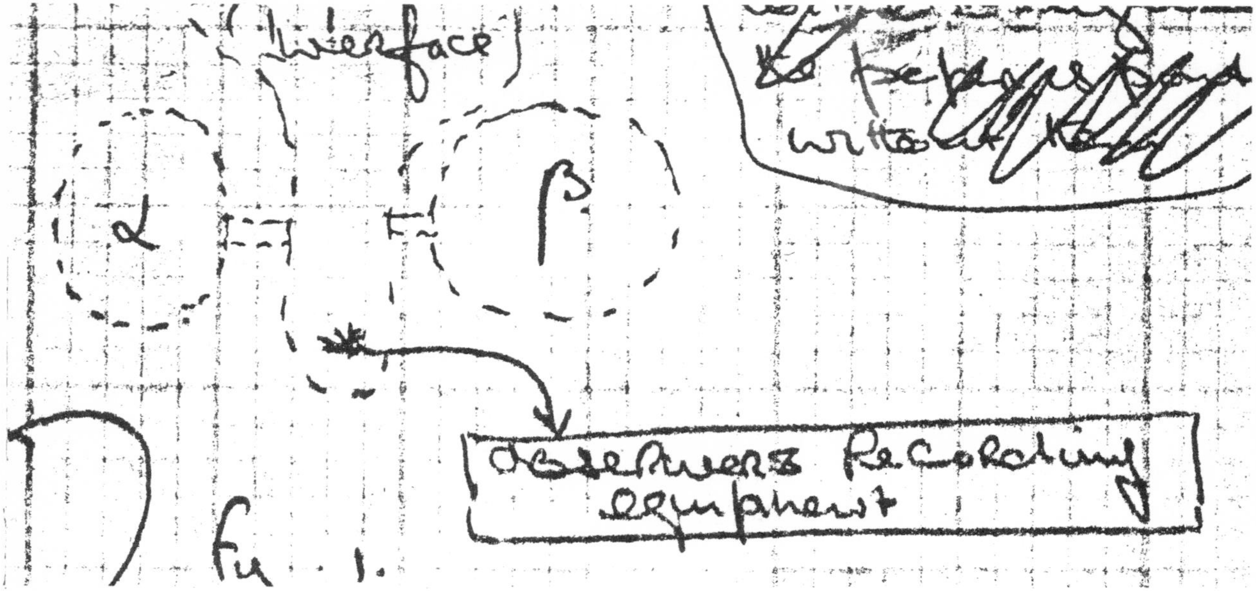

(interface)

α   β

to be passed on
without form

Observers Recording
equipment

Fig. 1.

2.1.3. It is crucial to the argument that *all* observations occur at such a spatio-temporally localized interface; the observer's measuring and recording equipment is, in the last resort, bound to it. But the interface is neutral regarding the type of interaction, if any, that takes place across it.

In Figure 1, which introduces the notation for distinguishing *M Individuals*, α may be a user of the architecture machine regarded as a biological unit and β the architecture machine regarded as a chunk of metal and semiconductor material. But α may also be a rat and β its experimental environment.

2.2. A *P Individual* is distinguished as a self-replicating and (usually) evolving *organization*. It is respectably and precisely defined in terms of an object language L and a relational domain R described in L by a description $D(R)$ with respect to which it *is* self-replicating. Here, self-replication is intended in the abstract sense of the theory of reproductive automata, as originally conceived by von Neumann (1968) and as recently developed by Loefgren (1972).

2.2.1. Though, in general, the domain may be allowed to grow systematically under the control of the given *P Individual*, we confine our attention to cases in which R is fixed. Under these circumstances, it is possible to specify domains with the property that if a given *P Individual* is viable (that is, is able to reproduce) on occasion n, then it is also viable at any later occasion $n + r$ (r finite) for R_i in R.[2]

2.2.2. It is assumed that a *P Individual* is active or that any conversation in which it is a participant does in fect proceed, that is, for each occasion, some topic relation R (a part of R or all of it) is actually ostended for discussion. Rather complicated but not esoteric conditions are imposed, in the full theory, to guarantee that this is so.

2.2.3. Typical *P Individuals* are people regarded as personalities—characters (in plays) executed by *any* actors, the performance of stable roles in society, the organization of coherent groups, factions, governments, cultures, and persistent ideas. A vertical cleft notation I is employed to discriminate *P Individuals* labeled *A* and *B,* as in Figure 2.

2.3. A *conversation* is taken to be the minimal situation for a meaningful psychological or, a fortiori, mechanical-psychological experiment. It consists of an activity involving at least one *P Individual A* and generating an *L* dialogue. On each occasion *n,* when the interaction is focused on a topic R_i of *R,* this interaction gives rise to a further *P Individual* called a *sprout* (growing point), which can be dissected into a portion S_A and a portion S_B with certain well-defined technical properties; namely, on occasion *n,* S_A, S_B are productive systems in respect of a surrounding R_i using the terms *productive* and *surrounding* in Loefgren's sense (1932) and at least one of them, S_A, (and possibly both) is reproductive both in the surrounding $< S_A$, $R_i >$ in the surrounding afforded by *A* (of which S_A is an externally delineated subsystem).[3]

2.4. The circularity inherent in this specification is quite deliberate. *P Individuals* are recognized by the existence of conversations, and the conversation itself is, on a *given* occasion, a further *P Individual* (the *sprout*). Hence, the form of the dialogue in a conversation is determined as an *L explanation* or *L modeling* operation, which is precisely the *reproduction of the sprout.*[4]

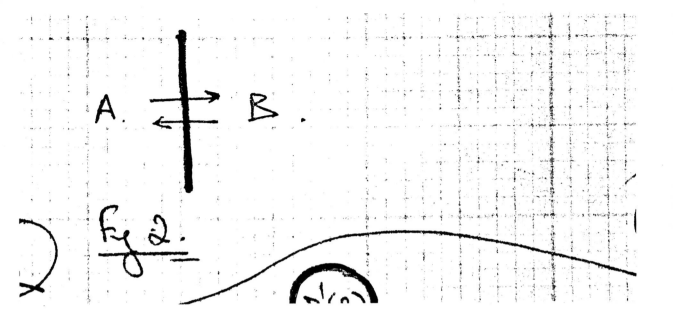

A. B.

Fig 2.

X

2.5. Conversely, a certain (to be described) complex of explanation cycles is the L image of a reproductive cycle, and these L explanations are split, by the dissection that yields S_A and S_B, into questions asked by A of B (or vice versa), which are answered in explanations given by B to A (or vice versa).

2.6. The reproductive cycles of P *Individuals* (the sprout included) are due to procedures executed in *some* processors; it is apposite to concentrate on the architecture machine *qua processor* and the *user's brain.* But it should be emphasized that a P *Individual* has no necessary spatio-temporal location, and procedures that constitute P *Individuals* may be executed in several M *Individuals* just as an M *Individual* may execute several P *Individuals.* In ordinary conversations many-to-many correspondences are ubiquitous. Stable *concepts* are frequently shared, and *memories* (which may be legitimate P *Individuals*) are distributed throughout society.

2.7. Conversations occur autonomously and are discovered or noted by accident. Most of these conversations take place in natural language; in the limiting case, $L* = L$. Hence, with certain exceptions like autogenous committee meetings and tribal rituals that perform a regulatory function, an observer is hard pressed to maintain the impartial poise of an external observer. Since it is important that he should do so in adjudicating the conversation as "intelligent" or "not intelligent," he needs to maintain a firm distinction between $L*$ and L.

3. The following remarks are thus confined to conversations *brought* into existence by an external observer who contrives some type of *contract* with any stable entity capable of understanding enough of L^* to agree to the contract and capable of interpreting L (of which the full semiotic is described in L^*). The nature of the entity that is party to the contract with the observer is, at this stage, left open.

3.1. In general, contracts are made with human beings or groups of them; in general, the observer speaks to (glances at, projects his voice toward) a human being or group in the sense of an *M Individual;* but at the same time, he negotiates the contract with a sentient creature, that is, the man or group regarded as a *P Individual* larger than the participant *A*.

3.2. The contract has the following clauses:

a. That the contracting entity will, henceforward, speak only in an object language L (in other words, the vocabulary of L will be used, and its syntax will be respected). Commonly, L is a mechanical language that does not involve verbal utterance.

b. That L will be interpreted with respect to a domain R, described as $D(R)$ (this is the semantic of L; it contains topic relations germane, for example, to architecture, geometry, and mechanics).

c. That the contracting entity will play a role, designated A. This is the pragmatic aspect of L or A's *intention* (for example, to be a *designer,* or, in selecting one R, in R, to carry out a particular design). In particular, "A seeks a goal" means either "A aims to bring about R," or "A learns to bring about R," for some topic relation R, in R.

d. That A will converse in L with a further entity B, that is, on each occasion n, A will aim for some goal; hence, some L expressions are used in an imperative or interrogative mode to pose and solve problems.

e. That the observer, for his part, will choose an L that is rich enough to accommodate the required questionings, commandings, answerings, etc.

f. That the observer will furnish a participant B (for example, the *heuristic* in the architecture machine) so devised that it will be *possible* for the other participant to realize the agreed-upon intention of playing the role of A.

4. In order to satisfy clause (6) of Section 3.2, an external observer must have an unambiguous representation of A. Because of that condition— because he wants to distinguish between a *concept* ≜ a goal-directed or problem-solving procedure ≜ the reproduction of a relation, such as R_i and a memory ≜ the reproduction of a concept, because he wants to judge the conversation "intelligent" or "not intelligent"—an observer finds it con- venient to avoid dilemmas of self-reference: for example, the notion of a program that "writes itself" or a procedure that "questions itself" or even the operational evocation of a self-reproducing system (so that the *sprout* of a conversation, which is a *P Individual,* can be represented as a prod- uctive pair, S_A, S_B). One expedient adopted for this purpose is to stratify L, that is, to specify $L = L'$, $L°$ where expressions in $L°$ refer to the bringing about of relations R_i (the solution of problems, the achievement of goals), and expressions in L' refer to the construction or learning to formulate and achieve goals or learning to solve problems.

5. The distinction between levels of discourse in the object language L', $L°$, is symbolized by a horizontal cleft —.

5.1. Moreover, once imposed, the stratification engenders two descriptions of R, namely, $D(R) = <D'(R), D°(R)>$.

5.2. $D'(R)$ is a grammarlike structure indicating *what may be known* or *learned*.

5.3. $D°(R)$ is grammarlike structure indicating *what may be done* (either by physical operations, to make a tangible model for some R_i in R), or by intellectual operations, to model R_i as an explanation—literally, of how to solve problems under R_i.

6. On making the distinction I and the distinction —, the observer declares the tableau of Figure 3 the conversational *skeleton*. This skeleton L and R are all described in $L*$.

7. To lay foundations for the representation required to satisfy clause 6 of Section 3.2 and, simultaneously, to exhibit levels L', $L°$, in L as levels of control, the spaces in the skeleton are filled by boxes (Figure 4) representing classes of goal-directed or problem-solving procedures, *Proc i* being a procedure that *brings about* ≜ *reproduces* a topic relation R_i.

7.1. The *superscripts* signify levels.

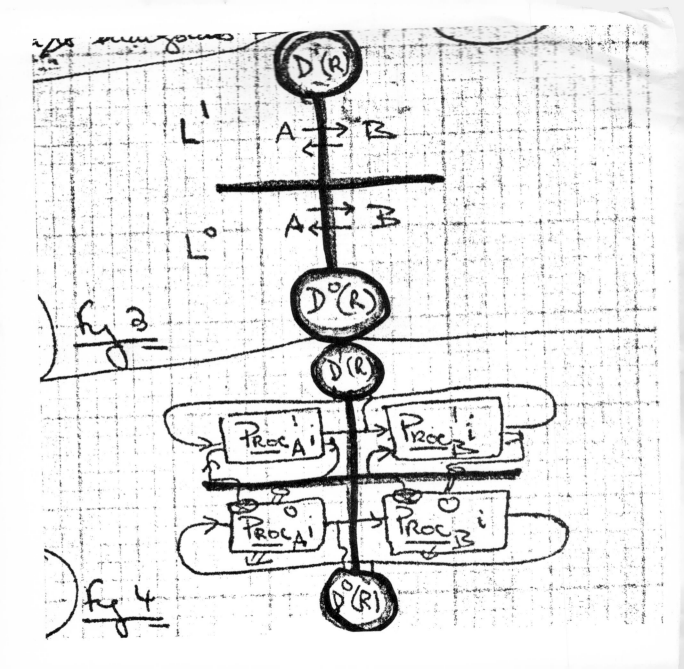

$D^+(R)$

L^1

$A \rightrightarrows B$

L^0

$A \rightrightarrows B$

$D^0(R)$

$D^i(R)$

| Proc A^1 i | Proc B^1 i |

| Proc A^0 i | Proc B^0 i |

$D^0(R)$

fig 3

fig 4

7.2. ♀ means "operates upon according to a hypothesis," and ⊗ means "gives a description (in the language appropriate to the level where the line terminates), which may or may not confirm the hypothesis."

7.3. Thus a complete circuit on one side of I , starting at ⊗, passing through — to a *Proc,* and returning by way of — and ♀ on the original *Proc* is a *causal* coupling, or, equivalently, it permits *reproduction* of the original *Proc.*

7.4. The unadorned, horizontal connections have a different meaning: they are *inferential* couplings, which, limiting cases apart, entail the notion of choice.

7.5. Hence, any complete circle (such as the line emanating from $Proc_A$ i to $Proc_B$ i and terminating on $Proc_A$ i) may be called a deductive chain.[5]

7.6. Finally, the lines to and from D' (R) and $D^{\circ}(R)$ indicate whatever is referenced by the inference, that is, whatever R_i in R is ostended by the participants A and B on occasion n.

7.7. Call this ikon (Figure 4) the conversational *paradigm.*

7.8. If one ikon is created by filling the spaces in Figure 3, then (obeying the proper rules) the process can be iterated laterally to yield a further *paradigm,* for example, the ikon in Figure 5. The motivation for doing so is noted in Section 2.1.1 ≜ to represent as much of mind as desired.

7.9. Parsimony alone dictates as few inscriptions as possible.

7.10. Figure 4 sufficiently represents the sprout of a conversation if R_i is ostended on occasion n (a P Individual $<S_A, S_B, R_i, n= <<Proc_A i>$, $Proc_A i>, <Proc_B i, Proc_B i>, n>$, where n itself may be a vector) and the full; requirement for understanding is satisfied if the form is iterated to the left until A is also a P Individual, even if devoid of S_B (a similar construction being possible, but not mandatory, for S_B and B).

7.11. To condense the notation, these iterated systems called *repertoires* of procedures (at level L' and L^o, available to A and B) are designated.

7.12. Repertoires are constrained by the rule that any such configuration contains a *sprout* on any occasion n (Figure 6).

8. The L dialogue across I implied by the existence of a *sprout* (specifically, by the ikon of Figure 4) is as follows:

8.1.
a. B can ask A to explain R and obtain an answer that *before* the end of occasion n matches *some* explanation B could have given in reply to the same question asked by A and, furthermore, A could have asked the question.

b. B can ask A to explain how he *knows* or is currently *learning* to explain R_i and obtain an answer that *before the end of occasion n* matches *some* explanationB could have given in reply to the *same* question asked by A and, furthermore, A could have asked it.

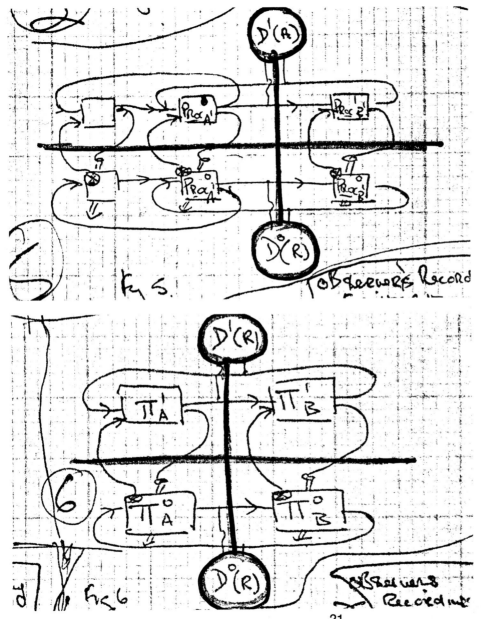

Fig 5.

Fig 6

OBSERVERS Record

OBSERVERS Recording

21

c. Since the closure condition is in force (Section 2.1.3), the possible explanations in (a) above are described in $D°(R)$.

d. Again because of the closure condition (Section 2.1.3), the possible explanations in (b) above are described in $D'(R)$.

8.2. Conversely, the joint holding of conditions (a), (b), (c), and (d) implies the sprout of a conversation, hence, a P *Individual*.

8.3. Likewise, this joint condition implies an *understanding* of R_i by A in which (a) is the L expression of a *concept* of $R_i \triangleq Proc_i \triangleq$ the reproduction of R_i, and (b) is the L expression of a memory of R_i ($Proc' i \triangleq$ the reproduction of $Proc°i$).

8.4. If these conditions are not all satisfied *until* the end of occasion n (recall from Section 2.2.2. that the series of occasions is *assumed*), then the ikon represents an evolutionary process called *learning* the concept ($Proc°i$) of R_i.

8.5. To obtain the general case, the entire argument is applied to the ikon in Figure 6.

8.6. That such systems exist can be demonstrated in the abstract; that the understanding they image can be appreciated by participants is a matter of experience.

9. But for the L dialogue satisfying (a), (b), (c), and (d) to be unambiguously recorded and adjudicated by an external observer calls for the further requirement, specified in Figure 1, that the cleft I shall

coincide with a spatio-temporally localized *interface* to which the observer's measuring equipment is attached; in other words, that Figure 1 is superimposed upon Figure 6 (say) so that the *interface* is in register with I and engulfs some physical representation of $D(R) = <D'(R), D^o(R)>$; A is in register with α, and B with β (Figure 7). If, under these circumstances, an observer *says* (in L^*) there is an *understanding*—that is, (a), (b), (c), and (d) are satisfied—then he deems the conversation *intelligent.*

Notice, however, that the form of interaction across the interface engendered by this construction is highly specific; it is L dialogue and could *not,* for example, represent the reactive interchange between a (laboratory) rat and its environment (whereas, in Figure 1 taken alone, it *could* do so).

10. An environment, in the strict sense reserved for this word in Section 2.1.1, can be added to the picture (Figure 8). It consists in a box U with the characteristics of a state and state transition system, as described in Section 2.1. The descriptors X_A are those properties *apparent to A* that tally with L^o predicates; its descriptors X_B are the properties *apparent to B;* its state is altered by the operations Y_A, that A may prescribe and describe in L^o (as m-tuples of values of L^o predicates), and the operations Y_B are those that B may prescribe. Hence, the environmental state is a function of two classes of variables, indexing the operator classes Y_A and Y_B. Its state on occasion n is relevant if it *instantiates* the relation R_i ostended at n. The members of X_A are those relations subordinate to R_i for which A has *memories* and which it *treats as* properties; a similar comment applies to X_B *and B.* A special interface V is used to localize transactions of this *causal* type.

23

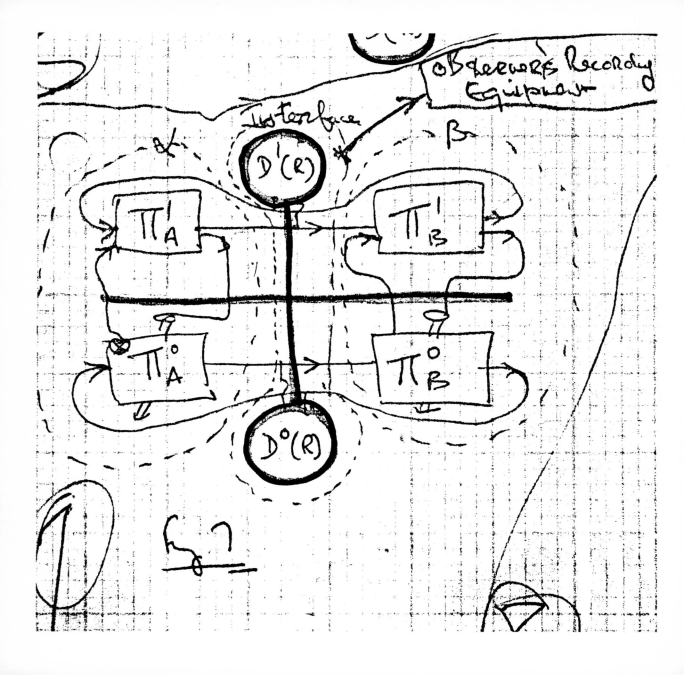

Observer's Recording Equipment

Interface

$D^1(R)$

α

B

π^1_A

π^1_B

π^0_A

π^0_B

$D^0(R)$

Fig 7

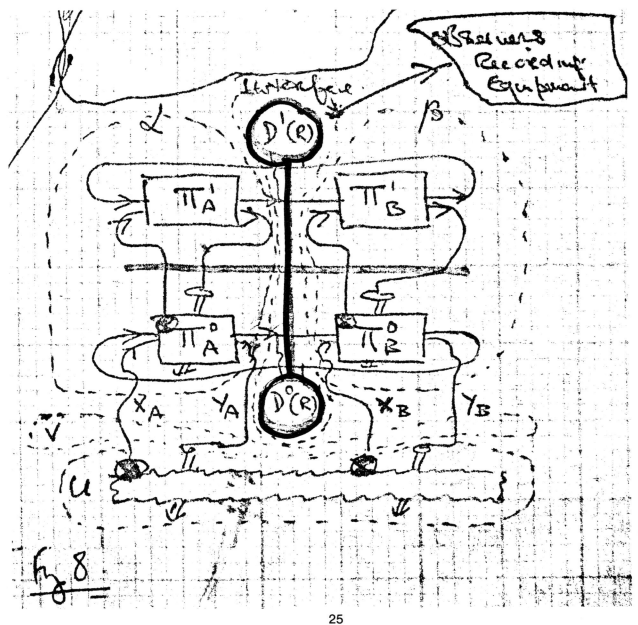

Observers
Recording
Equipment

Interface

α

β

$D'(R)$

π^1_A

π^1_B

π^0_A

π^0_B

$D^0(R)$

x_A

y_A

x_B

y_B

v

u

fig 8

Naive forms of behaviorism are solely concerned with observing *causal* transactions across *V* and are thus not very informative. In particular, no conversation occurs by virtue of these transactions.

11. The joint requirement that a conversation (see clause (6) of Section 3.2) exists and its cleft is in register with an interface is satisfied when A and B are conscious human beings, one of whom is a skilled interviewer (*B*, correlated with B).

11.1. Moreover, the same is true if the interviewer's capabilities are truncated by adherence to a heuristic (thus deleting the right lateral extension of *B* that generally represents *B*'s mind).

11.2. I have shown, by constructing a rather elaborate machine with liberal facilities for graphic representation of $D'(R)$ and $D°(R)$, together with arrangements to mark their constituents with tokens of aiming, access, working on, ostension, and exploration that *B*, in this minimal but adequate sense, can be the heuristic embodied in an electro-mechanical artifact. Using CASTE, the acronym for this equipment, it has been possible to investigate roles for different *P Individuals* (notably, *A = Student, B = Teacher*, and *A = Respondent, B = Interrogator*) and to plot, in considerable detail, the development of conversations and of the evolutionary component, which is regarded as *learning*.

11.3. Further, the closure condition can be relaxed so that a conversational domain may grow as the discourse proceeds, though not in an unlimited fashion.

11.4. With some minor augmentation, judged feasible after technical discussions with Negroponte's group, the Architecture Machine could, like CASTE, act with respect to *P Individuals* playing roles such as *Designer* and *Codesigner.* Our experience with the tutorial mode of CASTE suggests that this application would be well worthwhile. The outline interpretation for the Architecture Machine is shown in Figure 9.

11.5. In either case, the resulting conversation is deemed "intelligent" by an external observer since the conditions for understanding are secured by the regulatory B heuristic, which makes it possible for A to keep the contract he intends to keep (clause 6 of Section 3.2) as well as to maintain on the interface.

11.6. Said differently, the price paid for observation is that the external observer takes the conversation as his own environment in exactly the sense (Section 10) that the *P Individual* in Figure 8 takes U as its environment. The observer's description (analogous to but *not* at all *identical* with L expressions involving X_A, X_B) is an L^* description of L dialogue about R_i. This is what he records. To secure impartiality, he establishes a contract, which could be symbolized by *constant-valued* parametric arrows (analogous to but not identical with Y_A, Y_B) penetrating the uppermost process boxes adjacent to the cleft. To regulate the dialogue so that its conditions are satisfied on the interface (Section 11.5), he prescribes B, an interviewer or a machine, to act as his emissary, yet also as a participant.

12. Since one *M Individual* (B in Figures 6, 7, and 8) is a machine, the intelligence might be rated "partially artificial." The question of whether it is possible to achieve a "fully artificial" intelligence by making A (of Fig-

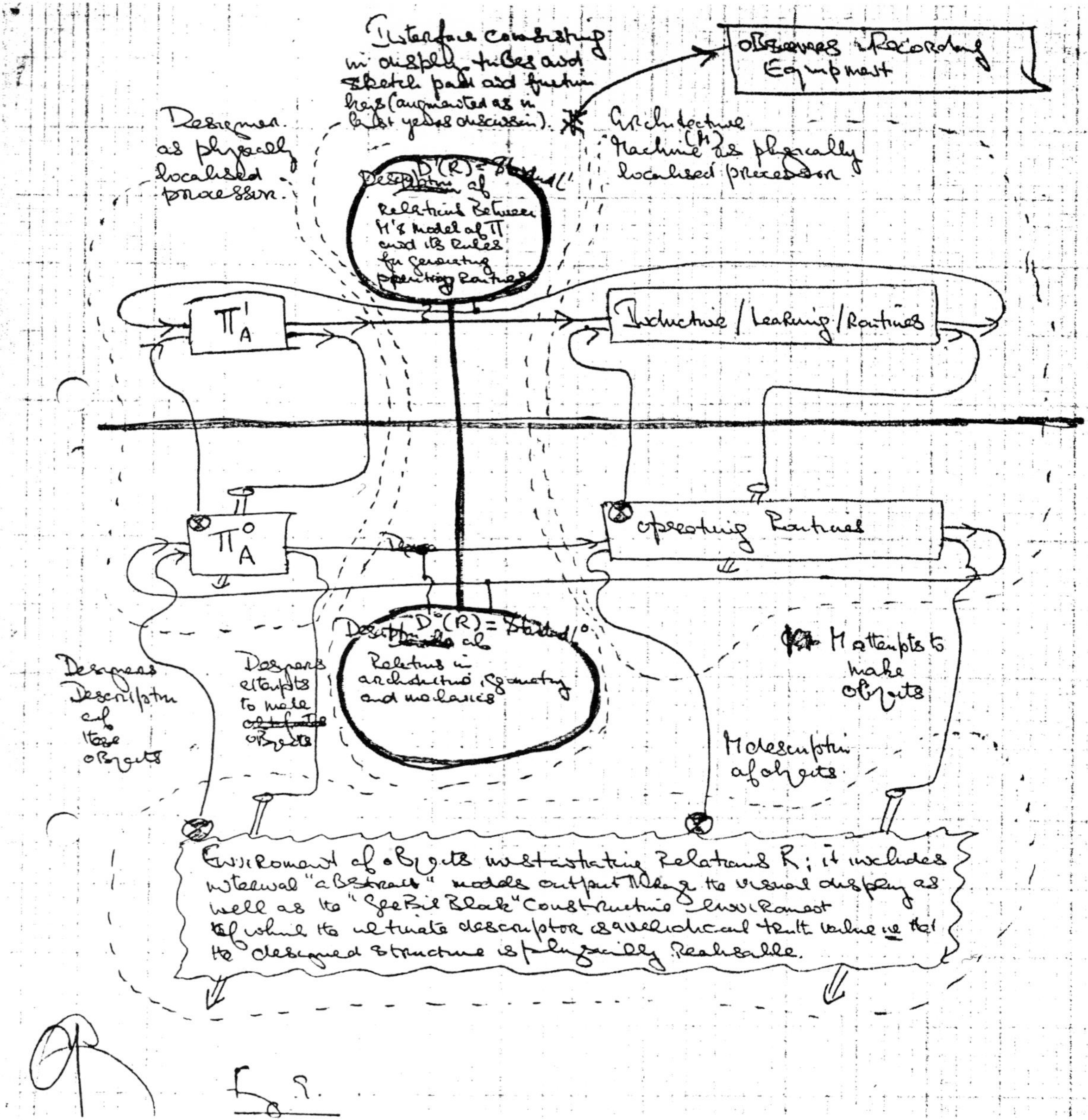
Interface consisting in display tubes and sketch pads and function keys (augmented as in last year's discussion).
Observers Recording Equipment
Designer as physically localised processor.
Architecture Machine (M) as physically localised processor
D¹(R) = Standard¹ Description of Relations between M's model of Π and its Rules for generating operating Routines
Π¹A
Inductive / Learning / Routines
Π⁰A
operating Routines
D⁰(R) = Standard⁰ Description of Relations in architecture, geometry and mechanics
Designer's Description of these objects
Designer's attempts to make objects
M attempts to make objects
M description of objects
Environment of objects instantiating Relations R; it includes internal "abstract" models output through the visual display as well as the "Seebil Black" Construction Environment of which the ultimate descriptor is a validational truth value re that the designed structure is physically realisable.

Fig. 9.

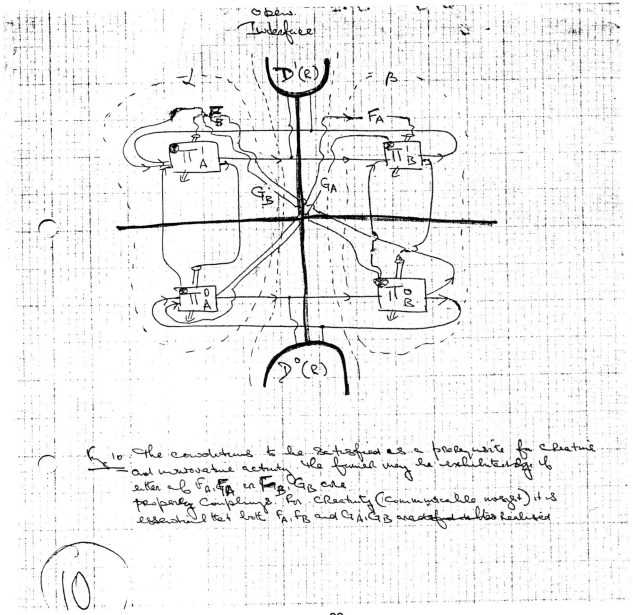

Fig 10: The conditions to be satisfied as a prerequisite for creative
and innovative activity the former may be exhibited of if
either of F_A, G_A or F_B, G_B are
properly couplings. For creativity (commucable insight) it is
essential that both F_A, F_B and G_A, G_B are defined whites realised

29

ures 6, 7, or 8) out of metal is stated in Figure 10. The connections F_A, F_B, G_A G_B, which allow A to take B as A's *environment* and/or B to take A as B's *environment,* are crucial to all manner of creativity and innovation; for, if these connections can be made, then a *P Individual* (the sprout of a conversation, at least) is an *observer* (Section 11.6) of itself. Once these connections are established, the closure condition is removed, the domain can expand (though not in an unlimited fashion), and, at the same moment, the stratification of L is lost, so that L may as well be L^*. If A and B stand for the brains of human beings, this trick is often played, and because of it, *P Individuals* are seldom fully correlated with *M Individuals*. I see no reason, in principle, why that trick should not be played with mechanisms, also. But, if it were, the mechanism would not be inanimate. Having this disposition, I prefer to avoid the qualifier "artificial" when speaking of intelligence.

1. In a coarse-grained account of the matter, a "natural law" is equivalent to a doctrine of "structural invariance." Considered in greater detail, it is possible to place natural laws in correspondence with regulatory principles that maintain and, as later, reproduce relations immanent in nature. This notion was mooted long ago (by Von Foerster, amongst others) and gives a nontrivial interpretation to causality, thus, for example, eliminating the confusion between *cause* and *enable*. The interested reader is referred to M. Bunge, *Scientific Research*, Vols. 1 and 2, (Springer Verlag, 1967) and requested to communicate with *L.* Perriera and *L.* Montiero (Dept. of Cybernetics, Brunel University or Centro de Estudos De Cibernetica, G.E.U.A. 53-9E Lisbon 5), who are systematically rewriting the principles of (near classical) physics in terms of feedback and regulator equations.

2. Throughout this paper it is assumed that the domain is of this type because heuristics exist for constructing such domains as relational structures with $L*$ description $D*(R)$ and L descriptions $D(R) = <D'(R), D^o(R) + $ *as in Sections 5.1, 5.2, and 5.3. It should also be noted that* $D*(R)$ *includes a set of* descriptors *for the graph or* entailment structure *express-*ing *what may be known* as well as the graph itself; thereby, for example, a real student can appreciate a topic relation in the context of others before he *knows* it or attempts to *learn* it. This class of knowable domains is much more restrictive than necessary. We have, for example, a CASTE-executed heuristic permitting evolution of the domain and can show that *this* is too restrictive. Though it can also be shown that there are limits upon knowable domains, or, at any rate, memorable domains, we have not yet done much empirical work to check that certain predictably immemorable relations are not, in fact, reconstructible.

3. Due to the special construction of the domain (Section 2.2.1 and its footnote and Sections 5.1, 5.2, and 5.3), R_i appearing in this expression covers all those relations needed by a given P Individual to learn R and thus to understand it. But, even with this construction, R might be learned in *many*, perhaps *infinitely* many, ways; that is, we are *not* characterizing domains as simple *hierarchies* of relations.

4. Though this statement is accurate, my theory includes several caveats and conditions. For example, the existence of a sprout on each occasion *n*; that the conversational domain $D(R)$ is so organized that it is possible to consider more and less comprehensive relations, R_i; and that the *sprout* selected on occasion *n* is a system that is reproductive and partitionable in a pair, S , S , with respect to a surrounding that is the most comprehensive of the R .

5. Notice that this usage makes *induction* simply a higher level of deduction (for example, if the L^o grammar admits statistical inference, according to Bayne's rule).

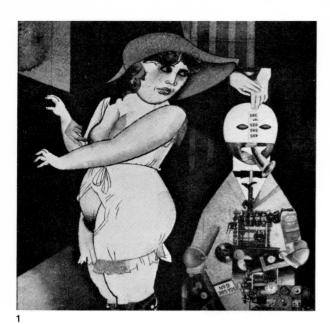

1

1 "Daum" marries her pedantic automaton George in May 1920. John Heartfield is very glad of it (Meta-Mech-[anisch]konstr[uiert]nach Prof. R. Hausmann). A dada watercolor, pencil and photomontage done in 1920. Original $16^1/_2 \times 11^7/_8$ inches, Galerie Nierendorf, Berlin.

2 Steam typesetter. Caricature from a 19th-century English printing magazine. Courtesy of Bettmann Archive.

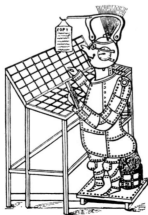

2

Why Intelligence?

Around 1968 I adopted the position that, if computers were to aid the evolution of architecture, they would have to be a class of machines that (we could generally agree) exhibited intelligent behavior. I took the stance that computer-aided architecture without machine intelligence would be injurious because the machine would not *understand* what it was aiding. This position is documented in *The Architecture Machine* (Negroponte, 1970) and in "The Semantics of Architecture Machines" (Negroponte and Groisser, 1971). It is a posture that results primarily from two anomalies that I believe to be inherent in and characteristic of architecture: *context dependency* and *missing information*.

Briefly, context dependency means that any axiom or rule can find a situation where it will fail or generate disaster when blindly executed as a truism. I do not believe that there are *truths* in architecture; all principles are qualified by *context*. Unfortunately, one cannot point to context or describe it. It is a property ascribed by an observer or by a participant as a function of *his* own personal experience and *his* state of mind at the time. In short, it is context that provides him the opportunity to give *meaning* to the event, principle, building, or whatever. "Context acts *as an operator* to assign meaning to the metaphorical signals we receive from the world, but it is not found in those signals. It is to be found, rather, in the consequences of our response to those meanings in that environment. 'Get undressed' does not convey the same meaning in a doctor's office as it does in the back seat of an automobile—but it would be a mistake to identify the background setting in either case as the context"

(A. Johnson, 1971). Context must be recognized by us in terms of our own behaviors or by a machine in terms of its behavior.

As an example of the antithesis, in discussing the computer simulation of urban dynamics, Jay Forrester (1969) concludes that: "It should be a model which, with proper changes in parameters, is good for New York, Calcutta, a gold rush camp, or West Berlin." But perhaps the contextual issues of culture, for example, are so different that this could not be true. Forrester will argue convincingly and with conviction that if he incorporates enough multiple-feedback loops and nonlinear relationships, his model will be comprehensive and complicated enough to embody what I am calling context. In other words, to Forrester context is to be found in the signals, not in you or me.

In contrast, one machine intelligence approach would be to embed (if possible) in a machine those devices that allowed Forrester himself to recognize that which allowed him to derive his parameters. This is particularly important in architecture where the contextual shifts are not as dramatic and overt as those between India and the United States. Instead, they are more subtle but no less important indicators shaped by site conditions, traditions, social setting, prior experiences, the whims of inhabitants, and so on. These are crucial issues if my architecture is to be responsive to me. Consequently, I postulate that the machine must be constructed in such a manner that its behavior gives us enough confidence to presume that it is acting intelligently and with common sense, that is, in context.

The second anomaly is in the theory of missing information. At the end of *The Architecture Machine* I stated that: "Part of the design process is, in effect, the procurement of this information. Some is gathered by doing research in the preliminary design stages. Some is obtained through experience, overlaying and applying a seasoned wisdom. Other chunks of information are gained through prediction, induction, and guesswork. Finally some information is handled randomly, playfully, whimsically, personally." The general fervor of so-called "design methods" research has been to remove the role of such devices as intuition and to ascribe a counter-intuitive nature to complex design problems. In some sense, I am saying the opposite: tools like intuition (sharpened by experience) are valuable and are often responsible for the major joys in architecture, and we should strive to bestow such devices on machines.

My position is that machines, like humans, will have to evolve these mechanisms by developing in time and with experience, each machine being as different from the next as you are from me. As an example of the vital role of experience in human design endeavors, consider the age of accomplished architects (as distinguished, per-haps, from successful architects). I would suggest that architecture has been an older man's profes-sion for reasons of experience (in drawing analo-gies, making inferences, generally handling miss-ing information) rather than of politics or of fiscal establishment. It takes a certain amount of time to witness a variety of situations wide enough to afford our successful dealing with ill-specified, context-dependent problems, as is the case in architecture. "In contrast, note that the design of a bottle opener or an airplane is based on almost

complete and reliable information and is inde-pendent of shifting contexts. The design of a plane does not change if the craft is to fly northbound or southbound or is to carry Italians rather than Englishmen. A bottle opener works as well on domestic beer as on foreign brews" (Negroponte and Groisser, 1971).

As a consequence of these two anomalies we, The Architecture Machine Group, took the route of attempting to make machines more like people inasmuch as they might exhibit a design behavior that would be responsive to both context and missing information and that, as such, could be viewed as intelligent behavior. Some people may find it insolent to ascribe or want to ascribe intelligence to machines; after all, intelligence is an attribute coveted by humans because it distinguishes us from other animals and certainly from "the artificial." Instead, we found this posture somewhat *self-defeating*. While the arguments for striving toward a machine intelligence can be made strongly, the convincing experiments to be conducted and the forthright exercises to be undertaken are, to say the least, elusive. Addition-ally discouraging is the fact that results as yet do not display intelligent behavior in any sense. We talk about heterarchies in the structure of knowl-edge, and we do not know how they are formed. We study context recognition, and we do not know how to see it. We look for human intentionalities, and we do not know how they are manifested. The result is that we build mundane gadgets and write primitive computer programs that have one thing in common: all the problems we tackle, and which are described in this volume, are problems with which we can experiment *modestly*, but which in their ultimate form would require a machine intelligence in order to be handled at the same level of accomplishment as by an onlooking human. In brief, every project described in the following chapters does something badly that humans do well. And only in a few instances can we argue with confidence that the particular experiment will lead to managing the broader problem. If we can build a machine that recognizes a pile of cubes to be a pile of cubes, will that help us achieve the recognition of a Swiss chalet in a pasture?

Two Approaches

In 1968 one could read all existing literature in English on the subject of "artificial intelligence" within one month. It now takes about six months. The field is still small and ill defined (as even the name suggests), and can be roughly characterized by two contrasting approaches to achieving a machine intelligence. One approach is to attempt to embed knowledge directly (both facts and methods for manipulating those facts) into a computer, in some sense to capitalize upon the time we, as humans collectively, have taken to learn these "facts." The other route is to understand and to impart to machines the learning process itself (which includes learning how to learn and, more important, the desire to learn) with the notion that machines could subsequently mature in a manner not dissimilar to that of humans.

The first approach is epitomized by the work of Minsky (1968) and his colleagues: "...to make a machine with intelligence is not necessarily to make a machine that learns to be intelligent.... In our present state it will be more productive to try to understand how people understand so well what they are told than to focus exclusively on what they discover for themselves." Or, more recently: "When we, ourselves, learn how to construct the right kind of descriptions, then we can make programs construct and remember them, too, and the problem of 'learning' will vanish" (Minsky and Papert, 1972). A consequence of this attitude is the need for well-formed descriptions of the world or that part of the world with which we choose to deal. Any experiment will be limited by the richness of the descriptive techniques (traditionally hierarchical, more

35

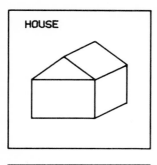

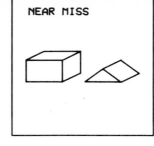

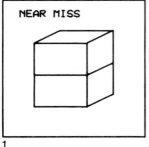

1 The four figures are from Winston (1970). The emphasis is on good description, in this case learned through example.

2 The representation of an internal structure for handling the input of natural language. Illustration from Roger C. Schank, Neil Goldman, Charles J. Rieger III, and Chris Riesbeck, "MARGIE: Memory, Analysis, Response Generation, and Inference in English," *Proceedings of the Third International Joint Conference on Artificial Intelligence* (Stanford University, Stanford, California, August 1973).

1

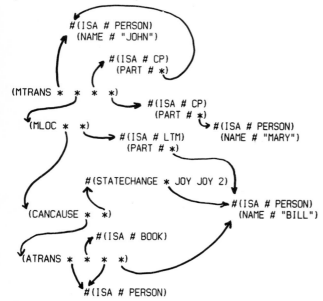

2

recently striving to contrive what have come to be called heterarchical structures). This paradigm for artificial intelligence assumes that the world can be viewed in well-classified parts, decomposable until a manageable chunk is found and solved and recomposable toward a "comprehensive whole."

This approach lends itself to tasks like game playing, theorem proving, and pattern recognition, all of which can be respectively partitioned, for example, into opening, middle, and end games; axioms, definitions, and subtheorems; lines, surfaces, and volumes. The approach is extremely appealing in that it can yield rapid returns, and it avoids the pitfalls of so-called "evolutionary" methods, so often misled by the results of parameter "twitching" found in most reinforcement or self-organizing systems. As an attitude toward artificial intelligence, it also enjoys the facility of single-minded *problem solving*, where the task is well defined (in the descriptive system), the tests for failure and success are well specified, and the "solved problem" has no side effects (Weizenbaum, 1972). The reader should be referred to the recent voluminous definitive work of Newell and Simon (1972). In the context of architecture, let's call this approach puzzle-solving; one should refer here to works of Eastman (1972c and d, for example) and his colleagues.

The second approach tackles learning and self-reference, recognizing that any conversation or interaction between machine and man or between machine and environment is altered by context, in particular by a domain of "relevant" previous experiences. In this approach one tends to experiment with dialogue and with the exploration of what Gordon Pask has called "sprouts,"

close in both time and space. The emphasis is on learning, heavily affected by the nature of the "interface." This does not imply emulating grammar-school drill and practice. What it does imply is a level of machine fumbling, error making, and self-observation (and reference).

This line of experimentation has less credibility today since it has produced very few results. A major problem of this route is that the world must be viewed more directly in its most complex whole, rather than severed into "manageable" chunks. This is because our response to the *complex whole* bears the context in which learning takes place and because intelligence is manifest in that response. Beyond stimulus/response psychology and the tyranny of immediate sensory control, intelligent behavior is exhibited only in cases where that "behavior is controlled by assumptions of the state of the world.... An example...is accepting an ice cream on the evidence of the retinal image which itself is not cold, heavy, sweet, or edible" (R. L. Gregory, 1970).

The two approaches may lead to the same end, but, for the time being, they must be recognized in terms of their effect upon formulating the questions. Loosely, the first approach can be called "problem solving," the second, "problem worrying" (S. Anderson, 1966). From the first, a sample question might be: Given the cryptarithmetic problem: DONALD + GERALD = ROBERT to solve, how can we most expeditiously explore the most likely solutions, rather than the entire 3,628,800 candidate answers? (Simon, 1969; Bartlett, 1958). From the second approach: How do we recognize a gesture or appreciate a joke in the context of a time, a culture, and a history (ranging from previous moments to a lifetime)? The first question is answered by building "search trees," for example, and employing heuristic techniques to avoid examining the prohibitively large number of solutions; one can imagine this taking place without machine learning but with embedded knowledge. The latter question, in contrast, cannot be answered with built-in knowledge; we must know what that knowledge (continually changing) *means* to us.

These two approaches are reflected in architectural applications, which show similarly divergent attitudes toward architecture and architecture aided by computer irrespective of a concern for intelligence per se. The first approach is epitomized by all of Christopher Alexander's work (even the recent patterns) (1968, 1969, in press) and more dramatically by Van Emden's (1970) view of complexity, which deals with subdivisions of tasks that lend themselves to "skillful" solution. Each goal and subgoal is formalized to the extent that one can say in a canonical format: "if C then A because P," where P is a recognized problem in condition C (Alexander calls it context), solvable by action A. The formalization itself requires that the problem P be small and, hopefully, context-less; otherwise the statement degenerates into: "if the meaning I ascribe to C can be maintained (or answered) by A because of *my* recognition of P...." If in contrast the problem is treated wholistically, it can be made manageable by viewing it in low resolution, in some sense squinting, rather than by decomposing it into precise parts. The process of abstraction in design is often used to uncover relationships hidden by the details of reality. Unfortunately, at this time the process of abstraction has examples only in human processes. This is because it requires making infer-

ences, drawing generalities, and making inductions, activities machines conduct badly, activities that may unearth Ps and Cs not discernible by examining the parts.

It is obviously too simplistic for me to propose two well-defined compartments and to stuff a project or an attitude into one or the other. Nevertheless, the two attitudes are conceptually different enough to signal polarities. It is much easier to work on problem solving, decomposition, and if-then-because than to tamper with issues of learning and meaning, processes that are intrinsically human and personal. The latter imposes an almost nihilistic attitude and philosophical despair inasmuch as the problem is so unmanageable and so evasive: there is just no calculus for metaphors.

The tragic aspect of this bipartition is that some communities of researchers have clustered about the poles to the extent that unsharable experiences have led to unsharable goals. In many instances, scientists in quest of understanding meaning and context have simply opted out and quit. The dominant work, both in computer-aided architecture and in artificial intelligence, is still in the first approach.

Language and Meaning

"...Language *is* just a set of format conventions" (Clowes, 1970). This comment is symptomatic of the paradigm that misled many researchers and dollars in the quest for automatic language translating machines. Now, researchers unanimously agree that language translation cannot be viewed as syntactic untangling and restructuring of format, that the syntax of a sentence is only a part, if not the smallest part, of understanding at the very first level. "The second level, semantic analysis, is concerned with the relationships of signs to the things they denote. A third level, pragmatic analysis, deals with the relationships between signs and their interpretation in terms of actions required" (Bobrow, 1968).

The two sentences "My mother cleaned the house" and "The house was cleaned by my mother" are syntactically different statements that would carry the same semantic and pragmatic interpretation, what Chomsky would refer to as the same "deep structure." Moran (1971) makes the observation that Christopher Alexander's "patterns" are similarly "deep structures" in architecture, while signaling the difference between the descriptive nature of natural language and the normative nature of the so-called "pattern language." In this way, we can account for or at least speculate on the fact that two buildings of the same "type" (a notion to be seriously questioned in itself) may look physically different but have a common "structure."

This common structure would be convenient, but unlikely. I propose that present theories of language, whether in artificial intelligence or in the few instances of computer-aided architecture, show no reason to be more productive than the automatic translation efforts of the late 1950s and early 1960s. I believe that the inadequacies result from two failures: (1) our lack of understanding of *meaning* and our insistence on searching for it in the language itself; (2) our treatment of language from the point of view of an external observer overseeing a conversation (usually through a single channel).

Why does a child understand spoken language so much sooner than he can speak it? Similarly, why is it so much easier to understand a foreign language than to speak it? The answer resides with where you get your information—from the highly self-referent context at hand. My own child at the age of one and a half understood perfectly well "Do you want to brush your teeth?" at 8:30 A.M., when he saw me wrapped in a towel after a shower. At 8:30 P.M., on my return from work, if I greeted him at the door with the same phrase, he would not know what I was talking about. Granted it is necessary to know some of the signs and symbols, the nouns and verbs, but the context at hand as defined by *both* the situation and his previous experiences is the prime conveyer of meaning. This is less true in discussing an algebra problem and more true in recounting a funny experience.

Avery Johnson (1970) provides a very telling scale for dialogue. His parameter is simply the distance in time and/or space of the "referent." At the one extreme is the telegram. At the other end is lovemaking, where "the referent is the participants themselves and their relation to each other." Computer scientists tend to stay at the very high end, benefiting from the fact that all definitions can be made a priori and symbolically; this is a

1

Love-making
Mother & Child
Physiotherapy

IMMEDIATE

2

Shared toys
"Hands-on
instruction"
Dual Controls

COMMUNAL

3

Environ-
mental
controls

ADJACENT

4

Air Traffic Control
Blackboard
Computer Graphics:
(Tablet, Light-Pen)

METAPHORICAL

5

Programming
Speech
Telegraph

SYMBOLIC

A scale of dialogue from Avery Johnson, "Dialogue and the Exploration of Context: Properties of an Adequate Interface" (dated 1970, unpublished). The scale moves from one extreme where the referent is common to both parties in time and space to the other extreme where it is remote and must be referenced symbolically. Figures drawn by and courtesy of Avery Johnson.

premise of the first approach. As you move down the scale, however, definitions become more and more vulnerable to situation and happenstance and dependent upon you and your experiences. Also, as you move down the scale, language is forced to become less singular in medium, demanding a plurality of gestures, facial expressions, intonations, groans, and the like. At the very bottom, the word becomes almost useless.

It has been suggested that pictures form a two-dimensional language (Narasimhan, 1970) in contrast to the one-dimensional aspect of spoken language. Can architecture be viewed as a three-dimensional language? If so, does it not follow that it too might be subject to contextual variations? Rather than viewing the built environment as an efficient corpus of concrete, steel, and wood, let us consider it to be a language somewhere in the middle of Avery Johnson's scale. This would imply that my behavior within the built environment and the meaning I attach to that environment are as important as (I really believe more important than) the physical thing itself.

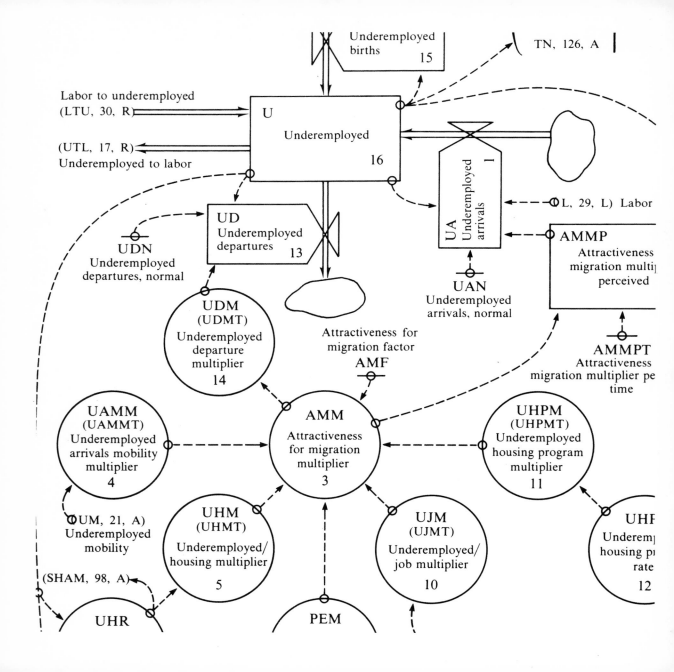

Section of Jay Forrester's
model of the "underemployed
sector" (Forrester, 1969b,
p. 134)

Models and Modeling

A road map is a model that can be queried to aid
in getting from point A to B (assuming they are on
the map). More literally, clay, styrofoam, wood,
and cardboard are used to build physical models
of the built environment to aid the pre-experience
of some aspects of that environment. Only recently, with the advent of computers, has it become
practicable to model human behavior (as well as
physical states) in intellectual activities. As such,
computer modeling has become extremely important to (1) test hypotheses and (2) simulate events.
In *each* case, it is necessary to *describe* some
states and some transitions. It is precisely the
description process that can both legitimize and
confuse the modeling procedure. It is for this
reason that I dwell upon some aspects of models
and associated attitudes.

In computer circles and jargon, modeling suffers
from being a procedure distorted (semantically
and pragmatically) by the individual backgrounds
of researchers. In some sense, any computer
program we write or any thought we may have is a
model. Some contend that procedures, algo-
rithms, heuristics, and so on, must be combined
in strict ways in order to qualify legitimately as a
model. I contend, however, that more important
than what modeling is and what it is not are the
consequences of alternative approaches to modeling, be it the modeling of the thinking process or
the modeling of the growth of cities.

There exist three general classes of models; each
contains very particular biases toward how we
observe that slice of the world and how we
represent it. To facilitate discussion, I am calling
the three models aggregate, essence, and reality.

43

The aggregate model is the most common. It is epitomized in the family of *Dynamics* (*Industrial*, *Urban*, and *World*; Forrester, 1961a, 1969b, 1972), which I mention as an example because it has been implemented with great care and expertise. However, the aggregate model is also found frequently in game playing, in picture processing and recognition, and in most exercises of artificial intelligence. The general characteristic of the aggregate model is the decomposition of events to be modeled into many unambiguous causalities, using human insights and expertise to achieve the proper compartmentalization. *Proper*, in this case, is defined as the most amenable (sometimes easiest to program) trade-off between the number of subprocesses and the number of linkages between them. On the one hand, one strives for an autonomy of parts with modest intercommunication. At the same time, one would like each submodel, in effect, to be as small as possible to ensure easy inspection (later) and conceptual clarity and precision (now).

The benefits of the aggregate model accrue usually in the making of it, rather than in its deployment. This is because it is necessary to scrutinize and to assimilate a procedure (like playing chess or planning fiscal policies) to such an extent that, irrespective of the resulting model, we end up knowing something more about the procedure itself. In the case of a well-formed aggregate model, fascinating results can be achieved, to the extent that our perception of the event itself is altered, and we must return to redesign or append the model to incorporate the new insight. This is good. In some way it is a Newtonian view in that the pieces that go together to compose the model can be individually contemplated, understood, and in the dilemma of

obvious (or not-so-obvious) failures, repaired. For example, if Forrester finds that the "underemployed/job multiplier" is forcing an unreasonable composite "attractiveness" in his urban system, he can simply twiddle the UJM parameter until the results match his views and, at the same time, map themselves faithfully into a general consensus of history.

The vulnerability of the aggregate model is twofold: (1) because it is at the mercy of the expertise of its designers, it can be no better than they; (2) it is prejudiced by what has and has not been included, intentionally or unintentionally. For example, Forrester's model for urban dynamics includes no suburbs, direct costs for programs have no effect on the tax rate, and the land area is fixed, supporting a constant density of construction. There is always the chance that these subprocesses, just as an example, could be added and some of Forrester's subprocesses left out, such that contrary results could be "proved." In other words, while we have learned a great deal from making the model, it is true that, in this kind of application (simulation), we can arrange matters to yield *any* result (with the inflated and injurious credibility ascribed to computers).

The essence model, on the other hand, makes no attempt to account for the whole through detail. It is quite specifically an abstraction, one that permits us to exercise more global processes in terms of our interpretations of their salient features. Models of the design process are often of this kind, the caricature being the homely analyze-synthesize-test model. While one can argue that they exist as essence models only because we do not know as much about the design process as we do about urban dynamics, I believe much stronger arguments lie in (1) the scope of the event, (2) the level of interactions with the "real world," and (3) the resolution or gain of observation. In the previously mentioned example of simulating urban dynamics, the problem was well founded in the sense that the inputs are data or measurements supplied or recorded in well-defined units. In contrast, models of the design process, for example, usually contain little boxes like tenant needs, political contingencies, environmental demands. These are parameters that cannot be predicted or measured unequivocally.

At first glance, the essence model appears to be a weak aggregate model. On further inspection, the appropriate analogue might be the floor plan (aggregate) versus the diagram (essence). As with the diagram, the essence model affords the opportunity to examine particular aspects of the whole at a level of abstraction necessary to allow general conclusions. As in the case of the second approach to artificial intelligence, the essence model loses its flamboyance in the problems of implementation because of the continual doubt that such-and-such is indeed a legitimate abstraction that captures the essence. Also, it is unclear to me how you build an essence model. Take the example of modeling the workings of and makings of a car. I can see how to describe it (ie: model it) in terms of parts and pieces, like axles and wheels, but I cannot see how to embody the essence of carness such that the adjacent diagram can be recognized as a car. A two-and-a-half-year-old child can recognize it! What kind of model does he have?

The last category of models skirts many of these issues in that the underlying scheme is: Rather than model a chunk of the world, use that chunk of the world for a model of itself. In other words, instead of modeling a city, use the city as a model of itself. The architectural counterpart is, in some sense, found in the use of full-scale models. In the following chapter, an experiment in "sketch recognition" will describe one kind of data structure that stores a positional representation of what lines were applied to paper. Another experiment, a "computer eye," looks at the drawing literally over the person's shoulder, that is, performs a redundant task. In the one case we have to construct a scheme for representing that slice of the world (piece of paper with lines); in the other case we use it directly.

This kind of model may appear to be simply a play on words. However, it acknowledges a device that we, as humans, use all the time in our daily activities and rarely consider viable for machines. That is using the world as memory. It allows us to attach whatever symbols we wish, apply whatever metaphors we like, and ascribe very personal meanings. In modeling and describing the world, computer scientists generally discount using parts of the world as memory and as models (if we can still call them that). One exception can be found in Feigenbaum (1963): "It is easier and cheaper to build a hardware robot to extract what information it needs from the real world than to organize and store a useful model. Crudely put, the SRI (Stanford Research Institute) group's argument is that the most economic and efficient store of information about the real world is the real world itself."

2

1

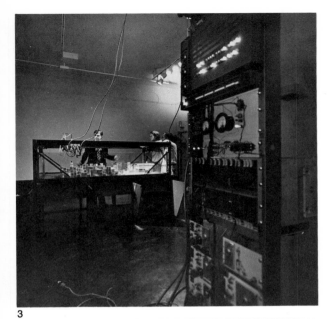

1 SEEK, part of the SOFTWARE exhibit at the Jewish Museum, New York, September 16–November 8, 1970. Its purpose was to show how a machine handled a mismatch between its model of the world and the real world—in this case five hundred two-inch metal-plated cubes. The mismatch was created by a colony of gerbils whose activity constantly disturbed the strictly rectilinear arrangement called for by the machine's model.

2 Gerbils were selected for their curiosity. The plastic box straightened blocks corner straightened blocks when SEEK discovered them to be crooked. A block slightly askew would be realigned. One substantially dislocated would be placed (straight, of course) in the new position, on the assumption that the gerbils wanted it there. The outcome was a constantly changing architecture that reflected the way the little animals used the place.

3 Steven Gregory and Museum Director Carl Katz (on the right) with the author on opening night

4 Opening night

3

4

Linkages with the Real World

Could an educated porpoise understand *Gone with the Wind*?

For a computer to acquire intelligence will it have to look like me, be about six feet tall, have two arms, two eyes, and an array of humanlike apparatus? The question sounds ridiculous. Furthermore, answers are impeded by two irrevocable conditions (at this time in history): (1) very few people (including you most probably) really and truly believe that machines someday might exhibit an intelligence equal to or greater than ours; (2) the question is too easily written off as sloppy romanticism and anthropomorphism.

I believe that the question is not ludicrous; on the contrary, it is one of the cruxes of the dilemma in which many of us find ourselves. It is clear that computers need a wide variety of sensory channels and a host of effectors in order to witness and manipulate "aspects" of the world, particularly those we use daily in our metaphors. However, to date, computers are by far the most sensory-deprived "intellectual engines." They are offered the richness and variety of telegraphese, with minor exceptions like computer graphics and a limited machine vision.

It is so obvious that our interfaces, that is, our bodies, are intimately related to learning and to how we learn, that one point of departure in artificial intelligence is to concentrate specifically on the interfaces. In the late sixties The Architecture Machine Group did just that, focusing upon linkages with the real world, specifically those that gave machines access to the physical aspects of the world. I cited in "The Semantics of Architecture Machines" (1970c) three goals for computers:

"(1) We want our machine partners to have the potential of perceiving those aspects of the physical environment that would become biased or incomplete when transmitted through other modes (such as a verbal description). (2) We want machines to be able to solicit information directly from the real world on the initiative of internal computations, rather than depend upon the intervention of a human designer and his conscious or subconscious interpretations of that information. (3) We want computers to be able to witness and handle concepts and relationships (and even experiences) that are concerned with those environmental qualities that human designers understand and handle through metaphors and symbols (which in turn are established from meanings gained through many sensing-effecting channels)."

The goals may be noble, and they may help to clarify the nature of the necessary experimentation. However, much in the same way as I have suggested that the puzzle-solving approach to artificial intelligence does not face squarely the issues of intelligence, playing with sensors and effectors similarly allows one to bide time, to skirt many issues, and possibly to avoid attaining any end. In some sense, we were driven by a blind faith that somehow these appendages would magically fall into place: "Our experiments are based on the hope that if machines are given the faculty for sophisticated interactions with the real world (people, places, pictures, and so forth), they can learn to develop their own design methods and methodologies, perhaps better than our own" (Negroponte 1970c and d).

The illustrations on the following pages depict some experimentation that has taken place over the past few years; they are limited to those experiments not described at greater length in the following chapters. In general, you will notice two classes of experimentation: high-resolution and low-resolution devices. What can you resolve with sixteen photocells? What can you recognize with a million addressable points?

These questions provide for interesting development of and experimentation with handsome gadgets. The initial question, however, remains unanswered. Does a machine have to possess a body like my own and be able to experience personally behaviors like my own in order to share in what *we* call intelligent behavior? While it may seem absurd, I believe the answer is *yes*.

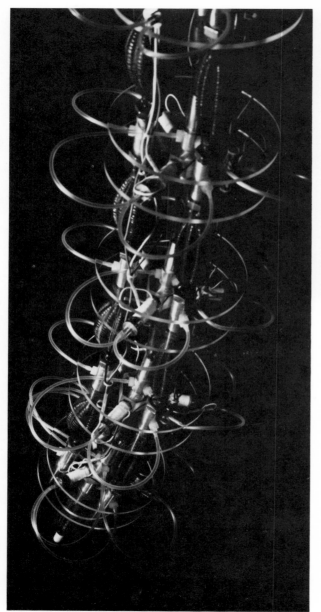

2

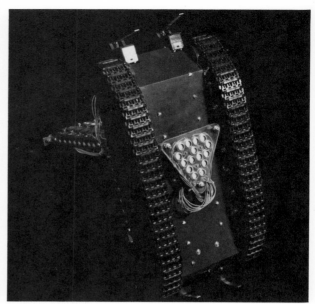

1

3

1 ARM, an exercise in transforming one coordinate system into another. The four groups of three pneumatic muscles allowed for small lateral displacements, barely enough to draw a capital A.

2 The belly of a toy tank called GROPE. As one of the earlier experiments in low-resolution machine vision, it holds an important place in Architecture Machine memorabilia.

3 A general-purpose interface that allowed 24-digital input, 16-digital output, and 16 channels of analogue input and output. This served as the interface between FORTRAN programs and student-built gadgetry.

4 A 16-photocell eye with 100mm lens

4

2 Computer Graphics

Introduction by Steven Coons

Computer graphics began some time before 1960, but it was Ivan Sutherland who first created a computer graphics system, and his system did exhibit some rudimentary aspects of intelligence. Unfortunately, almost everyone who followed Sutherland (including Sutherland himself, according to Negroponte) failed to see the central issue, and even today, some twelve years later, most computer graphics systems provide only an idiot-slave model of a fast draftsman who doesn't eat.

Sutherland's SKETCHPAD made modest but seemingly intelligent responses to the (graphical) actions of its human companion. It was capable of turning a crudely drawn quadrilateral into a perfect rectangle; it was capable of fitting together various separate objects into a composite pattern, even though the process might involve modification of the sizes, shapes, and orientations of the separate objects. In such an operation it was also capable of adhering to rules (constraints) about permissible and forbidden actions. In some of the situations the constraints made it impossible to carry out the scheme. In such cases the computer would "do its best" to satisfy the constraints while holding their violations to a minimum. In other cases the defining constraints might be insufficient to yield a unique result. In most conventional computer programming, such an insufficiency (such as lack of data, for instance) causes the program to halt without an answer. But in SKETCHPAD the computer in a sense supplied its own missing information and proceeded to give *some* result. After that, its human companion could accept the result or add more constraints to achieve a modification. SKETCHPAD had other capabilities like these, and this repertoire made it possible for the user to carry on a conversation with the machine that was, at least at a first level, intelligent. The machine didn't behave like a *complete* idiot; within its powers it took appropriate action.

Many, if not most, conventional computer programs seem constructed at what might be called the *level of specifics*. Much of SKETCHPAD was constructed at the *level of principles* (or generalizations). Most computers work at the first level; intelligent beings work at the second level.

Suppose I want an assistant (the intelligent machine) to find the square root of a number. It would be nice if I could point out to the machine that when the divisor and quotient of a number are equal, the divisor *is* the square root and have the machine take it from there. But perhaps that's asking too much (even for a human intelligence). But I could give one more hint: The square root of a number lies *somewhere* between an arbitrary divisor and the quotient. Now it would be nice if the computer could use this remark to construct its own algorithm for solution. Of course, no existing computer system can exhibit this kind of intelligence, which is at the level of principles, for we customarily write a program at the level of specifics for the idiot-slave that describes in complete detail every step to be taken and scrupulously takes into account every possible circumstance that could occur that would make the program fail. Sometimes in a complicated program it is impossible to predict that some combination of circumstances will cause failure, and then the machine is of very little help. It is possible that some existing programs have "bugs" that have never been detected because the "failure set" of simultaneous circumstances has never happened to occur.

The central issue seems to be how to endow the machine with that undefinable capability called "understanding." The evidence of "understanding" in humans as well as machines is some intelligent response that is "meaningful" and pertinent, although not necessarily "right." I am reminded of a child's explanation of the wind. His theory was that the trees waved their leaves and caused the wind. However "wrong" this is, it would be wonderful to have a machine intelligent enough to invent such an essentially logical idea.

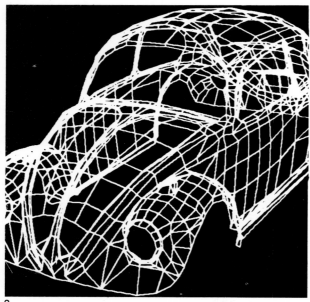

 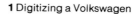

1 Digitizing a Volkswagen

2 Displaying the input as a connection of data points

3 Filling in the surfaces

4 Smoothing the surfaces. Illustrations courtesy of Ivan Sutherland and the University of Utah, Department of Computer Science.

On Seeing and Making Pictures

Steve Coons is the father of computer graphics. When I asked him to write the preceding introduction, I hinted that he should include a confession with respect to the disparity between his and his colleagues' early goals (as written) and experiments in their pioneering graphical systems. My purpose was to underscore some myths that I believe have deterred the progress toward making it possible to deal with computers in a congenial manner. While computer graphics has captured the fancy of brilliant scientists, it has enjoyed little application and the picture-making part of computer graphics has obscured some deeper issues.

If we look at the history of computer graphics we first find that it began in the early sixties exactly in parallel with another very important technological jump, time sharing. At M.I.T., time sharing was being developed at Project MAC, and computer graphics was being developed at Lincoln Laboratory, twenty miles away. Each effort was being conducted in ignorance of the other; both were concerned with *interaction*. Time sharing was aimed at producing a ubiquitous modality of interaction by multiplexing a large number of terminals off one big machine in such a way that each user could *interact* with his program at his leisure in a conversational manner and with the illusion of having a powerful and devoted computer at his service. Computer graphics, meanwhile, was striving to afford a new kind of interaction, one with pictures, one which could allow the user to discuss matters previously unmanageable by the interface, that is, the terminal or console facilities. The consequences of these simultaneous but independent efforts have been that (1) time sharing has been a poor host to graphics and (2) graphics has been exercised for the most part in an old-fashioned, big-machine paradigm.

The early papers about man-machine interaction (for example, Coons, 1963; T. Johnson, 1963; Sutherland, 1963) talked at great length about the potentials of graphical notations for providing a means for negotiating vague ideas with computers, notations that would not demand well-specified, syntactically exact statements. They also suggested that as a consequence of this looseness, of forming the problem as well as the solution in conversation with a computer, computers would provide a previously unseen *partnership*. The term "man-machine partnership" was proliferated and expounded, but I do not believe Coons, Johnson, or Sutherland took the term seriously. They were not proposing a partnership in those early days. Their paradigm was closer to a master-slave relationship, except that now the slave could draw.

This may explain why very little progress has been made on *interactive* graphics since the original fanfare and why most developments have been in making more realistic pictures and efficient data structures to describe them. A recent book on interactive graphics (Newman and Sproull, 1973) epitomizes my point. Very little work has focused upon the graphical abstractions and nebulous interactions commonly found in human discourse accompanied by graphics. The result is that picture making by computer has in fact not improved the man-machine partnership to any great extent. Dynamic graph making is probably the only widespread application of computer graphics that even begins to capitalize upon simple but powerful aspects of interactive

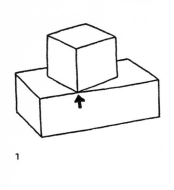

1

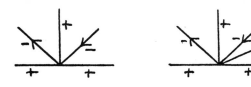

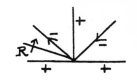

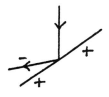

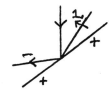

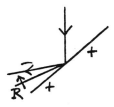

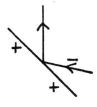

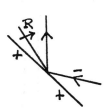

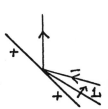

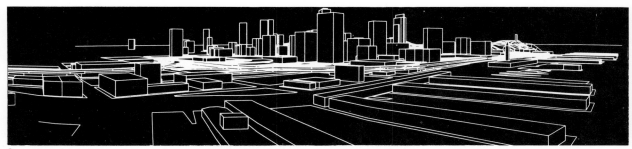

2

visual information. In the future we might see formidable application in the simulation technologies (Bazjanac, 1973).

The maneuvers necessary to get visual information into a machine are more difficult than those required to get it out. As a result, most graphic presentations are the result of internal computations or previously digitized input, rather than the result of a seeing or drawing device. (Art Paradis, President of Dynamic Graphics, Inc., calls this "computational graphics.") Most architectural applications are not graphical because it is so difficult to describe a building when one is forced to wait until the design is advanced enough to *amortize* the effort. The problem is somewhat paradoxical, because the longer one waits, the more difficult the "digitizing" becomes. It would behoove us to have an onlooking machine follow a design from the very early stages of conception to working drawings, with no explicit demarcation of "now we will put it into the machine." It does not mean that every designer must sit in front of one of these uncomfortable cathode-ray tubes. Why not have a machine look over your shoulder?

As far as I am concerned, machine vision and computer graphics are the same subject even though they have been so far relegated to totally separate groups of researchers in computer science. Machine vision has been the focus of a great deal of artificial intelligence work, but, like work in graphics, it has concentrated on realism and data structuring; the predominant work is in the decomposition of scenes into categorizable lines, planes, and volumes, most recently found in Waltz (1972). Very little work has been done on the recognition of abstractions and the consideration of vision as an inference-making behavior rather than simply as a data collection procedure. For example: How do we infer information about pictures? When does a circle with two triangles at one o'clock and eleven o'clock look like the head of a cat? These questions are in contrast to the goals defined by questions like: Can we see a French poodle on a shaggy rug or recognize a screwdriver on the surface of the moon?

To a member of a catless society *without catlike animals*, our diagrammatic cat might look like a monster. To a two-year-old child from Rome it will look like a cat with far less detail, because he has witnessed and understood "catness" in terms of salient and general features that can be characterized by abstractions. The child has seen cats from many attitudes and has developed what S. A. Gregory (1971) calls a "fiction" from which he can draw hypotheses (predictions) that it is or it is not a cat. Or, more appropriately stated in terms of picture making and recognition: *it is meant to be or it is not meant to be a cat.*

Intentionalities

I propose that a common oversight in the computer recognition and generation of visual material is the disregard for the intentions of the image. What I *mean* to say is more important than what I actually say. The intimacy of a dialogue can be in some sense measured by the ability of each person to recognize the intentions of the other. For example, in cases where people are not well acquainted and from different cultures, speaking to each other can become a profession (diplomacy) where it is very necessary to say exactly what is meant and to be well trained at understanding what is meant.

With two good friends, codesigners, husband and wife, this is not true. A well-developed working relationship is in fact characterized by one party's leaving a great deal of information for the other party to infer and assuming it will be inferred correctly. As Oliver Selfridge puts it, an intimate, interactive conversation is, in some sense, the lack of it.

Unfortunately, intentions can only be recognized in context, that evasive and omnipresent condition. But, in many cases, even the crudest definition of context (like "now we are going to talk about structures in architecture") can help what Kaneff (1970) has titled The Picture Language Machine. If you are sketching a plan and I know you are sketching a plan, even though some lines might replicate the schematic cat, I will do my best to assign to the lines a projective geometry or diagrammatic meaning associated with the built environment. However, if I know you are a lover of cats, there might be room (at some point) for equivocation, to the extent that I might have to ask, "Do you mean...?" There is nothing wrong with asking, but note that the need for asking is not necessarily a result of the level of detail, abstraction, or diagrammatic scribbling. The fact that most realistic rendering demands the same inference making and causes the same ambiguities is shown by trompe l'oeil painting and Ames experiments in the psychology of perception.

To make inferences about a statement requires a knowledge of the world. To make an inference about the intention of a statement requires some knowledge of the person making it. For me to begin to make inferences about your intentionalities, except at the very crudest level (of contradictions, slips of the tongue, mispronunciations, etc.), requires that I know you (even as slightly as knowing that you are American). That is, I need a model of you. Following some work with Gordon Pask, we proposed in "HUNCH—An Experiment in Sketch Recognition" (Negroponte, Groisser, and Taggart, 1972) that man-computer interactions should be supported by three levels of model. From the computer's point of view, these include: (1) its model of you, (2) its model of your model of it, and (3) its model of your model of its model of you.

The first level is a straightforward model of the user, ranging from his habits and mannerisms in sketching, for example, to his attitudes toward architecture. This model is continually exercised as a prediction device and supplier of missing information. Its validity is easily measured and tested in terms of the closeness of fit between the anticipated and the actual intention as manifest at some increment of time later (a millisecond, an hour, a year). Notice that in no sense can such a model be fail-safe; in fact, the very idea of fail-safeness itself is the wrong attitude toward the problem. In terms of implementation this model would be passive (and hence exhibit no inept behavior) at the beginning. After some period of time (with people this varies from personality to personality), this model is deployed to venture guesses and would inevitably make errors. Consider the process we go through in getting to "know" somebody. You will remember stages of attempting to make no predictions, times of wrong second-guessing, and later periods of "knowing" him or her. This is dramatically amplified if the other person is from another culture, ill-versed in your language.

The next level of model is the *computer's model of your model of it.* This is critical to inference making because one tends to leave implicit only those issues that one *assumes* the other party will understand (implicitly). This model grows out of a felicity of matches between the inferred information and the intended information. If, for example, the computer correctly assumes that you meant "door within the wall," it can draw the added inference that you *assumed* it would. Note that this model can only grow out of correct matches.

The last level of model may appear overly circuitous and somewhat fickle; however, it has unexplored (to my knowledge) implications for learning. It is the *computer's model of the user's model of its model of him.* In human relations, what I think you think that I think of you is as important as (and can be more important than) what I really think of you. I suspect that forthcoming research will reveal that this model is crucial to learning about people on a person-to-person level. This is because a deep acquaintance can

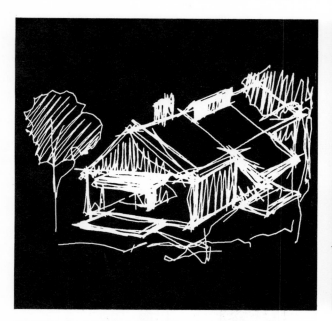

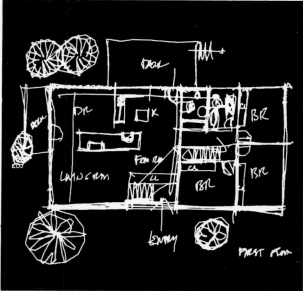

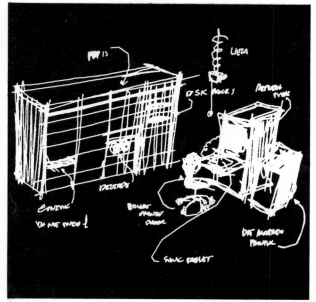

1

2

be described as a state of convergence between
this third level of model and the first. When your
model of my model of your model of me is almost
a replica of your model of me, we can say that you
know me; in terms of a human relationship, that
we have reached a level of confidence and trust.

Sketch Recognition

In a shocking and almost silly interview with Max Jacobson, Christopher Alexander (1971a, 1971b) recounted the following story:

"There was a conference which I was invited to a few months ago where computer graphics were being discussed as one item and I was arguing very strongly against computer graphics simply because of the frame of mind that you need to be in to create a good building. Are you at peace with yourself? Are you thinking about smell and touch, and what happens when people are walking about in a place? But particularly, are you at peace with yourself? All of that is completely disturbed by the pretentiousness, insistence and complicatedness of computer graphics and all the allied techniques. So my final objection to that and to other types of methodology is that they actually prevent you from being in the right state of mind to do the design, quite apart from the question of whether they help in a sort of technical sense, which, as I said, I don't think they do."

While I find notions of a "frame of mind...to create a good building" extremely distasteful (and paternalistic), I wholeheartedly admit that computer graphics is guilty of great complication and noise. In general, computer graphics research has been totally self-serving, aptly fitting Weizenbaum's (1972) analogy: "It is rather like an island economy in which the natives make a living by taking in each other's laundry."

The following section describes a specific experiment in computer graphics, one with which Alexander might someday be at ease: sketch recognition. The effort is particularly exciting (to me) because it allows for a wide variety of approaches (some contradictory), modestly executable, with the acknowledgment that the limiting case—a computer that can recognize any hand-drawn sketch with the same reliability as an onlooking human—will require a machine intelligence. The following pages report upon the salient characteristics of an actual computer program, but most of the major issues are far broader than the experience *can* admit. The reader should seriously wonder (as we continually do), If drawing is a two-dimensional language, does sketching have a syntax and semantics? Is any of HUNCH more than the syntactical processing of a hand drawing?

The founding work in computer graphics was called SKETCHPAD (Sutherland, 1963). While this was an effective name, in some way it polluted the notion of "sketching" in any sense of the word. In contrast to SKETCHPAD, "We view the problem of sketching as the step-by-step resolution of the mismatch between the user's intentions (of which he himself may not be aware) and his graphical articulations. In a design context, the convergence to a match between the meaning and the graphical statement of that meaning is complicated by continually changing intentions that result from the user's viewing his own graphical statements" (Negroponte, Groisser, and Taggart, 1972). Sketching can be considered both as a form of communicating with oneself (introspection) and as a form of communicating with others (presentation). In the first case the machine is holding the same pencil, eavesdropping, so to speak. In the second case you are sharing a piece of paper with the machine, and both of you are drawing on the same sheet, each with your own stylus. In both instances memory is the drawing

1 Examples of drawings made on the Architecture Machine as part of the so-called Cavanaugh experiment, designed to determine personalized drawing habits. Each figure is a computer display of every tenth point recorded by the data tablet.

2 The Sylvania data tablet

be described as a state of convergence between this third level of model and the first. When your model of my model of your model of me is almost a replica of your model of me, we can say that you know me; in terms of a human relationship, that we have reached a level of confidence and trust.

Sketch Recognition

In a shocking and almost silly interview with Max Jacobson, Christopher Alexander (1971a, 1971b) recounted the following story:

"There was a conference which I was invited to a few months ago where computer graphics were being discussed as one item and I was arguing very strongly against computer graphics simply because of the frame of mind that you need to be in to create a good building. Are you at peace with yourself? Are you thinking about smell and touch, and what happens when people are walking about in a place? But particularly, are you at peace with yourself? All of that is completely disturbed by the pretentiousness, insistence and complicatedness of computer graphics and all the allied techniques. So my final objection to that and to other types of methodology is that they actually prevent you from being in the right state of mind to do the design, quite apart from the question of whether they help in a sort of technical sense, which, as I said, I don't think they do."

While I find notions of a "frame of mind...to *create a good building*" extremely distasteful (and paternalistic), I wholeheartedly admit that computer graphics is guilty of great complication and noise. In general, computer graphics research has been totally self-serving, aptly fitting Weizenbaum's (1972) analogy: "It is rather like an island economy in which the natives make a living by taking in each other's laundry."

The following section describes a specific experiment in computer graphics, one with which Alexander might someday be at ease: sketch recognition. The effort is particularly exciting (to me) because it allows for a wide variety of approaches (some contradictory), modestly executable, with the acknowledgment that the limiting case—a computer that can recognize any hand-drawn sketch with the same reliability as an onlooking human—will require a machine intelligence. The following pages report upon the salient characteristics of an actual computer program, but most of the major issues are far broader than the experience *can* admit. The reader should seriously wonder (as we continually do), If drawing is a two-dimensional language, does sketching have a syntax and semantics? Is any of HUNCH more than the syntactical processing of a hand drawing?

The founding work in computer graphics was called SKETCHPAD (Sutherland, 1963). While this was an effective name, in some way it polluted the notion of "sketching" in any sense of the word. In contrast to SKETCHPAD, "We view the problem of sketching as the step-by-step resolution of the mismatch between the user's intentions (of which he himself may not be aware) and his graphical articulations. In a design context, the convergence to a match between the meaning and the graphical statement of that meaning is complicated by continually changing intentions that result from the user's viewing his own graphical statements" (Negroponte, Groisser, and Taggart, 1972). Sketching can be considered both as a form of communicating with oneself (introspection) and as a form of communicating with others (presentation). In the first case the machine is holding the same pencil, eavesdropping, so to speak. In the second case you are sharing a piece of paper with the machine, and both of you are drawing on the same sheet, each with your own stylus. In both instances memory is the drawing medium and the vehicle for looping into the physical world.

I am not suggesting that the heart magically tells the wrist something that embellishes a concept passing from mind to medium. I am proposing that a nebulous idea is characterized by not knowing when you begin a sentence exactly what you are going to say at the end. Furthermore, the final "phrases" are in fact flavored (for better or for worse) by my initial tack and my, your, or the computer's reaction to it. Consequently, in an act like sketching, the graphical nature of the drawing (that is, the wobbliness of lines, the collections of overtracings, and the darkness of inscriptions) have important meanings, meanings that must not be, but are, for the most part, overlooked in computer graphics. "A straight line 'sketch' on a cathode-ray tube could trigger an aura of completeness injurious to the designer as well as antagonistic to the design" (Negroponte, 1970a).

In contrast to most graphical systems, we have built a sketch recognition system called HUNCH that faithfully records wobbly lines and crooked corners in anticipation of drawing high-level inferences about...! The goal of HUNCH is to allow a user to be as graphically freewheeling, equivocal, and inaccurate as he would be with a human partner; thus the system is compatible with any degree of formalization of the user's own thoughts. Unlike the SKETCHPAD paradigm, which is a rubber-band pointing-and-tracking vernacular, HUNCH takes in every nick and bump, storing a voluminous history of your tracings on both magnetic tape and storage tube. HUNCH is not looking at the sketch as much as it is looking at you sketching; it is dealing with the verb rather than the noun. It behaves like a person *watching*

you sketch, seeing lines grow, and saying nothing until asked or triggered by a conflict recognized at a higher level of application.

Unlike a completed sketch, that is, a two-dimensional representation, what I have just described is so far one dimensional. In our specific experiments, the information is recorded serially at the rate of 200 X, Y, and limited Z coordinates per second. This coordinate information is augmented by measurements of pressure upon the stylus, from zero to fifty ounces. In addition to position and pressure the method of reporting X, Y, Z (that is, a continuous updating 200 times per second) is in fact a built-in form of *clock*, which provides the added and crucial features of speed and acceleration. At this writing, position and pressure (and derived speeds and accelerations) are the only recorded data; one can imagine measuring how hard the sketcher is squeezing the pen or taking his galvanic skin resistance.

Either on-line or upon command, HUNCH performs certain transformations on the stream of data and then examines it for the purpose of recognizing your intentions at three levels: (1) what you meant graphically, in two dimensions; (2) what you meant physically, in three dimensions; and (3) what you meant architecturally. Each category is progressively more difficult. They range from recognizing a square, to recognizing a cube, to being a new brutalist.

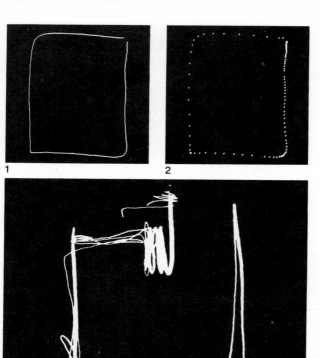

1 A square drawn from upper right

2 A representation of the points sampled at a constant rate. Note the bunching at corners and the relatively regular spacing in the rounded-off corner.

3 A scribble showing the measure of pressure in terms of line thickness. The display of line width is achieved by varying the focus control of a storage tube as a function of pressure (between 0 and 50 ounces) sensed by a tiny load cell in the stylus.

Graphical Intentions

This section describes the most primitive level of recognition, that which involves graphical intentions at the level of finding lines, corners, and two-dimensional geometric properties. For humans to "infer" these intentions is so easy and apparently uncontrived that it is difficult to convey the enormity of the computing task without embarking on a technical treatise of programming techniques. One major difference between the computer's problem and ours is that the computer is given the graphical information as a stream of points (indeed closely spaced but discrete) and does not "see" them as lines without some initial assumption making. Furthermore, it is forced to deal with the image sequentially. A revealing game is to take any line drawing and ask somebody to recognize what is depicted by viewing the drawing only through a small hole in an overlayed sheet that can be freely moved about (thus always hiding the whole picture except for what is seen through the hole). This is how a computer treats the image.

In a similar manner, HUNCH proceeds to construct two representations of the sketch while the user is drawing it, a one-dimensional data structure and a two-dimensional data structure. The first is a faithful record of how the drawing was created in terms of speeds, accelerations, pressures upon the pen (see adjacent illustration). The second is a two-dimensional bit map that is, in effect, a surrogate piece of paper. The two structures represent (redundantly) the original sketch, and they are kept intact at all times. All subsequent structures, either sequential or positional, are maintained above and beyond these original descriptions. They may be moved, manipulated, destroyed, updated, or reproduced forever. In contrast, the original sketch, as represented sequentially and positionally, is maintained as a faithful icon acting like the "real world" to which we can always return for another look. The bit map may be replaced by a vision system that looks at the sheet of paper, avoiding the need for surrogate paper. Another alternative under study is a raster scan display with a bit-per-point semiconductor memory, where the picture memory and display medium are one and the same.

The process of recognizing graphical intentions shifts between drawing evidence from one structure or the other. At present, it includes seven kinds of operations, each of which relies to different degrees on the two structures. The following paragraphs describe specific transformations in their most usual, but not necessary, order. Even though they are described as specific transformations with known inputs, it is usually the case that *several* guesses must be made and that several candidate resolutions must be carried through, building up evidence for and against. All the transformations are ridden with contingencies that cannot be handled in a rote fashion that puts all of one's faith in one guess.

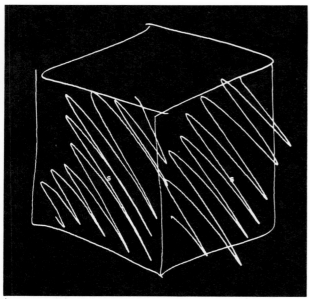

1 Cube with squiggles found on the fly, noted by the *S*s

2 A seven-point representation of the machine's guess at what the user meant. This drawing has 150,000 bits of raw data.

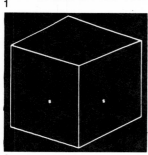

Diagrams

When one sketches, it is natural to intermingle elements that have a projective geometry interpretation (the intersection of planes, limiting contours, demarcations of patterns, etc.) with those that have a diagrammatic intent (symbols, arrows, letters of the alphabet, figures, etc.). Consequently, one of the initial passes at recognition is to separate the diagrammatic elements from the projective elements. There is no foolproof way of distinguishing, for example, arrowheads from rooftops. In some cases it is necessary to leave the ambiguity for a future operation to stumble upon and untangle with "higher-order" evidence.

Diagrams fall into two classes: those recognizable by shape and those distinguishable by gesture. An arrow, for example, has a distinctive topology and can be defined in the jargon of line types and joints. A squiggle, on the other hand, is a hand movement, meaning, for example, either shading or "to be erased." The recognition of the arrow is achieved primarily with positional data, whereas the squiggle is more easily found in the sequential stream, in terms of jerking hand motions. The adjacent illustrations depict the sort of weeding out that takes place at this stage. Note that the "positional symbols" are viewed at different grains (a form of zooming), and the squiggles are interpreted as "S's"— shading—or "rub out" commands (see adjacent figures).

Data Compression

Consider that at 200 coordinates per second a ten-minute sketch of a dog results in 3,600,000 bits of sequential data. A major role for any sketch-recognizing system is to compress this data for the purpose of transmitting it to other procedures or other machines. An ultimate case of data compression would be to take the 3,600,000 bits and transform them into: "short-haired poodle that looks like Spiro." A more modest transformation, in the context of architectural drawing, is to reduce the projective geometry elements to a list of nodes and linkages of straight lines and curves.

HUNCH performs this operation with uncanny success, guessing at the intended straight lines, curves, and corners. It achieves this transformation with two simple but powerful parameters of intentionality: speed and pressure. The adjacent figure illustrates the measures of intention in that the first square was drawn rapidly (and sloppily) and interpreted as a square, whereas the second was drawn slowly, hence with apparent caution and intent, and interpreted as an irregular figure with rounded corners. The correlation of speed and pressure to simple intentions yields a powerful measure of graphical "purpose." Nonetheless, it should be noted that these parameters are very sensitive to the hand of the individual designer and thus must be delicately tuned and tailored. This is achieved at first encounter by a simple exercise of: "draw me a this...or that...faster... slower" and later is revised on-line, ultimately (wishfully) in context.

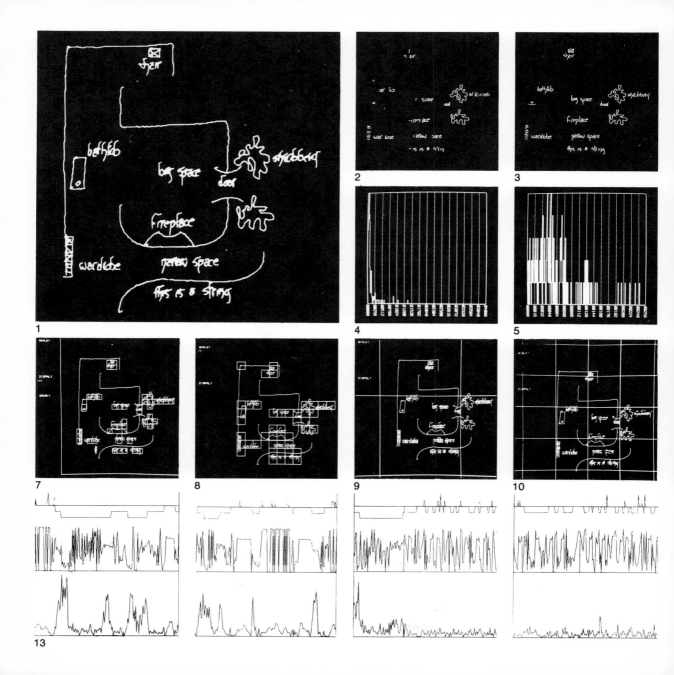

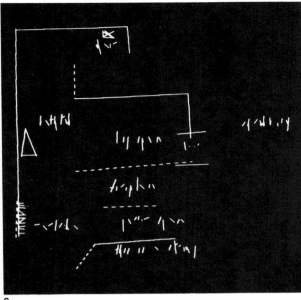

6

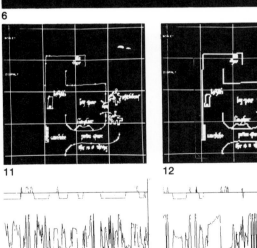

11   12

1 A sample test case for character and symbol finding

2 After filtering out all lines below 40. Note that some of the characters are lost, like the *F* in "fireplace" and the *T* in "this."

3 After filtering out all lines below 96. This finds all characters and symbols in this particular example.

4 A histogram of line lengths expressed in terms of the tablet's coordinates, 0 to 4096

5 A histogram of 0 to 240. This is used to cluster line lengths in an attempt to find characters.

6 A pass at line finding, which makes very little sense without the characters that have been removed. Notice that dotted lines are drawn when curves (or anomalies) are encountered.

7 Here the problem of character finding is treated as an adjacency problem, viewing the data on the grid, rather than in sequence. The picture is gathered in "windows" of a certain size (measured in the coordinates of the original data) and then subjected to a density (or population) test. This figure uses windows 20 bits by 20 bits and tags those with a density higher than 50. Observe that all characters and symbols are hit. However, some protrude from their "boxes."

8 Window is larger, 32 by 32, density is the same, 50.

9 Window is much smaller, 10, and density is 30, so high that only a few elements are found, for example, the drain in the bathtub.

10 Window is yet smaller, 4. Density is 8, and again, many characters are lost.

11 Window equals 4, density 6, and all characters are found, but also some of the nooks in the line quality.

12 Density and window size are the same, by definition encompassing the complete picture.

13 A graph of speed, change in arc/tangent, and pressure in 5 second intervals. Fourier transforms are necessary to begin to make sense of such localized data.

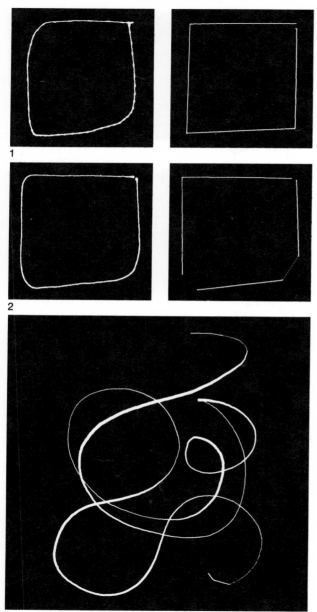

1 A rapidly drawn square and its interpretation by HUNCH

2 A slowly drawn square. Dotted lines mean that a purposeful curve was found.

3 A hand-drawn curve with pressure data before splining

1

2

3

Curve Recognition

A myth of computer-aided design has been that computer graphics can liberate architects from the parallel rule and hence afford the opportunity to design and live in globular, glandular, freeform habitats. I do not subscribe to this attitude. I believe that orthogonal and planar prevalencies result from much deeper physiological, psychological, and cultural determinants than the T-square. Partly as a consequence of this posture, The Architecture Machine Group initially and purposely ignored curves, feeling that straight lines and planar geometries could account for most graphical intentions. However, it is the case that in demonstrating HUNCH, the sketcher invariably incorporates curves in his *second* sketch, if for no other reason than to see what the machine will do.

Recently we have incorporated curve recognition as a subset of data compressing. The problem is twofold: to recognize and to fit. The recognition is a matter of distinguishing a hastily drawn straight line from a purposeful curve. As with the previous examples, speed and pressure provide the most telling evidence and form the basis for most heuristics. However, unlike finding corners and straight lines, recognizing curves requires a greater interplay between the two data structures, because taking derivatives of irregularly spaced points (without interpolation) can be very misleading.

Two approaches have been employed for curve recognition. The first (shown on the following page) is to try arbitrarily to straighten all lines with minor variations in parameter weighting. This causes minor variations in the straight line interpretations and wide variations in the curves because of the programming technique. The second approach is to concentrate on the derivatives (second and third) in the assumption that curves are less speed dependent and, by their nature, require more cautious application.

Curves are cumbersome graphical elements in the sense that neat ways for fitting and describing them in a simple "compressed" manner do not exist. Presently we represent them with a B-spline technique, a method that allows for a high level of curvature continuity and for a compressed representation that employs points that conveniently are few in number and do not lie on the curve. Illustrations on the next page show the effects of varying the order of the spline. For a more complete account of this technique the reader should refer to the thorough and definitive work of Richard Reisenfeld (1973).

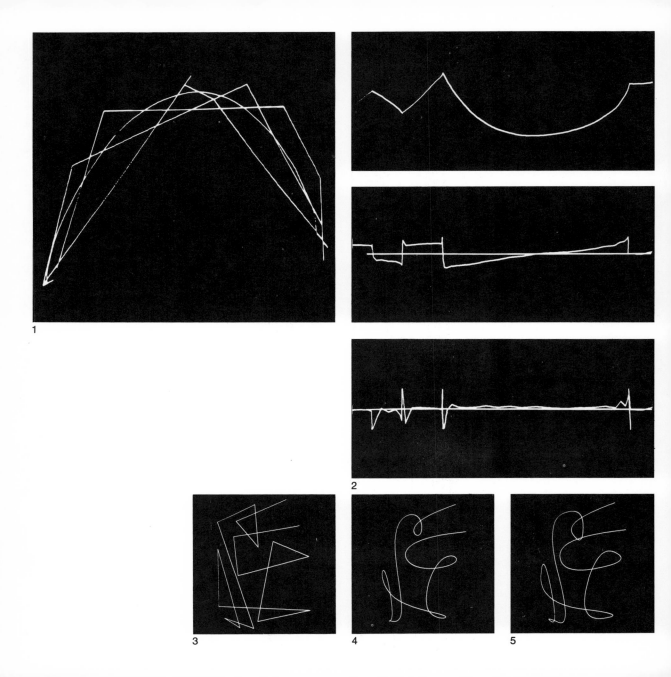

6

7

1 Three straight-line interpretations of a curve. Each results from a small variation of the "straight-line-finding" parameters.

2 The top curve is the graphical input entered from the tablet. The two lower graphs depict the first and second derivatives (taken from irregularly spaced data).

3 The "nodes" of a B-spline. These 17 points of data describe the following curves.

4 A fourth-order spline (note the cusp)

5 A third-order spline (where cusp begins to open)

6 A brand of Aunt Fiffy's house

7 Overenthusiastic latching

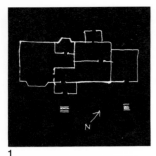

1

1 A house plan sketched on the tablet. The resolution of the dots is about four hundred points per inch.

2 The plan displayed in a coarse grain, a grid of 32 by 32

3 Each illustration shows the area defined by the preceding square at twice the resolution.

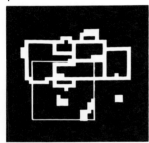

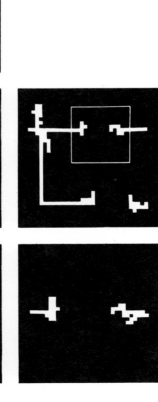

2

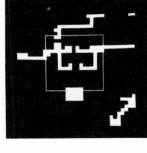

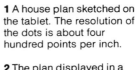

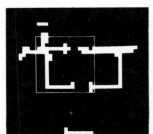

3

Latching

It is necessary to perform the task of latching, the process of guessing when a line is meant to be connected to a point, with as high a level of reliability as possible, because a single unlatched line can make the simplest figure topologically impossible (or implausible) in a planar or volumetric representation. In the early HUNCH days, we assumed that latching could give relatively consistent success when treated in a manner similar to finding corners; that is, we relied on speed and pressure to vary the range in which one would venture a latch. In fact, it worked quite well until a user drew small pictures or incorporated detail, like a window in a wall. In these cases the latching routines would be overenthusiastic and latch lines to all the nearby end points, making mullions look like starfish. This was because latching was intially achieved in a very narrow context. More recently (1973) latching procedures have been redesigned to look for patterns in the positional data. Heuristics employ features like repetition, closures, homogeneity, and density to provide evidence that a certain endpoint probably is meant to be attached to a certain other endpoint or line.

Latching is a very good example of a seemingly simple task that requires the full spectrum of human understanding in order to be achieved in a general manner. It is also a good example of the interplay between making a decision in order to know something and knowing something in order to make a decision. In connecting the vertices of an arrow it helps to know that it is an arrow in the first place. At the same time, arrowness is derived most easily from the connected figure. In short, latching epitomizes the problem which is a riddle with paradoxes and which is the cause of a despairing search for a handle on problems of recognition.

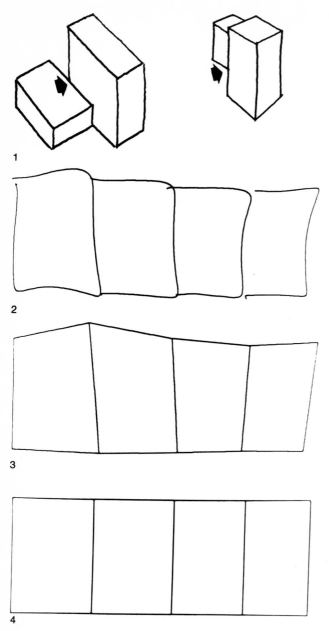

1 Characteristic T joints

2 Original sketch

3 Unconstrained interpretation

4 Implicity constrained
interpretation

1

2

3

4

Intersections

When a line is drawn that crosses or abuts another, the initial procedures do not locate the point of intersection. There is no reason to assume that any of the intersection points are actual data points in the initial stream. Finding intersections is a straightforward operation that has both significant and misleading results. It is often necessary to carry multiple representations, guessing when intersections are or are not important. For example, in the case of a five-pointed star, fifteen line segments and ten endpoints are returned. This distorts the concept of "starness," intrinsically a five-sided design.

Nonetheless, in most instances, intersections are invaluable for the recognition of higher-order features. One case is an intersection that contains one line that does not "pass through," for example, a T joint (see illustrations). This form of intersection will often be unlatched at a later time inasmuch as T's provide very strong evidence that one plane or body lies behind another.

Intersections have an interesting technical aspect in that finding them in a sequential representation (or nodes and links) is an exhaustive procedure that increases by the square of the number of lines. In a positional representation, on the other hand, that matter is settled in a trivial way as a result of being able to test for whether a bit is already turned on, while filling the bit map. What is important in this particular detail is the moving between one representation and another for the purpose of gaining simple access to information.

Implicit Constraints

Early SKETCHPAD experiments included constraint application and resolution such that you could draw two skew lines and apply the constraints of parallelism and similarity in length and observe the lines meander to equilibrium. Similarly, HUNCH supplies constraints; the only difference is they are initiated implicitly. At this writing they include horizontal/vertical, parallel/perpendicular, continuous, and over-traced. They are relatively straightforward computations (described in the adjacent figures); some involve local consideration, and some require a search of the entire image. One can imagine many more implicit constraints, and one can also imagine an evolving set of constraints resulting from a particular user's idiosyncracies and habits. These, too, would be a function of speed and pressure.

Overtracing, however, warrants special attention because it is a fascinating drawing behavior that can imply two very contradictory intentions: reinforcement or correction. In "yellow tracing paper operations," so familiar to students and practitioners of architecture, one tends to consider and execute contradictory but exploratory lines, with the result that the representation, if viewed in its entirety, would be a "nonsense artifact." It is also usually the case that, prior to overlaying more yellow paper, the most salient and ambiguous features are overtraced so that the translucency will cover the "noise." On opaque paper, the sketch often starts as light scribbles and construction lines and evolves into a black hodgepodge of many light lines with studied, purposeful dark lines.

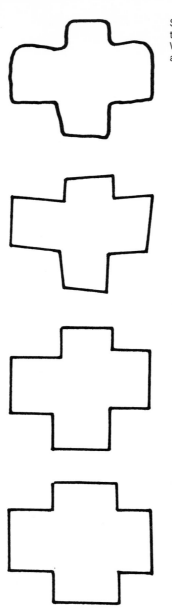

Stages of recognition and
transformation of a cross.
When does "crossness"
arise?

A simple way to handle overtracing is to consider it as a form of implicit erasure of the lines beneath (Ellis, Haefner, and Sibley, 1969). Or, equally simplistically, one could read the magnetic tape (that is, the sequential data) backwards, automatically giving higher credence to the most recently sketched features. Both methods work with surprising success (especially when reinforced by factors of speed and pressure). However, they overlook some of the important implications of overtracing. For example, highly reworked lines "may represent important (perhaps semantic) dispositions toward a design such as being 'concerned about,' 'sure of,' 'puzzled by,' and so on" (Negroponte, 1970c and d). This is important to save. To this end we store overtracings as a "feature" of the line even though the reworkings are removed in the resolved image.

Shape Recognition

At this point the reader should be discouraged by the disparity between seeking an artificial intelligence and enumerating simple geometric transformations. Nowhere has learning been involved. All previous operations are as syntactical as parsing a sentence or separating words in a speech. Shape recognition begins to raise more challenging questions—for example, At what point is a shape recognized?

An adjacent example depicts the transformations of a crosslike figure achieved in the order in which I have described them. Note that the last representation remains irregular (let's assume I meant a regular cross) in that the four wings are of different proportions. A first thought might be to append the additional implicit constraint of repetition of line length. This in turn could be mapped into the concluding transformation: CROSS (as defined rigorously by a figure with four equal...etc.). However, is it not more rewarding to look for "crossness" much sooner? "The very concept of 'cross' furnishes many of the graphical inferences that until now have been handled in some sense brutally" (Negroponte, Groisser, and Taggart, 1972).

The process of shape recognition is extremely circular in that the line finding is assisted by knowing the figure is a cross and, at the same time, shape recognition is assisted by having found the lines. We are many years away from being able to have a machine distinguish Aunt Fiffy's house from a north arrow.

Inferring a Third Dimension

How many people are aware that the general attitude of a cube is such that its silhouette forms a hexagon? Do we use such information to understand or to recognize the three-dimensional aspects of cubeness?

The retinal image is a two-dimensional representation that we constantly map into three dimensions with no overt intellectual effort. The psychology of perception is a voluminous field (with classic works like those of Gibson, 1951, 1966 and S. A. Gregory, 1973) that has provided some clues as to how *we* see. However, the traditional views of psychologists have been of very little help in making machines that can see or that can infer a third dimension. The reader interested in machine vision per se should refer to the founding works by Oliver Selfridge (1963) and his colleagues, the works of Minsky and Papert (1968), Guzman (1969), and a great body of papers emanating from the three centers of robotics: MIT, Stanford, and Edinburgh.

My own interest in machine vision has oscillated between low resolution and high resolution, between geometries and behaviors. One specific experiment is reported in *Machine Vision of Models of the Physical Environment* (1969). More recently my interest in vision has settled specifically on the inference making necessary to achieve three-dimensional information from a two-dimensional representation, such as a drawing. Notice that in the case of sketching, making inferences about the third dimension is somewhat easier than looking after the fact at a scene of, let's say, a pile of blocks. This is because one has the additional information of "construction sequence," which can be employed in heuristics

that make speculations like: this is connected to that, this is behind that, and so on. For example, on the next page of illustrations is a case where the horizon line "obviously" goes behind the block and, in reality, is continuous, though obstructed from this particular point of view. Guzman-like programs (after tediously piecing together the line segments without sequential data) develop evidence that the horizontals are connected by using heuristics that match T's, project lines, and observe the nature of interim regions. HUNCH, meanwhile, has the added invaluable information about the sequence in which lines were drawn. The likelihood is that the sketcher in fact drew the horizontal lines from left to right (if he is right-handed), stopping at the right edge of the block, lifting up his pencil (probably not very much), moving to the other limiting edge, and continuing to the right with the stylus touching.

The first task of inferring the third dimension in a drawing is to recognize the kind of projection. Is it a plan or a section? Is it a perspective or an axonometric? The two alternatives are distinctly different because the one group supports the illusion of three dimensions, whereas the other requires conventions, consistencies, and a combination of views or the additional cues of shading.

Let's consider axonometrics and perspectives first. They have fascinated researchers in computer graphics, in particular with respect to the removal of all lines and line segments that would be invisible from a given vantage point. The so-called hidden line problem has been exhaustively studied by L. G. Roberts (1965); Kubert, Szabo, and Giulieri (1968); Galimberti and Montanari (1969); Loutrel (1970); A. Ricci (1970); and, in a survey that proposed a new solution,

Encarnacao (1970). But it is not an interesting problem, because it is deterministic and blatantly solvable though complicated. It is much more interesting to consider the opposite problem: given a perspective, fill in the hidden lines. I say it is more interesting because (1) it is riddled with ambiguities; (2) there exists no algorithm that will work for all cases; and (3) it can be handled only with a knowledge about the physical world.

Figures on the next page show the operations of a program that takes HUNCH input, constructs an axonometric, and maps it into three dimensions with modest accuracy, using limiting assumptions. The primary operations include: (1) estimate the families of parallel lines; (2) find redundant points, stray lines, that is, HUNCH oversights in working in a two-dimensional frame; (3) axonometricize the figure, if necessary; (4) break *all* T joints; (5) project T's until they intersect a plane as defined by any two parallel lines that each belong to a different family but neither to the family of the projected T; (6) look for parallelograms; (7) furnish guesses at a third coordinate as a function of length and angle away from verticality; (8) project all horizontal planes to intersect any element that protrudes above.

Notice that the eight steps and functions are quite arbitrary; they represent an interpretation of desired results, not an interpretation of how we see. Each operation assumes a model of the world (it can be as simple as orthogonal) that imparts arbitrary legitimacy to the computer program in that it behaves with a nice precision. However, no matter how hard we try, we embed simplifying assumptions, and we can never be assured that handling the abstracted set of arbitrary three-dimensional figures will lead to handling the entire set. For example, we can limit the class of sketch to the extent of making this mapping just about deterministic (for example: contiguously arranged cubes on a flat surface). Similarly, we can broaden it to handle any collection of irregular polyhedra. In the latter case we find that we make implicit assumptions (as opposed to built-in limitations).

In contrast to axonometrics and perspective, plans and sections afford more unambiguous descriptions through conventions. They require, however, the additional task of piecing together sections and matching different views. Furthermore, an additional step of recognition is necessary: Is the slice horizontal (a plan) or vertical (a section)? Once again this is usually so obvious to the onlooking human that it behooves us to understand the essence of plan and section. I do not agree, for example, with the often-stated position that a plan and a section should be indistinguishable. Our physiology is such that we tend to witness the world in section but, interestingly enough, to remember it predominantly in plan. In addition, our sense of balance plays a major, unexplored role in the primarily orthogonal structure of human concepts about the physical world, as described by terms like *above*, *in front*, *right*, *left*, etc.

Unlike mapping perspectives into three dimensions, most energies in the recognition of plans and sections are devoted to the basic determination of which is a plan and which a section. A computer program must draw upon clues like steps, trees, and sloping roofs, and take advantage of such facts as: floors are usually horizontal. There will be cases where it will be unclear to even the most experienced architect whether the

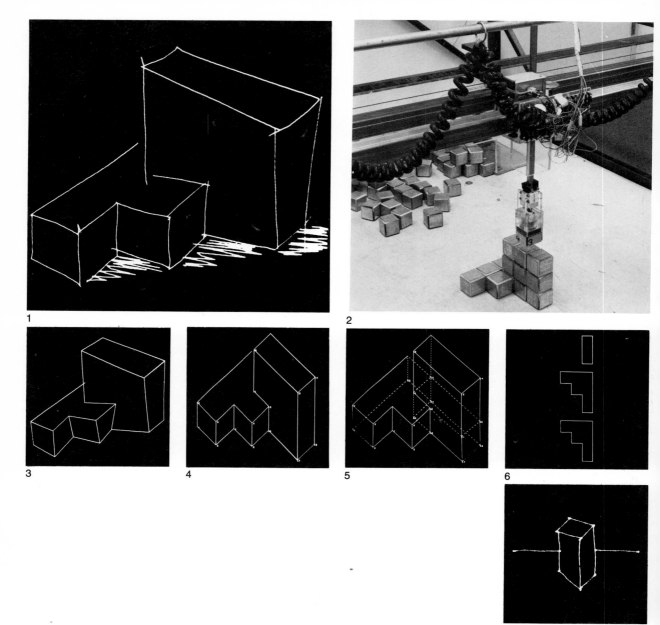

1

2

3

4

5

6

7

1 Drawing of a pile of blocks

2 SEEK builds an approximation (upon its return from New York)

3 Found lines

4 Lines pushed into predominant families

5 Hidden lines added with "shortest path" fit

6 Plans taken at ground and two upper levels

7 Horizon line

drawing is a plan or section. It would be wrong to expect a machine to do much better, but it would be right to expect it to *ask*.

The reader familiar with projective geometry techniques will understand that formats like those employed in mechanical engineering are quite a bit easier to correlate than the typical architectural set of drawings. Unlike mechanical engineers, architects do not share a general consensus of conventions for dotted lines, auxiliary views, and the like.

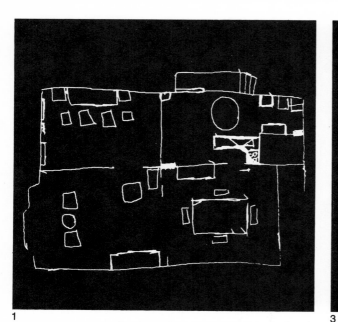

1

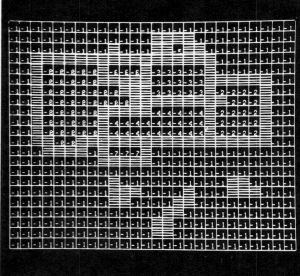

3

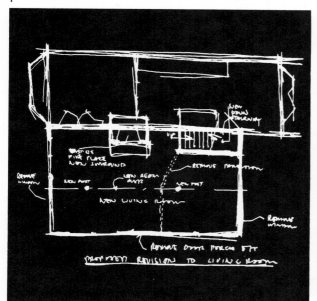

2

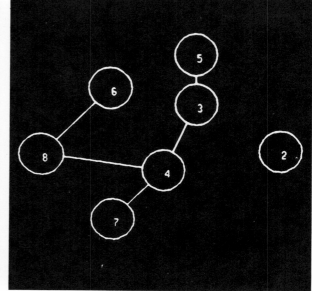

4

1 House plan drawn by novice designer

2 House plan drawn by "professional"

3 Gridded house plan

4 Planar graph of gridded house plan

Architectural Inferences

An architectural inference can range from recognizing the propensity to use cheap materials to assuming a life-style. "When we recall that the process will generally be concerned with finding a satisfactory design, rather than an optimum design, we see that the sequence and division of labor between generators and tests can affect not only the efficiency with which resources for designing are used but also the nature of the final design as well. What we ordinarily call 'style' may stem just as much from these decisions about the design process as from alternate emphasis on the goals to be realized through the final design" (Simon, 1969). And again, "If we see a building with a symmetric facade, we can be reasonably sure that that facade was generated at an early point in the design. If, on the other hand, we see one with many asymmetries, we will conjecture with some confidence that these asymmetries are the external expression of decisions about how to meet internal requirements" (Simon, 1970).

These two quotes may offend the professional architect; the notion of "style" belongs only to history and to a posteriori observation. However, if we replace the word *style* with *intent* and suggest that intentions are both implicitly and explicitly manifest in the method of work of the designer, the idea of looking for architectural inferences is more palatable; the problem is to infer what was meant versus what was done. By recognizing architectural implications, one can begin to say something about the past experience of the designer. This is because a large number of decisions are made through prejudice and preconception. Appendix 2 discusses at greater length the role of prejudice as a viable heuristic.

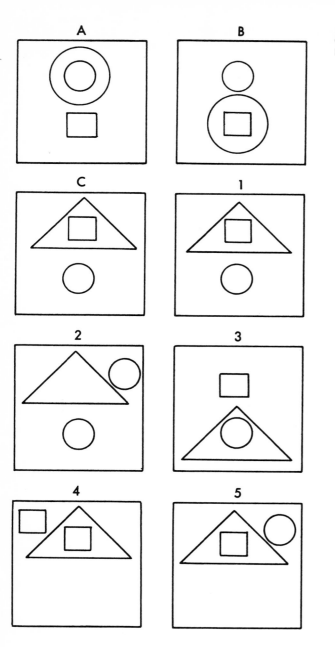

An example of the ANAL-
OGY problem taken from
Evans (1963, 1968)

One example of drawing inferences as a function of method of work can be found in an experiment associated with "plan recognition" (described in the next chapter). The "user" is asked to draw a plan of his house. We find two general methods of drawing such a plan. The first entails describing the external envelope and then subdividing it into rooms. The second involves "walking a line around," space to space, tracing out interior compartments as cells that interconnect. With some confidence we can make a rather wild guess that the first method indicates living in a detached house, for example, where one has the opportunity to witness the "whole" as set upon a plot of land. The second method is symptomatic of living in an apartment building, where one does not have the occasion to inspect the external envelope of one's own living space.

More formal examples of looking for architectural intentions can be found in hunting for tendencies to repeat elements, in recognizing a propensity to align boundaries, or in searching for playful and whimsical uses of angles and penetrations. These tend to be symptomatic of superficial constructs, especially when viewed as ends unto themselves. A deeper level of intentionality can be achieved in what Gordon Pask calls the "cybernetic design paradigm" by looking for unstated goals: "It should be emphasized that the goal may be and nearly always will be underspecified, i.e.: the architect will no more know the purpose of the system than he really knows the purpose of a conventional house. His aim is to provide a set of constraints that allow for certain, presumably desirable, modes of evolution" (Pask, 1969).

A principal means of recognizing architectural intentions will be to look for architectural attributes, rather than architectural properties, the physically measurable properties (Hershberger, 1972). Architectural attributes are measured in terms of our own experiences and are recognized in discourse by knowing something about the person with whom you are talking. To be sure, they are described by metaphors and analogies; they do not surface in the geometries of a sketch. To emphasize this point, I refer to Thomas Evans's early work (1963 and 1968) on the program ANALOGY as an example of one kind of difference.

The ANALOGY program tackles the so-called "geometry analogy" intelligence test: Figure A is to figure B as figure C is to which of the following? The adjacent illustrations describe a typical problem. The Evans program goes through four major steps: (1) the figures are decomposed into subfigures; (2) properties are ascribed, such as inside of, to the right of, above, etc.; (3) "similarity" calculations are determined to successfully map A into B; (4) the appropriate similarity is used to map C into whichever. The procedures are extremely complex; the program represents a historical landmark in the development of artificial intelligence. However, consider minor changes in some of the elements, as shown on the following page. They should alert us to a major difference between the geometric analogy and the "meaning" analogy between properties and attributes. It behooves us to ignore sometimes the formal counterparts and to recognize the simplest architectural intention, even a tiny step beyond geometry. But we really do not know how to do it in baby steps. It is indicative of the desperate problem of arriving at simple frontiers in artificial intelligence that appear to be extendable only in their most consummate form.

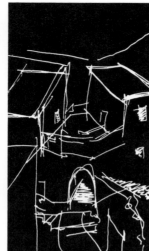

1 Illustrations from Richard Scarry, *Best Word Book Ever* (New York: Golden Press, 1970)

2 A target for sketch recognition

2

1

Why Bother?

In contrast to the unenlightening, recursive argument of "so what," "why bother" can be a particularly instructive question in the context of computers and, in particular, in the light of their continuously dropping costs. Historically, a well-supervised parsimony with computing power has forced us to bend our manner of conversation and warp it into a man-machine communication characterized by trumped-up, unnecessary levels of consistency, completeness, and precision. One is expected to be explicit and unequivocal with a computer; "it's like talking to a machine!"

Consider the previous example of recognizing whether a sketch is a plan or a section. The amount of code necessary to perform that task and the amount of ensuing computation are enormous. It might make a good programmer's doctoral thesis and require five to ten seconds of fast computing (in today's technology) to arrive at a reasonable conclusion. Would it not be easier to insist that the sketcher be required to exert the trivial additional effort of typing an *S* or *P* after completing his drawing? The answer is surely, Yes, it would be easier. The issue, however, is where to draw the line, even in the most timid, master-slave applications.

One extreme position is to adopt the SKETCHPAD explicitness: this is a line, this is its end, these two are parallel, this is an arc, and so forth. The other extreme is to consider all levels of communication as potentially as smooth, congenial, and free of explication as a conversation with a very intelligent, very good friend. I opt for the latter in toto on the following counts: (1) it is crippling to force an explicitness in contexts where the participant's equivocations are part of the function of design; (2) the tedium of overt, categorical exchange is counterproductive, unfulfilling for the speaker, and boring; (3) constructive and exciting responses are often generated by twists in meaning that result from the personal interpretation of intentions and implications; (4) finally, I view computer time as a *free* commodity to be allocated in the abundance necessary to make a rich dialogue, perhaps richer than we have ever had with another human.

3

Computer-Aided Participatory Design

Introduction by Yona Friedman

It is evident that the term *machine* has a general meaning and that it can stand for practically anything related to some temporal process. I mean by this statement that I can consider anything as a machine provided that this "anything" can have subsequent states (even if these states are all identical). A conclusion of this statement could be that a "machine" does not become a "machine" except because of me, who am observing it; I am submitted necessarily to a temporal process: life.

Obviously enough, these initial statements sound very abstract and very subjective (as do philosophical statements in general), and I don't intend to discuss them here. What I consider more important is to introduce this part of a book I like and to stay consistent in this introduction with my personal views and my own research; and for this purpose I had to underline the fact that no "machine" could be imagined that did not "contain" an intelligent observer. Thus I don't consider the "hardware" machine (or even the "hardware + software" machine) as *the* machine. I consider as "machine" only and exclusively a system containing "the machine and me."

The theme "computer-aided participatory design" is clearly contained within this definition, to which some restrictions can be added. First specification: In "computer-aided participatory design" there are two "partners" participating, namely, the "object to be designed" and me. Second condition: It is I who am the important partner. Third condition: The expression "me" (I) can stand for *any human being*, and any such particular human being *cannot be substituted* for any other one.

Thus we arrive at a quite simple statement about our topic: it signifies a "machine" composed of two "submachines." The first is "the real world

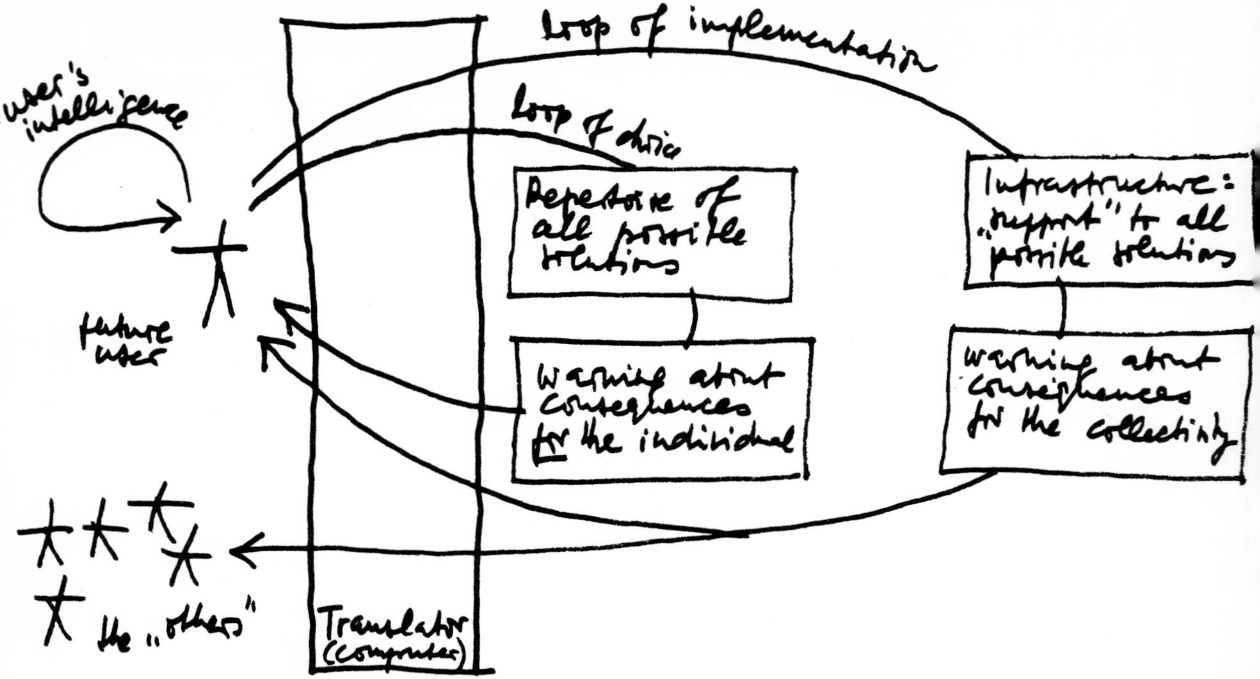

user's
intelligence

Loop of implementation

Loop of ethics

future
user

Repertoire of
all possible
solutions

Infrastructure:
"support" to all
possible solutions

warning about
consequences
for the individual

warning about
consequences
for the collectivity

★ ★ ★
★ ★
★ the "others"

Translator
(Computer)

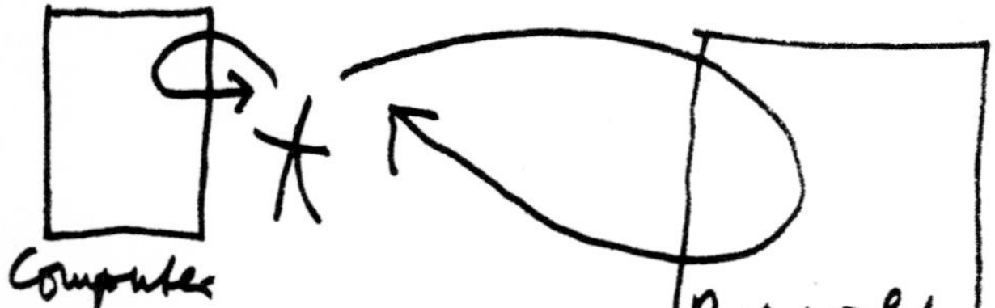

Computer

Computer
"paternalist" scheme

Real world

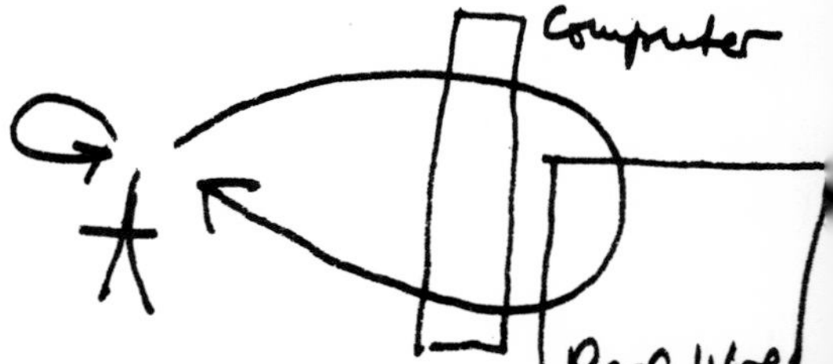

"non" paternalist" scheme

Real World

and the computer," and the second, "me and the computer." Otherwise expressed, the computer enters into the original machine as "translator."

Following this definition, computer-aided participatory design could be represented as a machine that would look like the adjacent diagram.

In this graph the computer functions as translator, as the provisory interface between the future user and the object to be designed (which will be a part of the real world) and between this object and another part of the real world that comprises the "other" human beings who might have some relations with the designed object. The relation wherein the computer does not come in as translator, that is, the relation between the future user and the "others," is not drawn in the graph.

Now, the interesting thing in this scheme is that it contains an additional loop, which is not observable by a person not belonging to the machine itself. I mean here the loop visualizing the process going on within the head of any particular future user. All values, preferences, and associations in this loop of the machine are arbitrary ones, which depend only on the personality of any particular future user.

Once we grant the existence of this part of the machine, we can consider the problem in one of the two ways I will sketch here.

The first one (which is the one designers today generally use) would be the one I label the "paternalist." In the paternalist organization, it is the translator (designer, expert, or computer) who establishes his own preferences and judgments, in the interest of a particular future user, after a learning period during which the translator learns the peculiar particularities of this future user. Thus the translator (in our specific case, the computer) would make some decisions for the future user, "with paternal benevolence," leaving the entire risk of potential errors for this future user to cope with himself.

The second way I call "nonpaternalist." In this case the translator makes no judgments or decisions and thus needs no learning period. It functions only as a sort of "speedwriter" denoting the tentative decisions of the future user and emitting a "warning" about expectable reactions of the real world upon each decision. In this case the learning period exists as well, but the learning is done by the future user, and it concerns the structural characteristics of the real world alone.

Simply stated, in the paternalist scheme the computer is associated with the future user, whereas in the nonpaternalist one it is a part of the real world.

I am opposed to the paternalist scheme, not only because of my personal moral attitude but principally because of the fact that the learning about the personality of the future user is less implementable than the learning about structural characteristics of the real world (not because the latter is less complex than the former, but because it is—by definition—more "structurable").

To conclude, I believe that the most interesting research theme open to our generation in the field of participatory design (computer-aided or not)—design meaning here constructive imagination of physical or nonphysical objects (for example, behavioral ones, like politics)—would be to investigate the possibility of a paternalist-nonpaternalist scheme, in other words, whether or not a machine (in the abstract sense used at the beginning of this introduction) could be conceived wherein both the intelligent observer (the future user) and the real world (the object of the design) would mutually learn about each other. I think that nearly all research people today are on this track, consciously or not.

There is no doubt that this research is going on. What its results may be, one cannot yet predict, and nobody knows whether or not a sort of symbiosis of machine intellect and human intellect is possible. If it is possible, we might find a new organ to interact with (much in the same way as we live in symbiosis with our own sensory organs), and we might become a different species. Today no one knows how such a thing would happen (or, indeed, if it can happen). I believe that no amount of research work is too much to explore such a possibility.

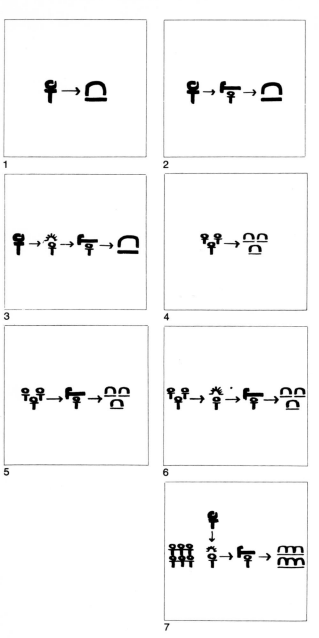

The illustrations are taken from *aap noot mies huis* by N. J. Habraken Amsterdam: Scheltema & Holkema, 1970. The captions are translated from Dutch and abbreviated from their appearance in *The Responsive House*, edited by Edward Allen (Cambridge: MIT Press, 1974).

Nowadays man lives in an unnatural relationship with his domicile. This artificiality becomes apparent when we know which types of natural relationships exist. There are six natural types of relationships. The seventh form of relationship brings into being non-homes."

1 The first . . . is the simplest; the occupant builds his own house with his own hands."

2 The second type of individual relationship is that in which the craftsman . . . offers his services. This relationship was very often responsible for housing in western history.

3 "The third type of individual relationship is that in which the architect acts as intermediary between occupant and craftsman . . . There are very few who can afford this type of relationship. . . ."

4 The first collective type of relationship is that in which the community builds collectively the houses it needs, and does this without delegating the labor to craftsmen."

5 The second collective type differs only by the delegation of some or all tasks to craftsmen.

6 "The third collective relationship is that in which the community and craftsmen do the actual building. The architect acts as the specialized intermediary."

7 "The seventh relationship is a nonrelationship. None of the previous types of relationship are found in mass production building. This seventh type is characterized by the fact that the occupants really take no part in it. They are unknown during the process of decision which leads to the production of dwellings."

"It is for this reason that in the last diagram nothing reaches the architect from the group of the 'anonymous multitude' of people. The architect is commissioned by another specialist who is no more the occupant than he is."

User Participation in Design

The idea of and need for user participation in design have surfaced in the past five years as a major (and fashionable) element in both design education and professional practice. A recent synopsis can be found in Nigel Cross's (1972) *Design Participation*. This interest in participation follows from a general feeling that architecture, particularly housing, has been inadequate and unresponsive to the needs and desires of its users. One cause for this seems to be that the design of housing is in the wrong hands, that is, in the hands of an outside "professional," rather than of the resident. The question is: Can the resident participate in or control the design of his own house?

The concept of user participation can be traced back centuries in indigenous architecture. In contemporary architecture and planning it is generally credited to Paul Davidoff's "Advocacy and Pluralism in Planning" (1965). Some architects view participation as a form of giving up, capitulating to the individual who knows less than the expert but is willing to live in his own mess. Others see it as the most promising and sensible, if not the only, approach to ensuring responsive physical environments. The subject is, to say the least, controversial. Ironically it is generally studied and pursued by designers who view computer-aided design as an antipodal effort, as a tool for the military-industrial complex only.

The underlying assumption of user participation is that individuals and small groups (a family, a neighborhood) know what they want or, at least, can learn what they want. The concept further assumes that they can apply this understanding in

concert with a "competence" to realize designs for the built environment. The results are an apparent (though not necessarily real) democracy in decision making, the consequence of which is ideally a responsiveness in architecture. This approach shortcircuits many of the traditional roles of the professional planner and architect regardless of whether he views himself as what Horst Rittel (1972) calls the doctor planner, the egalitarian planner, the needs planner, or the decisions planner.

Consider two other examples of what can be viewed as the design of shelter: the design of automobiles and the design of clothes. In the case of the automobile most of us will agree that we personally do not know enough about combustion and mechanics to design our own cars. While exceptions like the Sunday mechanic and amateur car racer exist, most of us are satisfied with the existing selection of foreign and domestic cars, whether we view the automobile as a means to get us from here to there, as a status symbol, or as an extravagance. Therefore our participation in design is limited to supporting political lobbies to force Detroit to make cars safer.

Clothes in some respect are at the other end of the spectrum inasmuch as I am confident that you and I can design and make our own clothes if we have to or want to. But clothes, unlike cars, require simple tools and involve materials that are generally easy to manipulate. At the same time, the low capital investment in materials and the high volume of the market allow for so many different kinds of clothing that anyone can find articles both that he likes and that are relatively unique within his circle of acquaintances. Note that our concept of "fit" is not demanding (most women's dresses come in only sixteen basic sizes). When we are fussy we can employ a tailor to make our clothes fit better though not necessarily to be better designed.

Houses are somewhere between clothes and cars. They are not as expendable as shirts but are more manipulable than cars. There is a greater variety of kinds of houses than of cars, but any city offers less variety than the most meager haberdasher.

The questions of this chapter focus on housing (which represents 85 percent of the built environment). The general thesis is that *each individual can be his own architect*. The participation is achieved in association with a very personal computing machine. Somewhat in contrast to Yona Friedman, I believe that a "learning period" with such a machine would be necessary, during which the machine would not make judgments and decisions but would ask telling and revealing questions and attempt to understand what *you mean*.

Three Attitudes toward Participation

There exist three quite different perceptions of what user participation really means in architecture or to architects. I will list the views in an order that moves progressively further away from the notion of a trained architect as "expert."

The first attitude is epitomized by the often heard comment: "We need more information." This is usually characterized by a program to solicit more complete information about what future users will need and want and what they have as present attitudes toward their residential environment (Sanoff and Sawhney, 1972). The attainment of such information is usually followed by "scientific" methodologies for manipulating and overseeing the new wealth of information in a manner that most effectively reveals kernels of truth, generalizations, and invariants. Conclusions are evaluated in terms of the probability of success and are exercised with, for example, computer simulations and "enhanced decision making" techniques. The architect, by reason of his training, is still the final judge of design alternatives. "There are better and worse ways to pursue design objectives. As professionals we are supposed to be experts in design. Otherwise we are nothing" (Rubinger, 1971). Or: "I would suggest that the most important area is that of social design; i.e.: the design of institutions and the deliberate control of life style, which so far seems to have been inherited..." (Jones, 1971).

A second attitude toward participation, almost equally protective of professionalism, is focused upon fiscal and political mobility; it is often called "advocacy planning." My interpretation of advocacy planning includes generating enough leverage for the neighborhood group, for example, to be heard and seriously considered by planners and architects in order that their needs will be reflected in plans for renewal and development. This is usually implemented in the form of a professional person or persons urging a body of "decision makers" on the behalf of a certain larger group; it is rarely the case that the individual citizen gets more than the most indirect poke at a plan. He is usually appeased with minor forms of self-government: operating the local welfare establishment or attending a PTA meeting. Or, in the context of building, he and his kids might have the opportunity to participate in the building of a playground.

The third approach, the Yona Friedman paradigm, is to go all the way, removing the architect as translator and giving the inhabitant what Wellesley-Miller (1972a) rightly calls control. In short, each person becomes his own architect. He is forced to become intimately involved with viewing the consequence of one alternative versus another. The analogy put forth by Yona Friedman (1972b) is illuminating: Consider an illiterate society that had only a few public writers who, perforce, would be required to employ printed standards when writing personal letters for all the individual clients. In contrast, the public writer could be eliminated by public education.

I propose to set aside the first two approaches; I do not consider them serious forms of participation. They are timid endeavors of deprofessionalization, and they have in common the retention of a new kind (perhaps) of expert or, to use Goodman's (1972) term, a "soft cop." The third approach, on the other hand, is a do-it-yourselfism that completely removes the architect and *his*

previous experience as intermediaries between my needs (pragmatic, emotional, whimsical, etc.) and my house.

It should be noted that this third approach cannot be easily examined in the context of today's urban landscape. We have very little precedent, for example, of physical shifts taking place continually, on a day-to-day or week-to-week basis, in the way this approach might afford. At the same time, it raises some very serious issues like: Would people really want to design their own homes? What are the advantages of designing versus choosing? Are we losing positive inputs by removing the personal previous experiences of the human architect? How do such experiences differ from conceivable machine experiences? Is this really an architecture without architects, or are we really implying a new breed of surrogate architects?

Paternalism, Middlemen, and Risklessness

When I graduated from architecture school I sincerely thought that I knew better how others ought to live; I knew this as a result of my five years of training. After all, in school we studied methods for supporting "life styles," articulating "patterns of living," and educating the unaware citizen. It did not occur to me that upon entering practice and in the guise of peddling an expertise, I would in fact be foisting my values upon others. It would not be a case of reckless autocracy; rather, it would be a pervasive and evasive set of restrictions that would result from the good intentions of being comprehensive, orderly, and empirically correct.

I remember one professor telling me that architecture is a form of social statement, that any building I ever designed ought to be the manifestation of profound symbolic comment. Isn't that both presumptuous and irresponsible, and, to say the least, paternalistic? While such attitudes may be applicable in a special context of building, I propose that they are generally inappropriate and a frequent cause of unresponsive architecture. The problem can be phrased in a simple question: Can an expert have expertise in goals and values, or is expertise per se limited to means?

Father knows best for a long time. However, after a while he begins to lose credibility rapidly. Inconsistencies and unexplainable "musts" make the original institution of paternalism more and more suspect to a child; the doubt probably starts as early as age one or two. Nonetheless, for a long time the issue of Father's rightness is less important than the comfort of knowing he is around. In this sense, it is interesting to question the role of the architect in terms of comfort and confidence; can it be embraced in a machine and thus avoid the potential orphanage of participation?

Another question: If the architect as middleman is translating your needs in a built environment via transformation procedures seasoned by wisdom and his ability to "pre-experience," what side effects and distortions take place in the process of this interpretation? How much of the deformity is positive in, for example, generating goals that you would never have thought of yourself? What do we lose when he goes away? Can a computer provide it?

As a last question, consider the issue of risk. Can you seriously trust that someone who has no ultimate personal stake in the built artifact will do his utmost to achieve your personal and complex goals? An impelling motivation in most labors is in the consequence of doing a bad job. In contrast, the architect is released from all risk after his particular chunk of the built environment is built. The hazard to his reputation is slight, for he will be judged by colleagues and observers who do not have to live in what he has built and who will use extraneous criteria as the basis for criticism. In other words, the architect gets off scot-free, as innocent as the author of a bad novel.

Indigenous Architecture as a Model

Positano, Mykonos, Gasin, and Mojacar are typical sites of an indigenous architecture that has fascinated and held the admiration of architects. Rudofsky (1964) provides a wide-ranging set of illustrations that dramatically display an "exciting" architecture, which is specifically the result of citizens designing and building their own homes. This has been achieved without the help of architects, explicit master plans, or explicit zoning (or computers). How did it happen?

At first glance, most indigenous architecture appears to be the result of purely "local" activities: a house added here, a path extended there, and so on. However, upon examination one finds "global" forces, which act in a very real sense as elements of town planning and which ensure an overall unity. Typically these are found in the availability of building materials; for example, a locality that lacks timber achieves spanning by means of masonry domes, or one that lacks stone limits its structures to one or two stories. In other instances, these forces are found in climatic conditions, manifest most obviously in the whiteness of houses to reflect the heat, less obviously in the purposeful crookedness of streets to break the wind. In still other cases, the unifying forces are compelling traditions, which often support building conventions that had previous (but now defunct) environmental causes.

Forces such as these are the basis of a "vernacular." They provide a unifying pallet of materials and design conventions, what Friedman calls the "alphabet" of the "language." They act much in the same way as the proposed information process of Friedman (1971):

"With the elimination of the designer (the professional one) from the design process—by vulgarizing the 'objective' elements in the process, and by introducing a simply understood feedback concerning potential consequences of individual decisions on the whole—the paternalistic character of the traditional design process will disappear. The enormous variety of emotional (intuitive) solutions which can be invented by a large number of future users might give an incredible richness to this new 'redesigned' design process."

How can we simulate (if we want to) these conditions in an industrialized society? Strict zoning, more severe building codes, one building system (imposed by law), or a regulation that you must use brick are certainly not the appropriate measures; they lack the subtlety of natural forces within which a richness is conceivable. The answer must lie in the so-called "infrastructure," a mixture of conceptual and physical structures for which we all have a different definition or interpretation. I refer the reader to Yona Friedman's two most recent books: *Realizable Utopias* (1973) and *Society=Environment* (1972). And while I am continually alert to the need for such subtle but preponderant forces, for my purposes here I would like to assume an infrastructure composed of a resilient building and information technology and ask what role there might be for a machine intelligence acting as a personal interface (not translator) between this infrastructure and my ever changing needs. I recognize it is a big assumption.

Before venturing a machine intelligence position, I would like to examine the indigenous architect as an archetype and to scrutinize his behavior beyond commending his picturesque results. He

1

2

did not need an architecture machine; his environment was simple and comprehensible, punc-
tuated with limited choices and decisions. He no
more needed a professional architect than he
needed a psychologist or legal counselor. To
understand him, let us consider three representa-
tive (but not categorical) features of indigenous
architecture.

The first is the naming of spaces. In this sort of
architecture, the rooms tend to be about the same
size, often as large as the technology or timbers
will permit, and they rarely have names. A place
to eat is often somebody's place to sleep, and
cooking is frequently done in more than one room.
This implies that a multiplicity of activities can be
conveniently housed in similar spaces, and there
is very little generic meaning to "bedroom" or
"living room." The generics seem to reside in
"sleeping" and "eating" and "cooking," and we
can extrapolate (tenuously perhaps) that they
have a *large common intersection*, larger than we
tend to believe.

A second feature that deserves comment is the
apparent ad hoc growth of the dwelling unit.
Usually a dwelling unit is limited to a small
number of rooms and might be added to in the
event of offspring. In Greek island societies the
dwelling is passed down as dowry; a larger house
is often divided in two and the boundary allowed
to oscillate between the shrinking of one generation and the growing of another. Rooms are
frequently passed to a contiguous house,
entrances sealed and opened as required. These
local expansions and contractions result from a
permanency of home with which most Americans
are unfamiliar. In an industrialized society, the
pattern is to sell your house and buy a bigger one,

105

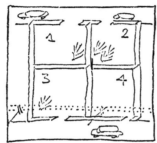

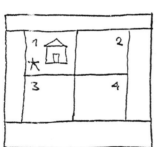

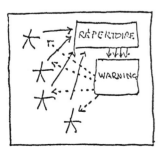
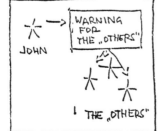

5

6

1 The story of Mr. Smith:
I *had an idea* about my house.
I *translated* my idea into bricks.
This is my house, the *result* of my "translation."
I made a mistake in translating, which I did not discover until I *used* my house.

2 The story of Mr. Wright:
I had an *idea* about my house, and I *explained* it to the builder.
The builder misunderstood me. The result is that my house has no door to the garden.
Every time I want to use the garden, I have to get there through the window.
My mistake was in not explaining *more explicitly* to the builder what I wanted him to build for me.

3 The story of a neighborhood:
Each of us had an *idea* about his house.
We tried to *explain* our ideas to an architect, but there were so many of us that there was *not enough time* to explain our ideas sufficiently.
The architect *translated* our ideas into an idea of his own.
He liked his idea but *we* did not like it.
And it is *we* who have to use these houses, not the architect!

4 The story of another neighborhood:
Each of us had *his own idea* about how to live.
Our architect did not listen to us: he knew everything about the "average man."
The apartments he built were designed for the "average man."
But we are *real* people, not average at all. We are not comfortable living the way our architect likes to live.

5 A different kind of story:
Each of us has *his own idea* about his house.
Fortunately, there is a *repertoire* of all possible houses.
Fortunately also, there are *instructions* about what to expect from each kind of house.
Each of us can make his own *choice*, using the repertoire and the instructions.

6 Each of us can thus *plan* the home of his *choice*, based on his own *idea*.
In order to build our homes, we each need a lot, an access road, a water main, a power line, and so on. This is the *infrastructure* that supports each house.
John wanted to build on lot 1. The others agreed...
...After making sure that John's choice of location *did not hold disadvantages* for them.
Here the stories end.

then later, a smaller one. I can remember (but not reference) the statistic that the average American family moves every three years.

The third observation, perhaps the most important, comes from my personal experiences of living on an Aegean island. It appears to be true that the local residents of an indigenous environment are unanimously dissatisfied with their architecture. Glass slabs are their metaphoric goals as much as, if not more than, the little white stucco house is mine. My electric typewriter has as much meaning as a Byzantine icon. Perhaps this can be explained in terms of communication technologies, by arguing that the local resident would be content, at a level to which we aspire, if he had not witnessed the electric toys of our times through magazines, television, and the passing rich tourist. However, a more deep-seated issue is the breadth of experience shared among these people. It is the case that they have in fact had very similar experiences among themselves and consequently carry nearly similar metaphors and share personal contexts. I am not saying that individuality has been squelched; I propose that the spectrum of experiences is small and may be accountable, in part, for this dramatic level of participation, so far not achieved in industrialized societies. It is quite clear that in faster-moving societies our personal experiences are phenomenally varied. This is why we have a harder (if not impossible) problem. This is why we need to consider a special type of architecture machine, one I will call a design amplifier.

Design Amplifiers

Before I begin I feel obliged to tell you that The Architecture Machine Group has worked very sporadically and without much success on this problem. The notion of a "design amplifier" is new and might provide an interim step between the present and the wizard machine, the surrogate human. I use the term "amplifier" advisedly; my purpose is not to replicate the human architect, as it may have been five years ago, but to make a surrogate *you* that can elaborate upon and contribute technical expertise to *your* design intentions. This allows us to consider and possibly see in the near future an option for computer-aided design that presumes "informed" machines, though not necessarily a machine intelligence.

There is an inherent paradox here. A design amplifier will have no stake in the outcomes of joint ventures; hence it must act truly as an extension of the 'future user.' Does this in turn mean that the machine intelligence necessary to support richness of dialogue will in fact be counterproductive to the participation because this same intelligence, like that of the human architect, would fall prey to the ills of translation, ascribing meanings of its own? In other words, does the intelligence required to communicate contradict the notion of informed amplification? I would draw your attention to the analogy of a good teacher who fosters an intellectual environment in which you discover for yourself in comparison to the one who drills facts and proclaims principles. As such, let us consider aspects of a design amplifier in terms of a somewhat dual existence: the benevolent educator and the thirsting student, all in one.

There are two categories to consider: (1) What does the machine know? (2) How does the user deal with what it knows? These questions are particularly interesting because the most obvious paradigm is in fact the least rewarding. The most obvious method would be to construct a machine with a vast knowledge of architecture and to view the user as an explorer of this knowledge through a window of his needs and the medium of some sophisticated man-machine interface. An example of this is found in most computer-aided instruction systems where, for example, the machine *knows* arithmetic and the child manipulates the machine in a more or less prearranged exploration, witnessing *yes*es, *no*s, *do*s, and *don't*s.

A more exciting approach applicable to a design amplifier can be found in the recent work of Seymour Papert (1971a, b, c) and his colleagues. In brief, their theory is that computer-aided instruction should be treated as the amplification and enlightening of the processes of learning and thinking themselves, rather than merely presenting and drilling specific subject matter. To achieve this, the computer is treated, in some sense, as an automatic student *by the child* (see also Ackoff, 1972). In the Papert experiments, the six- or seven-year-old youngster has the opportunity to give a "behavior" to the computer via a simple but powerful programming language called LOGO. Whether the behavior is to be manifest in reversing a string of characters or having a turtle draw a polygon, its misbehavior reveals "bugs" and, most importantly, contains cues for ameliorating the system. The child observes the process by which he learns, and the notion of *debugging* is suddenly put in contrast with the penalties of *error making*. Furthermore, the child is learning by doing (by playing). "You

can take a child to Euclid but you can't make him think" (Papert, 1972).

If you are an architect, how many times have you heard, "Oh I wanted to be an architect but was no good at drawing" or "I wanted to be an architect but was terrible at mathematics"? If you are not an architect, have you ever said something like that? In the same way that your saying "I am no good at languages" is contradicted by your living in France and learning French (or in the case of math, having Papert's mathland), one can consider a designland where one learns about design by playing with it. The underlying assumption is that, while you may not be able to design an efficient hospital or workable airport, you can design your own home, better than any other person.

You already choose furniture, paint walls, and select decors for your house. If the building technologies supported the notion, what knowledge would you lack in order to move up a scale to allocate space and decide boundaries between indoors and outdoors? Or, to pose almost the same question another way, What does an architect know that a contractor doesn't? The answer may be found by briefly partitioning the design process, separating what you might call talent from competence (an apprehensive but telling disjunction). The ensuing argument is based upon the assumption that the symbiosis between future user and machine is so strong that "talent" is in the eyes of the resident and competence in the hands of the design amplifier. This is in dramatic contract to previously stated (by me) positions!

Note that comfort and confidence (and credibility)

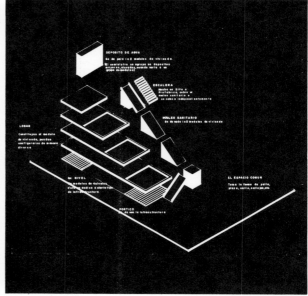

1

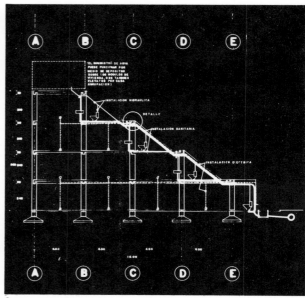

3

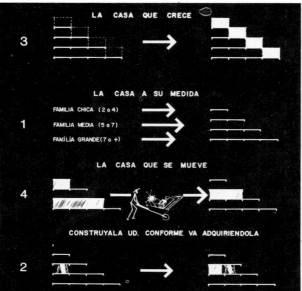

LA CASA QUE CRECE

3

LA CASA A SU MEDIDA

FAMILIA CHICA (2 a 4)

FAMILIA MEDIA (5 a 7)

FAMILIA GRANDE (7 o +)

1

LA CASA QUE SE MUEVE

4

CONSTRUYALA UD. CONFORME VA ADQUIRIENDOLA

2

2

DEPOSITO DE AGUA

ESCALERA

NUCLEO SANITARIO

LOSAS

1er NIVEL

EL ESPACIO COMUN

PORTICO

4

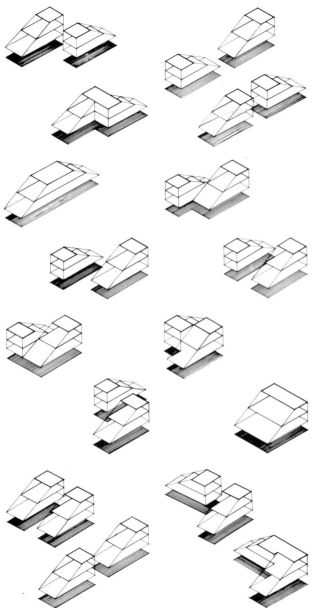

1 A model of the possible outcome of a participatory design and building system

2 A selection and construction sequence

3 The sanitary core and detail

4 The stair and circulation components

5 Possible configurations. Note that the structural system combined with the building methods removes any possibility for conflict between the needs of the individual and the amenities of the group. Photographs courtesy of Carlos Tejeda, Miguel Yanez, Carlos Barrenechea, and the Iberoamericano University, Mexico City.

5

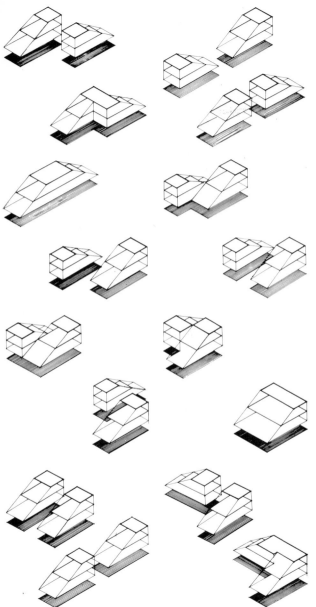

1 A model of the possible outcome of a participatory design and building system

2 A selection and construction sequence

3 The sanitary core and detail

4 The stair and circulation components

5 Possible configurations. Note that the structural system combined with the building methods removes any possibility for conflict between the needs of the individual and the amenities of the group. Photographs courtesy of Carlos Tejeda, Miguel Yanez, Carlos Barrenechea, and the Iberoamericano University, Mexico City.

5   111

An overview of ARCHI-TRAINER, a computer tutorial developed by Chris Abel at M.I.T., which presents the user with thirty-six houses to choose from. The purpose of the computer program is to allow a user to become acquainted with the "constructs" of another person (embodied, in this case, in a machine).

embrace a recognizable competence. Aside from a profound knowing of the user, there are certain operational "expertises" that can oversee interrelationships measured in such terms as British Thermal Units, kips, or feet per second. In a very real sense, these are simple computing tasks and, beyond correctness (which is simple), the checking must reflect only timeliness (which is not so simple). The closest I can come to a design amplifier is URBAN5, which did have "competences" and did try to effect a timeliness in the surfacing of what we called conflicts and incompatibilities (Negroponte and Groisser, 1967a and b; 1970). However, it should be recognized that URBAN5 was the ultimate paternalist; it suffered from (among other things) being directed to serving the architect, not the resident.

Architecture Machine

Two Loops

Following Friedman's simple model of two loops, one with me and one with my neighborhood, let's examine some aspects of each in terms of automation. The reader should refer to the extensive works of Friedman, found in the bibliography, but should be cautioned about the particularly French notion of a "*banque de données*" or what he calls "a repertoire." It is somewhat misleading taken at face value because it assumes a menu-picking activity rather than a design activity. The offerings of a menu of solutions obviously cannot exceed the combinatorial product of the parts (which may be enormous). Friedman, unlike many researchers in France, escapes this particular constraint by making his repertoire (*banque de données*) contain topologies that do not have a metric. It is the user's adding of this metric that affords the limitless variety.

The first loop is private. It must be self-sustaining in its powers to maintain the user's attention, ask intelligent questions, and provide broad commentary. It must tread the thin line of distinction between making suggestions and being a bully, between criticizing and insulting, between navigating a search and directing it. Friedman (in personal conversation) makes a distinction by calling the computing organism a "consultant," implying a "knower" at your beck and call, paid to help even if he may not agree with your personal premise. The connotations of *consult* are illuminating in the sense that the underlying skill is uncluttered by metaphorical distinctions, but it is also disturbing inasmuch as one must seriously question whether proficiency can be shared without dialogue requiring metaphor.

115

Möbel, die Ihnen beim Entwurf helfen sollen

Wir haben hier die wichtigsten Möbel einer Wohnung maßstabgerecht abgebildet. Richten Sie Ihre Entwürfe damit ein. Dann merken Sie noch rechtzeitig, ob etwa ein Raum zu klein geworden ist. Zum Schluß können Sie die Möbel fest einkleben und auch eigene dazuzeichnen. Das müssen Sie aber nicht. Einen Einfluß auf die Entscheidung der Jury hat das in keinem Fall. Sie bewertet nur den Grundriß.

Wohnbereich

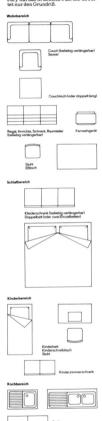

Couch (beliebig verlängerbar)
Sessel

Couchtisch (oder doppelt lang)

Regal, Anrichte, Schrank, Raumteiler
(beliebig verlängerbar)

Fernsehgerät

Stuhl
Eßtisch

Schlafbereich

Kleiderschrank (beliebig verlängerbar)
Doppelbett (oder zwei Einzelbetten)

Kinderbereich

Kinderbett
Kinderschreibtisch
Stuhl

Kinderzimmerschrank

Kochbereich

Spüle
Doppelspüle
Küchenschrank-Einheit
(beliebig aneinanderreihbar)

Geschirrspüler
Kühlschrank
Elektroherd
Waschmaschine

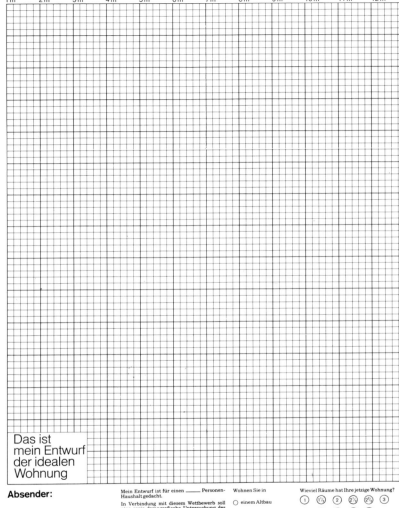

| 1m | 2m | 3m | 4m | 5m | 6m | 7m | 8 m | 9m | 10m | 11m | 12m |

Das ist
mein Entwurf
der idealen
Wohnung

Absender:

Vor- und Zuname

Ort

Straße / Platz

Mein Entwurf ist für einen _____ Personen-Haushalt gedacht.

In Verbindung mit diesem Wettbewerb soll eine sozio-demografische Untersuchung der Wohnwünsche der Bevölkerung vorgenommen werden. Für diese Befragung wären uns die folgenden Angaben, um die wir Sie bitten, von großem Wert.

Alter des Einsenders:

Familiengröße:
(Zahl der Personen)

Wohnen Sie in

○ einem Altbau
○ einem Neubau
○ einer frei finanzierten Wohnung
○ einer Sozialwohnung

(Zutreffendes bitte ankreuzen)

Wieviel Räume hat Ihre jetzige Wohnung?

① 1½ ② 2½ 2½ ③
3½ 3½ ④ 4½ mehr.

(Zutreffendes bitte ankreuzen)

Wenn Sie Mieter sind, wie hoch ist dann Ihre jetzige Miete (netto, ohne Nebenkosten wie z. B. Heizung, Treppenhausreinigung)?

_____ Mark Miete im Monat.

Zahlen, die Ihnen sagen, wie teuer Ihr Entwurf kommt

Die Qualität eines Entwurfs hängt natürlich auch davon ab, was es kostet, ihn zu verwirklichen. Wir haben deshalb in einer Tabelle zusammengestellt, wie teuer unter Umständen Quadratmeter Wohnung mit zeitgemäßer Ausstattung sind, wenn man sie kauft oder mietet. Dabei haben wir einen Kaufpreis von 1800 Mark und einen Mietzins von 6 bis 11 Mark pro Quadratmeter angesetzt (je größer die Wohnung, desto niedriger die qm-Miete). Das entspricht dem derzeitigen Preisniveau in einem Stadtteil wie Wandsbek.

qm	Kauf	Miete
30	54 000	330
40	72 000	400
50	90 000	450
60	108 000	510
70	126 000	560
80	144 000	630
90	162 000	690
100	180 000	750
110	198 000	810
120	216 000	880
130	234 000	940
140	252 000	970
150	270 000	1000
160	288 000	1060
170	306 000	1110
180	324 000	1150
190	342 000	1180
200	360 000	1200

Fünf Tips von Architekten für alle, die mitmachen

Wir haben Architekten die Frage gestellt: Was muß ein Laie unbedingt wissen, der eine Wohnung entwerfen will. Die Antwort: Nichts — bis auf eine Handvoll unumstößlicher Regeln. Hier sind sie.

1. Kinderzimmer sollen stets auf der Sonnenseite der Wohnung liegen.
2. Ein Kinderzimmer muß mindestens acht Quadratmeter groß sein. Dann kann das Kind darin schlafen und Schularbeiten machen. Soll es in seinem Zimmer auch spielen können, sind zwölf Quadratmeter gerade ausreichend.
3. Eine Küche soll niemals unter 1,80 Meter breit sein. Und selbst dann kann man nur an einer Längswand Schränke aufstellen.
4. Eine Loggia (Balkon) muß eine Tiefe von wenigstens 1,50 Metern haben. Ist die Loggia schmaler, kann man den Liegestuhl nicht mehr beliebig aufstellen.
5. Zimmertüren (nicht die Haustür) haben im allgemeinen eine Öffnungsbreite von 80 Zentimetern.

Das ist alles.

Unsere Anschrift:

Schicken Sie Ihren Entwurf bitte nur an diese extra von der Post für den Wettbewerb eingerichtete Adresse:

Hamburger Abendblatt-
WESTBANK-
Wettbewerb

„So wollen
wir wohnen"

2000 Hamburg 100

1 Advertisement which appeared in a Hamburg newspaper. Headline reads: "We want to live like this." Some of the text reads: "Furniture that should help you with your design." "Architects and architectural students are not allowed to participate." "Five tips from architects...." Unfortunately, the bulk of the text is devoted to prizes and jury.

2 A building scheme that allows for participatory arrangement and rearrangement as families grow and shrink. Illustrations courtesy of Professor Jos Weber, Hamburg, Germany.

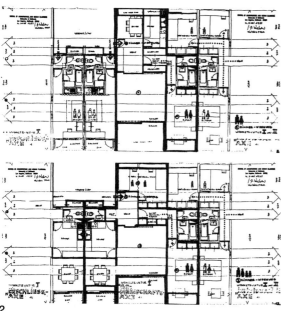

2

The closest example of the first loop implemented in a computer program is ARCHIT (Rorick, 1971). The following is an excerpt from one conversation.
Computer:
Shall we discuss the dining areas?
User:
Yes.
Computer:
Who does most of the cooking in your family?
User:
Carol.
Computer:
I would suggest that the dining area for your everyday meals be in the same room as the cooking area so that everyone can socialize while meals are being prepared and Carol won't be isolated in the kitchen. Don't you agree?
User:
Yes.
Computer:
How often do you want these occasions to be formal (that is, other than casually joining you for dinner) in times per year?
User:
12.
Computer:
Keeping these answers in mind, do you feel that you need a separate dining area for more formal occasions?
User:
No.
Computer:
How many people do you want the everyday dining area to accommodate including company?
User:
8.

At this point the reader should be appalled. The computer program has browbeaten the user into not wanting a dining room and short-circuited the deeper patterns of living that may keep Carol in the kitchen quite happily away from everybody. The program has exhibited an illusion of intelligence and "knowingness" and, in this example, done all the talking! Unfortunately, I do not have a more positive example to offer (but am working on it). A blatant flaw in ARCHIT-like programs is the desire to rapidly pinpoint an "architectural program" via direct yes/no, one/two questions. Inference making and indirect procedures should be used, not for the purpose of making life difficult (for the computer), but for the purpose of soliciting more complex and revealing patterns of living. We must avoid initiating dialogue by asking questions because the questions perforce flavor the answer. The next section describes a simple experiment in inference making, one that avoids asking questions.

In contrast to the "inner" loop, the "outer" loop is a great deal easier to conceive. Its purpose is to flag local perturbations when a desire of mine conflicts with an amenity of yours or of the group at large. A simple example would be a construction of mine blocking light or view from a portion of your house. Such functions assume that the machine is all-knowing about geometry, particular desires, and complicated rules (which is relatively easy). It also assumes, like any law-arbitrating system, the ability to exercise rules in context (which is not so easy). In managing urban spaces we already have the example of zoning ordinances and the vicissitudes of seeking variances.

The general scheme would be a network of many (one per person) design amplifiers working in concert with a variety of larger "host" machines, machines that could direct questions to other amplifiers or could answer those related to more global matters. An advantage of this layout is the opportunity, hitherto impossible, for personal negotiations within a regulatory framework that could capitalize upon the special-case amenities that are important to me and are available for negotiation. For example, my roof surface could serve as your terrace without inconvenience to me because it happens to be above services and functions that would be disturbed by noise. Or, I might not mind your cantilevering over my entrance, as the reduction in light would be more than compensated by the additional shelter I happened to want. While these are simpleminded examples, they reflect a kind of exchange (even bargaining) that is not possible in present contexts. They assume two parties, but this could be extended to complex and circuitous tradeoffs: if $A \rightarrow B$, $B \rightarrow C$, $C \rightarrow D, ..., \rightarrow n$, $n \rightarrow A$. We begin to see the opportunity for applying three-dimensional zoning standards and performance standards in context, a feat that I propose is manageable only with a large population of design amplifiers that could talk to each other and to host machines.

Plan Recognition

A typical exercise in computer-aided design is the generation of two- and three-dimensional "layouts" from a set of well-specified constraints and criteria. The classical and most recent experiments can be found in Bernholtz (1969), Eastman (1972a), T. Johnson et al. (1970), Liggett (1972), Mitchell (1972b), Mohr (1972b), Quintrand (1971), Steadman (1971), Teague (1970), Weinzapfel (1973), and Yessios (1972b). The underlying and common thread of all these works is the framework: input of "problem specification" and output of physical description. This section considers an experiment that seeks to do the reverse: input of a physical description (through recognition rather than specification) and output of problem specification. The goal is to recognize a structure of relationships and attributes in contrast to asking for a description.

In the context of participation, the purpose of this experiment is to initiate a dialogue by raising issues (not necessarily questions) drawn from inferences derived from a plan of the "user's" present house. Preceding sections and previous chapters suggest a profound man-machine acquaintance, one that would take a long time to achieve, perhaps years, and one that would have certainly a much wider application than assisting you to be your own architect. In the same way as the machine intelligence paradigm is self-defeating, the acquaintanceship approach to dialogue also could stymie progress and impede initiative in that it is difficult, if not impossible, to seriously consider a modest experiment without ending up with goals to match human dialogue and friendship. The following experiment is a sample point of departure and, as such, it should be viewed only

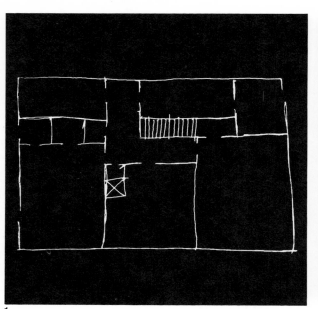

1

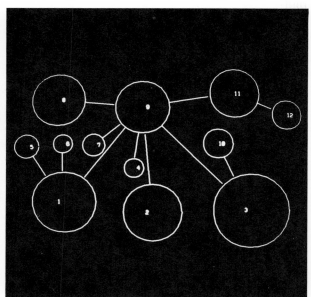

2

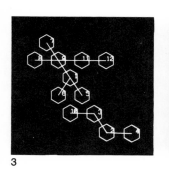

3

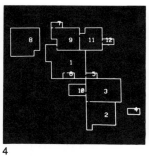

4

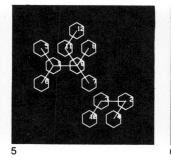

5

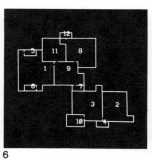

6

1 House plan sketched by novice

2 Mapping of preceding house plan into planar graph

3 A hexagonal resolution of the graph

4 House plan generated from 3

5 Another alternate graph

6 House plan generated from 5

as a mechanism that will lead to conversation, not as a means of generating house plans. The prime feature of this approach is that it can remain silent and attentive at first (without "tell me this," "answer that," "say this," etc.), can timidly venture comment, and then can vigorously interact (if all goes well). This is in contrast to the otherwise necessary tedium of questions and answers that must be employed to immerse the user and to introduce the machine.

In this experiment the user is simply invited to draw a plan of his house. He does this with ballpoint pen and regular paper without the burdensome paraphernalia of most computer graphics (the hardware is described at somewhat greater length in Appendix 1). It can be arranged that the user be completely unaware of the attention or observation of the machine. Remember that the user is not an architect and probably draws very badly; he may very well have never drawn a plan of his house before. It is interesting to note, however, that the most inexperienced sketcher suffers from the lack of two skills, neither of which really matters (at first): (1) He is bad at maintaining constant proportion and scale, as exhibited by his inevitably running off the side of the paper. (2) He is not sure-handed enough to draw straight and forceful lines. However, he is, curiously enough, extremely adept at describing physical relations and juxtapositions, from which we can extract adjacencies and linkages and can construct, for example, graph representations like the planner graph grammar used by Grason (1971).

The initiation of the dialogue is achieved by mapping the physical plan into a relational structure (like the adjacent graph in figure 2) that does not have a metric (hence the initial unimportance of scale). The structure then is used to generate other solutions, assuming that the structure is underconstrained as a result of recognizing only a subset of the relations. It is much like only half-listening to a story, extracting an incomplete theme, and developing a new narrative (with similar structure). The other plans (that is, the machine's story) reveal physical arrangements that have enough commonality for the user to make interested comments and for the machine to pose interesting questions. *Interesting* is defined here as leading to an increase in the user's realizing and understanding architectural implications and an increase in the machine's apprehension of the particular needs and patterns as manifest by what the user has now.

The plan recognition program, SQUINT, employs the services of HUNCH. In particular, it exercises the feature of zooming in and out of the positional data, traveling within the spectrum of very low and very high resolutions. The preceding chapter illustrates the sort of range; the grain varies from 1,024 rasters per grain to a one-to-one correspondence. And, at any grain except the finest, the percentage of "hits" can be viewed as a gray tone.

As happens with HUNCH, the noble intentions of SQUINT become reduced to very straightforward operations. Simple properties are recognized from the limiting boundaries of spaces and the penetrations of the boundaries. The first step is to look for the total number of bodies in the sketch. While there is usually one, this initial observation is necessary, if for nothing else than to save memory by compressing the positional data to exclude the "white of paper" that lies outside the sketched plan. The recognition of discrete bodies is

achieved by a "flooding" process that creeps in from the sides of the paper, flowing around obstructing lines at a grain appropriate to ensure that it does not seep through doors and windows. Subsequent to flagging all flooded bits, the remainder are accounted for in a similar flooding technique, starting at any point. If all points are not accounted for by the first two floods, then there must be more than one body, and the procedure needs to be repeated until all points are tagged. It is the responsibility of later routines to decide whether the multiple elements in fact represent two autonomous disconnected sections of a house, for example, or whether in reality the additional figures are diagrammatic elements: north arrows, lettering, doodles, or coffee stains.

Following the location of the silhouette(s) of the plan, rather similar procedures wander through internal subdivisions from one space to another, at one grain or another, a little bit like an expandable/shrinkable "mouse" meandering through a maze. Most sketching techniques will allow for internal spaces to be attained at the finest resolution. However, some sketching techniques include the demarcation of door radii and steps, which would impede passage of our "mouse" if the lines were considered boundaries (which they are not). These are the interesting cases; one must look for cues and develop evidence that, for example, such-and-such is probably a tread and not a chimney flue or this is probably a jamb and not a sill. Some of these situations are particularly difficult to deal with, where, for example, in one case the misinterpretation of a one-step level change resulted in guessing that the entire circulation of the house passed through the guest closet. This extreme example may appear to be a violent programming oversight.

I must repeat, however, that there will *always* be conditions of such ambiquity that will require even the onlooking human to ask. I further insist there is nothing wrong with asking!

Irrespective of whether the user has ascribed names to spaces, the program will give its own names in order to have an internal nomenclature of nodes and links. The labels can apply to traditional names (if you insist) like "bathroom" and "bedroom"; to orientations like north, windward, or view-oriented; or consist of schematic titles like space A, B2, or 732. The labeled nodes of the structure are linked with either categorical *yes/nos* or graded values of an attribute like access/circulatory, visual, acoustical.

The subsequent mapping into an alternate floor plan has been done by Steve Handel and Huck Rorick (illustrated in Appendix 2). Rorick's experiment appends the somewhat extraneous but interesting feature of adding heuristics that represent his view of what another architect might have done. In the specific case illustrated he has developed heuristics for overlaying a third dimension upon the plan following the vernacular of Frank Lloyd Wright, generating a variety of Wrightian roof forms. Though this is contradictory to the full level of participation suggested by Friedman, it is fun to speculate that a representation of a deeper structure of my needs could be manipulated and displayed in the formal jargons of various famous architects, perhaps even Vitruvius or Viollet-le-Duc.

We should not forget that the user of "computer-aided participatory..." is not an architect. "Plan recognition" might imply to some a more formal approach than is intended. The reader should be referred, if he is interested in the morphologies of floor plans, to the original works of Levin (1964), Whitehead and Eldars (1964), Casalaina and Rittel (1967), and the most recent work of Weinzapfel (1973). However, remember that these systems assume the driver to be an architect.

4

Intelligent Environments

Introduction by Sean Wellesley-Miller

Idle speculation on intelligent environments is usually of the "what if" sort that quickly enters the realms of science fiction. Need, economics, and even theoretical, let alone technical, feasibility are banished to the real world where they, together with architecture, presumably belong. The result is some amusing speculation seemingly guaranteed to be unrelated to any major issue of the day and designed to upset all but the most iconoclastic of wet dream architects by its frivolity. We are about to enter a parallel universe that happens to be your home. The very idea seems time bound; it belongs to the psychedelic sixties in a way that brings to mind a futurist of the fifties forecasting a helicopter in every backyard by 1975. The energy crisis, environmental pollution, political bugging, and all the other sad facts of the sober seventies are set aside. Viewed in these terms the investment of "intelligence" in the man-made environment seems a surrealistic dream of doubtful desirability, unlikely to be realized.

Yet is it? "What if" despite her banishment, necessity herself, that well-known mother of invention, is pushing us in that very direction? It is certainly not too difficult to build a case along these lines. Imagine—it has been done—an on-line traffic monitoring system that informed you at each traffic intersection of the relative traffic densities along each branch. Such a system could save motorists considerable amounts of gasoline while wasting very little energy to operate. We would also have a real-time transport map of the city which, correlated with energy densities, land uses, and so on, would probably tell us more about urban dynamics in six months than we have learned in years.

It has been calculated that if MIT installed a minicomputer (we plan to do it) to watch the campus load profile and regulate all lights, fans, radiators, and thermostat set points on MIT's antiquated and sprawling campus, it would pay for itself in energy and labor saved within days.

Both of these examples are progeny more of the base and unassuming thermostat married to the common counter and so blessed with memory than of a "machine intelligence." Yet they are happening for sound economic resons. It would seem that after a century's preoccupation with the physiology of buildings we are beginning to become involved with their metabolism and are even starting to develop rudimentary nervous systems for them complete with sensors and actuators. The ganglia will thicken.

Some motels no longer heat up all their rooms in one go. Rather, guest rooms are heated up to match anticipated (binomial) guest arrivals according to a variable sequence that also considers external weather conditions and room groupings. A minicomputer is used to predict arrivals and determine room heating sequence to minimize overall energy requirements. The same system also handles registrations, personal services, accounting, and room security, including keeping tabs on the color T.V. sets.

A major lumber company is constructing an experimental greenhouse that will be directly responsive to the tree seedlings it contains. Thermocycles, photoperiod and intensity, ventilation and nutrition rates, and so on, are all determined by the plants themselves in a growth-monitoring/equipment-activating adaptive logic system. The nursery "learns" about its protégés, mothering them to maturity. Maybe the plants will be so much happier that they will grow in one year by an amount that used to take two.

All this may still smack of the thermostat but the response parallels that of an elevator. The reason is that the system in the last example is exploring a possibility-space according to a hill-climbing routine rather than giving a predetermined response to a predicted situation. Its response is nontrivial in that some "learning" is involved and the form of the response is not predetermined. Its behavior is purposeful if not intelligent.

However, if, in addition to sensors and actuators our environment had a functional image of itself upon which it was able to map actual occupant activity, it would not only be able to monitor and regulate environmental conditions but also to mediate the activity patterns through the allocation of functional spaces. In short, it would know what was going on inside itself and could manage things so as to, say, maximize personal contacts, minimize long distances, conserve space, handle lighting or what have you on a day-to-day or hour-to-hour basis to provide a more efficient and gracious environment. It would also be able to observe the results of its interventions. Now, for "a functional image of itself" substitute "my model of me"; for "activity patterns" substitute "my model of you"; then, given that we have two adaptive systems interacting with each other, can "my model of your model of me" be so very far behind?

So far all these examples deal with the behavior of statistical groups in relation to physical conditions. Cybernetic cities, helpful hotels, solicitous greenhouses, and parsimonious campuses are still a long way from the living room.

Because of solid waste disposal problems, water shortages, overloaded utility nets, and the energy crisis, a number of essentially self-sufficient houses are on the drawing boards. They are heated and cooled by solar radiation, can share their heat, are powered by wind turbines, photovoltaic cells, and methane generators and may provide 70 percent of their occupants' food supply through integral greenhouses and aquaculture systems. The umbilical cord with the control utility nets has been cut. All the external control practices now have to be internalized. At the level of energy flows and mass transport they are completely responsive closed-loop systems tied into the same natural processes that drive the rest of the biosphere. The control system will have to decide on the best way to use available resources to meet the occupants' requirements. The house becomes essentially an environmental regulating device mediating between its inhabitant and the external environment. As the functions handled autonomously increase in complexity and interconnectedness so the response will become more personal. One can imagine integrated self-sufficient homes providing horticultural management, dietary planning, and waste recycling (including uranalysis checks?); energy control, environmental comfort, and medical care; water recycling, hygiene, and maintenance and valet services; personal security, acoustic and visual privacy, and space planning advice; information processing facilities tied in with communications, and so on. Developments in building materials at the thermophysical and mechanical levels will provide multistate materials capable of quite radical transformations. The superimposition of end functions (illumination, silencing, warming, cooling, softening, supporting, accommodating, and so on) and process control (sensing, sampling, actuating, controlling) tend to emphasize material responses. We are talking more of artificial domestic ecosystems capable of intelligent responses than of computer-controlled conventional homes. Buildings that can grow and upgrade themselves, that open up like flowers in fine weather and clamp down before the storm, that seek to delight as well as serve you.

How far this will or can go is open to argument but the fact remains that the concept of a physically responsive environment is being turned from dream to reality by the force, appropriately enough, of environmental circumstances themselves. We are making buildings more context responsive, and in doing so we should not forget that a building's final context of response is the needs and senses of its inhabitants.

"Intelligent" environments, responsive to you and me and the outside world, may well happen. Responsive environments at a gross functional level already exist.

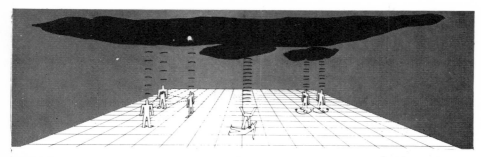

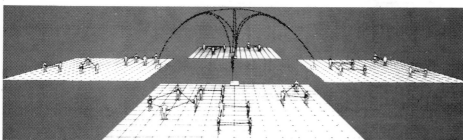

1

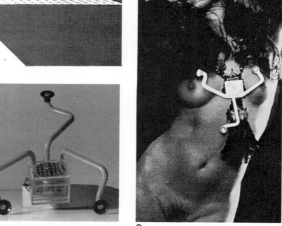

2

3

1 "Sounding Mirror" (1970), a light-sound transducer invented by Juan Navarro-Baldeweg that creates a sounding environment (musical notes or oscillations of varying frequencies) responsive to people's spatial configurations. It can be attached to the body and has three photocells oriented right, left, and front. Participants carry small flashlights which they direct at others to create a sonic representation of movement and personal interaction.

2 One application of the Baldeweg device

3 A pneumatic structure built for recreational purposes

Responsive Architecture

As a profession undergoes philosophical, theoretical, or technical transition, words in the vocabulary of the particular movement take on very special and sometimes distorted meanings. In some instances a word will slip into technical jargon with so many oblique and personal connotations that it can be effectively used in conversation only with those "out"; in "in-jargon" it is too misleading. For example, when I was in school in the early sixties, the term *a building* was anathema. To design "a building" implied everything from fascism to romanticism, from making profits to foisting whims. Similarly, in the late sixties, the adjectives *flexible*, *manipulative*, and *responsive* have received a wide variety of conflicting definitions and interpretations with examples of flexibility ranging from the cafetorium to the teepee.

While it is too easy and not productive to make one's own definitions and then to declare who has and who has not adhered to them, it is revealing to distinguish general thrusts associated with each attitude, irrespective of the adjective you may use. For example, the term *flexible* has generally followed the spirit of Mies van der Rohe's "less is more" in the sense that, when two activities have a large intersection (in set, mathematical, theoretical terms), we design for the few "ands." The "exclusive ors" are compromised, if not ignored, for the purpose of cohabitation of the two activities. Just as with any conduct, one maintains flexibility by making as few commitments as possible.

The term *manipulative*, on the other hand, implies effort committed to making a close fit for each

131

activity by providing for change and alteration that can range from closing a curtain to moving walls. Each state of a manipulative environment is in a very real sense nonflexible. To achieve a multiplicity of uses, the environment must undergo a physical transformation, large or small, at the behest of the users. What is important to my following arguments is that this change, that is, manipulation, is an *overt* action directed by the user(s). The manipulative environment is a passive one, one that is moved as opposed to one that moves.

In contrast, *responsive*, sometimes called *adaptable*, or *reactive*, means the environment is taking an active role, initiating to a greater or lesser degree changes as a result and function of complex or simple computations. There are very few examples of this kind of architecture. This chapter considers extreme examples of responsiveness, in particular those behaviors that could become manifest in homes of the future and be viewed as intelligent behavior. While the following sections speculate about the pros and cons of an intelligent environment in terms of specific experimentation, you should attend to your own notions of what it might be like to "live in an architecture machine" because, unlike the following discussion, your ideas will not be flavored by technical *can*s, *could*s, and *might*s. Furthermore, there is some very serious question as to whether we really would want our environments, particularly our houses, to be responsive. While the case for responsive traffic systems or responsive health delivery systems can be made easily (hence not covered in this chapter), the case for a responsive living room only can be made after satisfying very personal questions of life style.

The typical introduction to responsive architecture is made with the thermostat. Eastman's (1971) "Adaptive Conditional Architecture" carries the analogy to great length. I believe that it is the wrong analogue. In Eastman's essay it leads to the objectionable process-control model for architecture, a decode-interpret-translate decision structure with old-fashioned feedback loops evidenced in the most common oil burner. In contrast, let us start with another analogue, perhaps the only other: elevators.

As in designing a heating system and equally unwisely, it would be possible to build a predisposed system. By this I mean a system that has a pre-established model of the world and operates without taking further samples. In such a case, it would be necessary to study the vertical circulation patterns of an existing building with careful enough measuring and monitoring to build a deterministic or stochastic model of vertical movement. With such information it would be feasible to construct an elevator system that had no buttons but would stop frequently enough at the right places and go frequently enough to the right places so that everybody would be serviced at some level of satisfaction. This, of course, is how a public transportation system works and, as is the case with public transportation, there exists a synergistic bending of one's own timetable to meet the bus or subway schedule, and, perhaps, a means of altering (by an authority) the routing and frequencies to meet calendar needs.

While such a system might work satisfactorily for an elevator or heating system (especially if the inhabitants did not know better), it is vulnerable to inefficiencies because it cannot satisfy the immediate demands of the users or respond to sudden changes that invalidate the model. Note that the addition of buttons to call for service allows for the complete removal of a model, that is, a schedule. The elevator system must be designed to meet limiting, worst cases as measured, for example, by tolerable wait limits (usually 20 to 30 seconds) at peak times (morning arrivals, in the case of office buildings). Once the elevator is installed, if use changes (a restaurant added on the top floor, for example), the tolerable limit may rise or fall for particular stations on the vertical chain. However, the response to my call will always be the direct result of the machine's sensory inputs.

What happens in the case when I ring for the elevator to go down and it arrives full? I must wait and ring again. More sophisticated elevators, however, take the previous modelless scheme and add, once again, a model. But this time it is not a schedule but *a model of appropriate behavior.*

In the simplest case, a load cell is imbedded in the floor of the vehicle to sense the total weight of the passengers (a safer measure of elevator population than whether yet another passenger can fit on). This information is incorporated in the simple algorithm: if weight exceeds some maximum, ignore all further calls until some passengers disembark. It should be noted that such elevators do exist and, to my knowledge, this is one of the few examples of trivial-but-serious computing in everyday physical environments.

But now what happens in the following case? A full elevator is traveling down and one passenger is not going to the bottom, but to the fifth floor, let's say. At the same time, on the fifth floor there are two passengers who have rung to go down. In this situation, a very sophisticated mechanism is necessary if we wish the elevator to be able to notice the problem and to request that the two decide who the single newcomer should be or that both wait for another cab.

From this point it is possible to extrapolate and to fantasize to the extremes of a courteous elevator, a suggestive elevator, a humorous elevator. In the same breath, we can wonder about the eventuality of its being grumpy, poking fun, or trying to befriend influential passengers by giving them more personal and efficient service. These are not preposterous possibilities; perhaps they lose their validity in the nature of the particular example. I propose to exercise such notions of responsiveness in the context of a house. Maybe a house is a home only once it can appreciate your jokes.

Ménage à Trois

The founding notions for an intelligent environment are in Brodey's (1967) "Soft Architecture: The Design of Intelligent Environments." More recent reflections can be found in Avery Johnson's (1971) "Three Little Pigs Revisited." Neither paper, however, presents convincing examples or gives the slightest inkling of a picture or description of how such a system might work. This is because there are no examples, there are no pictures, in short, there are no historical precedents of intelligent environments. Space capsules, cockpits, and any environment that consists solely of complex instrumentation are *not* the correct metaphors.

The proper metaphor is the family with a new member in it—the house. Absurd, repugnant, perhaps wicked, but the idea deserves serious scrutiny not only because there are important issues like privacy at stake but also because it may be the most rewarding, exciting, and amenable of all conceivable forms of living. What does Johnson (1971) mean and what are the implications of his position: "We must build environments that invite their playful participation so that their self-referent knowledge of their community will grow..."?

Big Brother is not only watching, he is measuring your pulse, metering your galvanic skin resistance, smelling your breath. No. Those belong to the paradigm: "An adaptive process for architecture is made up of: A sensing device, a control algorithm, a change mechanism, and a control setting" (Eastman, 1971). This attitude is typified in the sofa that alters itself to "fit" the body aloft and that initiates soporific music and smells at 10:30 P.M. This view is wrong because it is ignorant of context, because it is generative of a complacency hitherto unseen, and because it does not account for what Gordon Pask has titled the *you-sensor*.

When I return at night and ask my wife to put the whatchamacallit youknowwhere, she most surely knows exactly what I mean and where I mean. She knows because she knows me in terms of all the models and models of models previously discussed and because she can use this information in the context of my facial expressions, the weather outside, and whether we are going out to dinner that night. At the same time, her response is in the context of her own intentions, and her level of commitment to one behavior versus another is achieved by our participating *in the same events with the same objects*.

Transposing a similar *responsiveness* to the physical environment suggests that it, too, must have purpose and intentions, and it must have all the paraphernalia required to build the necessary models of me and to use them in context. In brief, it is not a regulatory control system, it is an intelligent system.

Recognition

The simple sensing-effecting model of computation that views a processor receiving signals from its sensors and emitting responses with its actuators is not appropriate to making responsive architecture; it is the downfall of the thermostat analogy. The problem with this model, as illustrated in the adjacent figure (taken from Eastman, 1971b), is that the consequences of inputs are determined strictly by a feedback loop, no more responsive than (and equally as regulatory as) the governor of a steam engine. The model is inappropriate for two reasons: (1) the "control algorithm" in the feedback loop can issue effector changes as a result of what has been sensed, but it cannot initiate changes in its own criteria; (2) the behavior of the system resides at the interface; not self-referent, it is oblivious to the important inputs of observing its own responses. This second reason is stated more elegantly by Avery Johnson (1972): "In order to elicit *meaning* [my italics] from any data entering our sensorium, it either must have arisen as the consequence of our effector (outgoing, active) interaction with the course of the information, *or at least imply an interaction* [italics in original] in which we might engage with some other."

In the feedback model a "policy" is necessary for the control algorithm and the control setting. For example, a simple policy might be: 72 degrees Fahrenheit and 50 percent humidity. The setting states the policy, and the algorithm maintains it. If, however, we should find a better policy or need special revisions (because someone is ill or in a draft), we must change the control setting, thus revising the parameters of the controlling algorithm. Can this be done implicitly?

If we move one step back and revise the goal structure and replace the policy of 72 degrees and 50 percent humidity with a new policy, "maintain a comfortable temperature and humidity," we not only have to consider varying parameters; implicitly or explicitly we must also consider which parameters to include at which times. In some situations a much cooler temperature might be appropriate, and in other instances the tolerance of "fit" of temperature is so large that it becomes unimportant. Can a machine handle this?

A final step back might be to view the goal of responsive architecture to be the support of the "good life" as defined by our individual tastes for a mixture of action modes: sleeps, eats, drinks, voids, sexes, works, rests, talks, attends, motor practices, angers, escapes, anxiouses, euphorics, laughs, aggresses, fears, relates, envies, and greeds. The table on the following page is from Iberall and McCulloch's (1969) "The Organizing Principles of Complex Living Systems." In this last case, the responsive system must know me. To this point it might have been possible to tune a passive device, singularly concerned with the manipulation of a handful of criteria within complicated but well-stated contingencies: if this and if that or that, then this and this. In this last case (and, I believe, in the one before) we definitely need the you-sensor.

The mechanism necessary to recognize enough features to distinguish you from me is formidable. As a particular example, I am drawing upon the master's thesis of Mark Lavin (1973) on GREET, a doorway that recognizes who is passing through it. The experiment has many implications that exceed the scope of the example; however, in

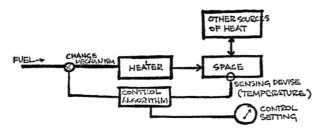

1 From Eastman (1972)

2 Table from Iberall and McCulloch (1969)

1

Action Modes

Sleeps 30
Eats 5
Drinks 1
Voids 1
Sexes 3
Works 25
Rests (no motor activity, indifferent internal sensory flux) 3
Talks 5
Attends (indifferent motor activity, involved sensory activity) . . 4
Motor practices (runs, walks, plays, etc.) 4
Angers 1
Escapes (negligible motor and sensory input) 1
"Anxious-es" 2
"Euphories" 1
Laughs 1
Agresses 1
Fears, fights, flees 1
Interpersonally attends (body, verbal, or sensory contact) 8
Envies 1
Greeds 1

Total . . . . 100% ± 20%
of time involvement

2

today's technology, it is the epitome of the you-sensor. At the onset of the experiment we must deny the recognition mechanism of inputs from any overt action *required* on the behalf of the person passing through the door. As soon as we ask him to speak (to get a voice print) or to touch a door knob (to measure galvanic skin resistance), we might as well give him a key with the thirty-two (four bytes!) notches necessary to distinguish any person within the entire population of the world. The recognition should take place without counting on any single or small set of "faithful inputs."

There have been several experiments in people recognition, especially face recognition (Kelley, 1970; Bledsoe, 1966—with the sordid application of sorting mug shots). What they have in common is the requirement of strict protocols for "being seen" and, more importantly, the examination of high-resolution information. Unique (to my knowledge) in Lavin's thesis is its use of low-resolution information. He observes only a few crude but telling features: height, weight, stride, foot size, and profile.

These features can be recorded all at once to produce a point in *n*-space (where *n* is between five and seven, in this example). A statistical pattern recognition approach would be to look for the intersection of an *n*-dimensional blob to see if it is you or me or either of us. In the latter case of finding two blobs, the machine has to guess or to measure accurately (if it is worth it) a closeness to the "center of blob" as defined, perhaps, by a history of successful distinctions of you from me.

A more promising approach would be to treat the problem much more heuristically (a method and

attitude discussed in greater detail in Appendix 2). This approach does not require looking at every feature at once. It examines a small number of "telling" ones that provide clues and strategies for examining or not examining others. For example, the adjacent figure shows a profile reported by GREET to the Architecture Machine. It obviously indicates that the parameter of weight ought to be considered marginally, but not ignored (because there is a whole class of people whom it could not be, probably, because their own weight is higher than that of the person carrying whatever).

We can add to the procedure a description of the room to which GREET is the door and knowledge of environmental conditions outside. If it is the only entrance and if I have passed in one direction, it is *unlikely* that I am passing from the same direction. Or, if it is snowing outside, the *likelihood* of heavy shoes must be considered. Similarly, knowing my habits and idiosyncrasies can be incorporated into a powerful recognition system with low-resolution inputs.

It should be realized that there is a major difference between distinguishing a small number of people (let's say five or ten) from all other people in the world and recognizing one out of a known population of a hundred or two hundred. The latter is easier and is what the Lavin experiment is testing. It should be understood that this is only one form of you-sensing, not necessarily the most efficient or, for that matter, the most ethical. There are some serious issues of door-tapping and jamb-snooping that can raise havoc with our privacies.

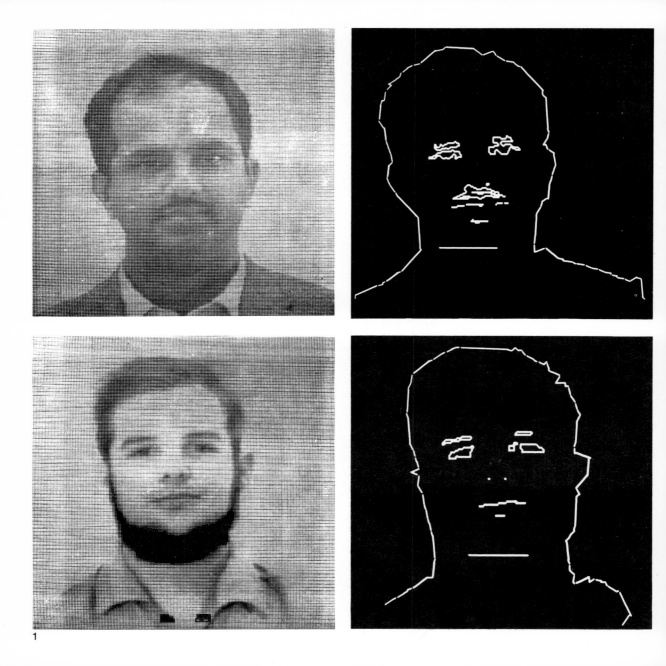

1

2

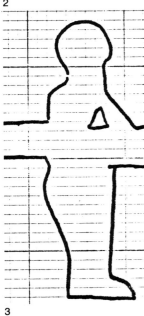

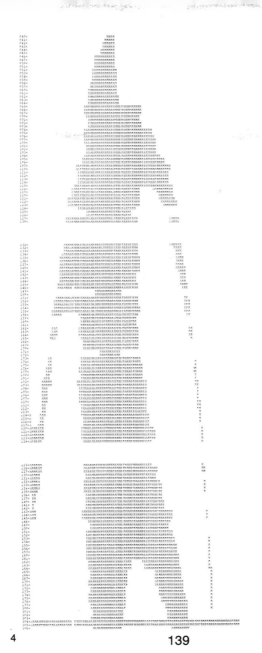

1 Faces and machine "contours" taken from Kelly (1970)

2 GREET. It used 280 photocells for profile detection. This illustration does not show the platform used for sensing weight, stride, and foot size. The project was curtailed prematurely.

3 Man with a two-by-ten

4 Profile of Andrew Lippman

3 4 139

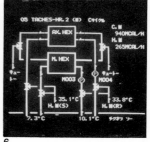

5

6

4

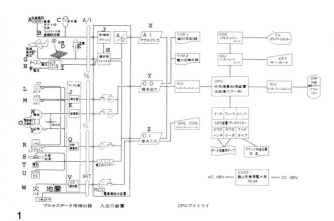

1

INPUT	PRESSURE, QUANTITY OF WATER, TEMPERATURE, QUANTITY OF GAS, VOLTAGE, ELECTRIC CURRENT, SOLAR RADIATION, WIND DIRECTION, WIND VELOCITY, ATMOSPHERIC PRESSURE, ELECTRIC POWER, POWER RATE, TIME, EARTHQUAKE, FIRE

DIGITAL/ANALOGUE CONVERTER

COMPUTER	ARRANGEMENT, OBSERVATION, JUDGEMENT, PRESERVATION, CALCULATION, COMMAND, MEMORIZING ESTIMATED DATA

OUTPUT — RECORD (TYPE, TAPE) — INDICATION (VIDEO) — INFORMATION (KEYBOARD) — OPERATION (C/O) — CONTROL (A/O, C/O)

JOB

| DAILY REPORT, BILL, DATA COLLECTION, OPERATION AND ACCIDENT RECORDING | TIME, DATA INDICATION, EQUIPMENT MALFUNCTION INDICATION, SCANNING OBSERVATION | PROCESSING ELECTRIC CUT OFF, DEMAND CUT, OUTDOOR AIR DAMPER, GENERATOR CAPACITY | CYCLE CHANGE, ECONOMICAL RUNNING, HEAT ACCUM. RUNNING, SCHEDULE RUNNING AND CORRECTION | AIR COND., RISING UP RUN, ROOM TEMP., PERIMETER WATER SETTING, PUMP NUMBER & WATER WHEEL CONTROL |

EFFECT — EFFORT DEDUCTION — INFORMATION PROCESSING — OPERATION RELIABILITY — COMFORT, AIR CONDITION

2

3

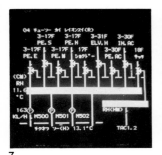

7

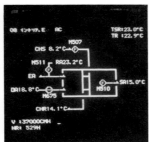

8

The adjacent figures illustrate an integrated environmental control system for the Osaka Kokusai Building, completed in February 1973. The architects and contractors were of Takenaka Komuten Co. Ltd., Osaka, Japan. Illustrations are courtesy of Takenaka Komuten and Mr. Makio Otsuju, who showed me the systems and helped me assemble the figures.

The hardware is composed of an 8K minicomputer, 131K magnetic drum, and a variety of typewriter and video displays. Note that the actual graphic displays are in color, regrettably not reproduced on these pages.

1 A flow chart of the system's operation. The translation concentrates on sensors and effectors: A, platinum resistance; B, temperature sensing in rooms, ducts, ceilings, and concrete; C, water temperature; D, solar radiation; E, water flow; F, wind velocity, direction, and atmospheric pressure; G, voltage; H, current; I, transformer; J and K, controllers; L, pumps; M, fans; N, subsidiary heat; O, compressor; P, main heat; Q, automatic adjustment devices; R, fan coils; S, hot water supply; T, electric supply; U, gas supply; V, fire alarm; W, fire and earthquake sensors; X, analogue inputs; Y, digital outputs; Z, digital inputs.

2 Block diagram of system

3 Control room with minicomputer in background

4 Closeup with projection display on

5 Display of water cooling and warming capacities, including performance coefficient (4.2), condensation temperature (36.4°C) and evaporation temperature (6°C).

6 Cool and warm water temperatures on their way in and out. Cool water lines are displayed in blue, warm in pink

7 Cool and warm water conditions in the middle stories

8 Indication of running conditions on the east side, including average room temperature (23.0°C), room temperature at the moment (22.9°C), return air temperature (23.2°C), outdoor temperature (18.8°C), cool water temperature in (8.2°C); cool water temperature out (14.1°C); and supplied air temperature (15°C)

9 Section of the building

10 Ground floor plan

Captions assembled from material translated from Japanese, courtesy of Mr. Masanori Nagashima.

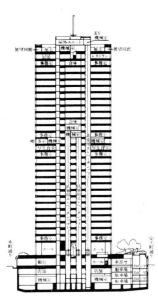

9　　　　南北断面図

10　　　2階平面図

141

1

2

3

1 Inflatable for walking on water. Photograph courtesy of Sean Wellesley-Miller.

2 Inflatable for children's play. Photograph courtesy of Sean Wellesley-Miller.

3 Inflatable that responds to sunlight, ambient temperature, and body movements. Photograph courtesy of Timothy Johnson and his students.

Responses

Speculation on or enumeration of exemplary responses by an intelligent environment is where this notion becomes rather suspect and the goals become flimsy. We can easily dream up operational and informational responses that could be handled by a good computer terminal or loyal household robot, but they would not meet the definition of what we are calling responsive *architecture*. When we look at responses that have been suggested (in the literature) for architectural behavior, we find the most banal illustrations, reminiscent of second-rate light shows. Even Brodey (1967) offered hackneyed images: "If the heartbeat accelerates, the room becomes redder (for example); if his breathing deepens, the room takes on a richer hue. As the hue intensifies his heart may beat faster in response to the stimulus (the strength of the color which changes with his feelings). This personalized total environment will be capable of producing a profound experience without brain damage." I only hope so.

What sort of behavior can the physical environment exhibit? I propose two classes of behavior: reflexive and simulated. The first is a motor, visual, olfactory, or auditory response that takes place as a part of space, reflecting a purpose. We have very few examples of even the simplest sort. Electric doors, rotating stages, and motorized partitions are not good examples because they are activated by yes-no, overt commands; thus they are no more interactive than the turning on of a vacuum cleaner. We find more valid (but still not too illuminating) examples in the Rolls-Royce engine whose grill is composed of louvers that automatically open and close as a function of the heat of the engine and the ambient temperature or the greenhouse that opens and closes a glass roof for the comfort (as determined by us) of the flowers. But these are process-control, decode-interpret-encode procedures of the thermostat variety. Do we have any better examples? "Self-organizing controllers can maintain (for example) average light levels or favorable brightness differences in the context of the weather, time of day, and the difference between your mood and that mood which was anticipated. The radiation or absorption of heat in direct exchange with the surroundings can be made relevant to your activities and to the thermodynamic conditions available. The acoustic properties of the inner spaces can be caused to enhance the privacy of a tête-à-tête or the mutual involvement of a larger gathering. Walls that move to the touch—relevant to the function of support or moving back in retreat—that change color and form: streamlining themselves to the wind or shrinking down when unoccupied, are all possible within the state-of-the-art technology" (A. Johnson, 1971).

Johnson's vision is vulnerable in detail. What is a self-organizing controller in this context? How do we recognize mood? What encompasses the enhancement of mutual involvement? But the theme is instructive in its description of a participating, courteous (as he calls it) environment with goals of a higher order than 72 degrees Fahrenheit and 50 percent humidity. Nevertheless, are not most of the responses going to come from voice output? The gesturing nature of reflexive responses is still difficult to imagine (and even find relevant).

The second kind of response, what I have called "simulated," is easier to envisage. One can imagine a living room that can simulate beaches and mountains. One can fantasize experiencing the chills of Mt. Everest and the heat of the Congo within a simulatorium or within extrapolations of Sutherland's (1968) helmet that include sound, smell, and touch. One of the reasons that simulated responses may appear easier, more wholesome, and less troublesome than reflexive ones is that they are naturally relegated to play and entertainment and most probably will not intrude into the pragmatic, serious activities that are the cornerstones of our daily lives and the Protestant ethic.

At this point, two other forms of response warrant elaboration: operational and informational. They are not exhibited through architectural gestures and transformations. However, at present they afford the most convincing examples of computers at home. For example, operationally, we can imagine the home of the future having surrogate butlers and maids embedded in all walls and floors or clunking about in bodies of plastic or steel. They would make beds (when it was recognized that you were not returning to bed), prepare the food (stepping aside on occasions when you enjoy cooking), and clean the house (distinguishing between throwing away broken glass and discarding a diamond). Such a robot would be a wonderful device, the joy of American housewives, and for reasons of safety (as suggested by Edward Fredkin in personal conversation) it ought to bark.

Informationally, the notion of responsiveness becomes even clearer. Unlike the household robot, my machine would know me on a more abstract and individual level. As an example, consider a suggestive television set that could recommend interesting viewings in knowledge of my tastes, my present mood, and previous engagements for the evening (which might lead to the television's taking it upon itself to record the program for me to view later). In the same spirit, we can speculate about synopsizing radio-news machines that could command a mixture of graphics, text, and voice output to present the news either on request or in terms of my interests. Or, finally, consider any information terminal or wall surface to which I can verbally pose questions on subjects ranging from the weather, to the stock market, to the likelihood of a particular political turn of events.

Putting all of these responses together begins to reveal a picture, however unclear it may be. We can start to imagine a dramatically different relationship between ourselves and our houses, one characterized by intimate interaction. Fanciful wondering can lead us to rooms that giggle, doors that fib, or windows that fidget. Or maybe concepts like "room," "door," and "window" are anachronisms. Just as the previous chapter removed the architect-middleman, maybe the notion of intelligent environment removes the contractor-middleman, and the design process and building process become one and the same, continually in operation. Out of what will a self-reproducing autogenic environment be made?

On Materials and Memory

Sant'Elia's 1913 plans for Milano 2000 were a direct extrapolation from the industrial revolution, from a glass to a concrete Crystal Palace. In some sense, today's research and development in the field of "building technology" is still no more than a similar, direct outgrowth of the ways of the industrial revolution, a way of thinking that has long been superseded in most other disciplines by a cybernetic, informational, computational, or whatever you want to call it, revolution. The industrial revolution brought sameness through repetition, amortization through duplication. In contrast, information technologies—soft machines—afford the opportunity for custom-made, personalized artifacts. This opportunity, however, has been ignored for the most part by industrialized building systems (for which Dietz and Cutler, 1971, provide a comprehensive overview).

Nevertheless, there are some researchers (for example: Allen, 1974; Schnarsky, 1971; Wellesley-Miller, 1972) who see the chance for custom-made environments more reflective of personal needs, implemented with techniques of industrialization, augmented by computing systems. In studying intelligent environments one must look at these pioneering efforts because, aside from the ethical validity of intelligent environments, there are serious questions about the materials of which all this shall be made. There seem to be two types of construction in the infancy of invention that lend themselves to physical responsiveness. I will refer to them as the "softs" and the "cyclics."

Brodey's original 1967 article was subtitled "Soft

contracted

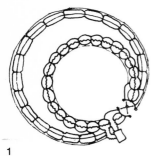

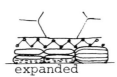

expanded

1

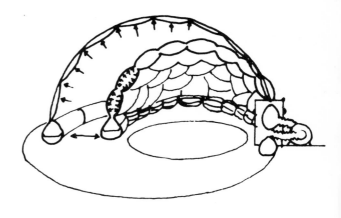

2

1 When the photocells are tripped in order A-B air is pumped from the cushions to the interior. When they are tripped in reverse order B-A air is pumped from the interior to the cushions and the play space contracts within three minutes. Designed in 1968 by ERG, Amsterdam. Diagram reconstructed by Sean Wellesley-Miller.

2 A structure in the process of unfolding itself. Photographs courtesy of Sean Wellesley-Miller and his students at MIT.

Architecture." I believe that some researchers have pursued studies that have suffered in their very conception of taking the term "soft" too literally, brutally transposing it from a computational paradigm to a building technology. Brodey himself takes the term too literally. He lived in a foam house, and his ex-partner, Johnson, plays with plastics, or so he states (1971): "To date a few of us have been working and playing with plastic films and foams, and with compressed air and other expendables." I believe that the "softs" are an important vehicle to responsiveness, but they must be studied with great caution. In the same way that I refute computer graphics' proliferating Gaudiesque architecture, I worry about the obvious materials of "responsive architecture" foisting a soft-Soleri, or globular, mushy architecture. Not everybody wants to live in a balloon.

Soft materials, like inflatable plastics, are presently the most natural material for responsive architecture, because they exhibit motor reflexes through simple controls. Sean Wellesley-Miller at the forefront of this technology once built a child's crèche whose entrance contained the photocells necessary to count the kids entering and exiting. With the total population of children always known, he wired his compressor to inflate and deflate the structure in proportion to the population: the more children went in, the bigger it became; as they left it would shrink until finally collapsing for the night.

The computations necessary to control the size of the crèche are hardly symptomatic of intelligent behavior, but the response *is* architectural, and the material has indeed not afforded the opportunity for dramatic change. However, I do not agree that: "The construction of this kind of sophisticated pneumatics takes us into the realm of living

147

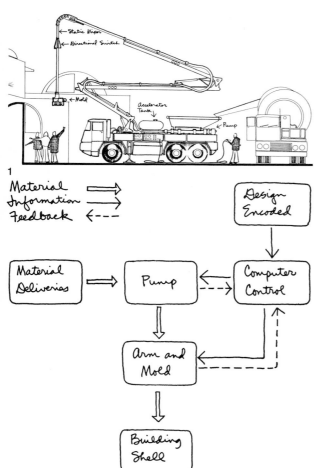

1

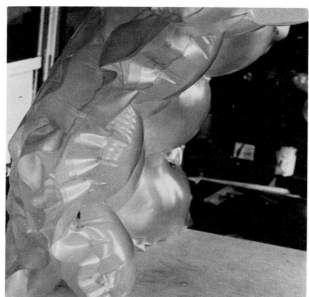

3

Material ⟹
Information ⟹
Feedback ⟵ - - -

Design
Encoded

Material
Deliveries ⟹ Pump ⟵ Computer
Control

Arm and
Mold

Building
Shell

2

4

1 The free mold concept. The mold supports and propels itself upon the wall, controlled by microwave and laser beams. The directional switch senses the movements of the mold and causes the hose-handler to follow above it. An accelerator is metered into the mix by means of a static mixer. Illustration by and courtesy of Edward Allen.

2 A flow chart of Edward Allen's continuous construction process

3 A cellular structure

4 A web/plenum structure

things and ecology" (Hamilton, 1972). I do agree with Rusch (1972): "Such 'soft architecture' is only one alternative. 'Hard architecture' can be responsive as well.... However, 'hard architecture' is almost by definition harder to make responsive, so it is no mystery why soft materials, air, light, and sound have formed Brodey's pallet. The unfortunate result is that we do not tend to see his work as particularly relevant to 'architecture.' "

There is a particular aspect of pneumatics that (to my knowledge) has not been explored, that is so far untapped, and that is an innate property of the large class of inflatable structures: cellular structures. This property is memory. Some of the adjacent illustrations (taken mostly from Wellesley-Miller) show physical structures that can move and even walk about as a result of carefully scheduled sequences of local inflations and deflations. In a limiting case (depicted on the preceding page as well) the fabric could be a flat sheet with an upper and lower row of cells and a weblike plenum. By appropriately inflating and deflating selected lower and upper cells, the mat can be made to assume any freeform shape or actually move across the ground. However, what is more important than this malleability and mobility is that the pressure states of the cells are its memory. One can sample the cells and know the shape. In other words, form is memory. Of course it would be equally possible to have an electronic computing mechanism "remember" which cells were inflated when and to what degree (and to query the computer). But it is more suitable to have pressure-sensing devices in each pneumatic cell, letting them be memory, because this makes it possible to have the structure respond locally to body movements and interactions. In this manner we could directly push and pull upon memory. This can be extrapolated to exercises of cellular automata, in three dimensions, having the structure dance about.

The notion of memory is not limited to inflatables; it can be extended to "hard" architecture. A potentiometer in every door hinge or a sliding resistor in every window can also be viewed (mildly) as devices for giving the environment memory. If planes could disappear, move aside, or expand themselves, such a memory would be more revealing. However, it is much harder to make stone, brick, and stud walls move or change themselves than it is to control inflatable structures. Not only is it difficult to conceive of the motor reflexes themselves, but the impediments of mechanical systems tend to make the most simple dwelling into a monolithic, immutable unit. It is no surprise that we have no historical precedents.

The other approach to responsive materials, what I have called the "cyclics," considers "architectural" responses in a coarser time grain, relegating the moment-to-moment responsiveness to informational and operational features. The underlying assumption is that we can develop a continuous construction and destruction process. I am not referring to "Kleenex architecture" that can be disposed of and readily replaced. I am referring to an ever-continuing building process as suggested by Allen (1970; 1974). He is trying to create Safdie's fantasy: "Ultimately, I would like to design a magic housing machine.... Conceive of a huge pipe behind which is a reservoir of magic plastic. A range of air-pressure nozzles around the opening controls this material as it is forced through the edges of the pipe. By varying the pressure at each nozzle one could theoretically extrude any conceivable shape, complex free forms, mathematically non-defined forms. People could go and push the button to design their own dwelling" (Safdie, 1970).

Edward Allen is working on just that and more. The "more" is the important feature because it is the necessary dissembling process (not mentioned by Safdie) that makes this notion viable for the premises of responsiveness. The magical material needs the supplementary feature of being reversible or, at least, digestible by a house-building bug. In the event that a "bug" could crawl about extruding and eating up chunks of my house, much like spinning a web, I can envision architectural transformations taking place on an hour-to-hour or day-to-day basis (versus month-to-month, as Allen views it, or year-to-year, as Safdie implies). This would be a viable route to physical responsiveness, reminiscent of royal traditions of building pavilions and structures for a gala event, vulgarized to building a jalousie porch to peruse *Reader's Digest*.

Addendum

I have avoided discussing aspects of machine learning in this context, where the machine is the house. Previous chapters have included some comments about machine learning, particularly in the sense of modeling a participant (and his models). Similar models are necessary for a viable responsiveness. My house needs a model of me, a model of my model of it, and a model of my model of its model of me. We know less about how to do this for a house than for a sketch-recognizing machine.

We must experiment with more caution in responsive architecture than is necessary with mechanical partners that have relatively singular purposes. The nonintelligent, stubborn computer that mailed twenty thousand copies of *Time* magazine to the same person is obviously not desirable. Similarly, we do not want the ultrasonic dishwasher to emit a freak frequency that turns on the television whose luminance will cause windows to open and shades to close. At the other extreme, we do not want a genius-house that invades our privacy, bullies us about, nags, belittles, and is grumpy or rude.

Unfortunately the two extremes do not lie on a smooth continuum to which we can point and say that it is here we should place our targets. Instead it is a complicated set of nonlinear trade-offs that will vary from person to person, from family to family, resting, for the most part, on the feasibility and advisability of a machine intelligence. The question will arise: Can a machine learn without a body? A house has a body of its own; will I be able to laugh at its jokes? As R. L. Gregory points out in his "Social Implications of Intelligent Machines" (1970): "What happens when the internal fiction of a machine is very different from the human brain-fiction?... One can imagine a class of machines which work quite mysteriously, with non-human fictions, to give us answers without justifications we can understand. Some people might trust such machines, much as they trust cars though they have no idea how the steering wheel is connected to the front wheels. But would it be possible to phrase questions appropriately to such machines?"

Epilogue

An Allegory

I have heard versions of the following story on several occasions, and I have told varying versions on many occasions. For these reasons I am no longer sure where I first heard it or of its original form or from whom (though I tend to think it was Seymour Papert). The story, nonetheless, has close analogies in the historical development of architecture as assisted by computers. The story is about a machine. It is called the string-and-ring machine.

There exists a classic combinatorial problem in mathematics called the *traveling salesman problem*. It considers N geographically distributed locations interconnected by "roads." The problem is to find the shortest route that will take a salesman to every city with the shortest possible mileage without going through any city twice. Note that the problem has important practical applicatons in the routing of pipes, wires, and communications networks. Consequently it has been studied at great length (Bellmore and Nemhauser, 1968; Arnoff and Sengupta, 1961; Karg and Thompson, 1964; Dantzig, Fulkerson, and Johnson, 1959; Croes, 1958; Gomory, 1966; Flood, 1956; Heller, 1955; Little, Murty, Sweeney, and Karel, 1963; Lambert, 1960; Morton and Land, 1955; Roberts and Flores, 1966; Raymond, 1969; Wootton, 1969; Srinastava et al., 1969; Rothkopf, 1966). "Although some ways have been found for cutting down the length of the search, no algorithm has been discovered sufficiently powerful to solve the traveling salesman problem with a tolerable amount of computing for a set of, say, fifty cities" (Simon, 1970). Consider that the number of alternative routes is $N-1$ factorial (which for fifty cities is greater than 3×10^{64}).

Another version of the problem, equally well studied (Beardwood, Halton, and Hammersky, 1959; Dantzig, 1960; Butas, 1968; Dreyfus, 1969; Hu, 1968; Hoffman and Markowitz, 1963; Hu and Torres, 1969; Nicholson, 1966; Mills, 1968 and 1966; Pollack and Wiebenson, 1960; Peart, Randolph, and Bartlett, 1960; Verblunsky, 1951), is to find the shortest path from one given point on the network to another given point. It is the history of this particular version of the traveling salesman problem (usually referred to as the shortest path problem) that I wish to break into "generations."

The first era is the obvious application of a machine to a task unmanageable by a human and is characterized by an exhaustive search for all possible solutions. Note that this method does yield the optimum solution, because all alternatives are searched (and there happens to be only one goal, shortness of path). This was the era of exhaustive searching.

The second era of approach to the problem is characterized by the following attitude: Let the machine do what it is good at doing, let the man do what he is good at doing, and provide the two with a smooth interface such that they can work effectively. Hence, a typical solution would be to display on a cathode-ray tube the map of N cities and have the human operator of the console point at a "reasonable" set of nodes that lie between A and B. The machine's task is simply to sum up the mileages and display the total. Continuing, we allow the user to alter his routing interactively so that as he moves the line of travel he receives a constant updating of the new mileage. In this manner he can "massage" the route and within a short period of time come up with a "very good" route (conceivably the optimum).

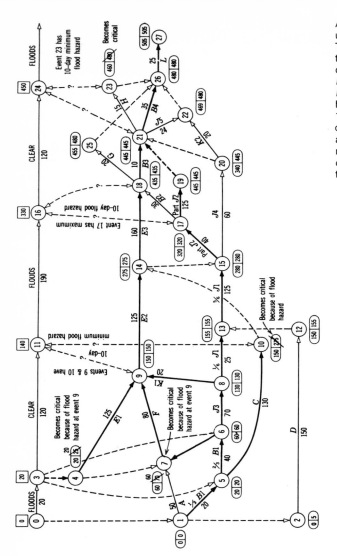

A typical critical path method used in construction practice. The particular example is of the construction of a rock fill dam taken from *Critical Path Methods in Construction Practice*, Antill and Woodhead, New York: Wiley & Sons, 1965. Note that, to the chagrin of CPM enthusiasts the string and ring machine cannot be run backward. That is, it cannot compute the longest trip distance.

The third era of the problem is characterized by wondering just what the human was bringing to the problem that the machine could not possess itself: what pattern-recognition abilities and, particularly, what heuristics? Hence, the approach of the third era was to develop heuristics that could limit the search, reducing the alternatives to a few thousand or even a few hundred reasonable ones. We can imagine such rules of thumb as: It is probably not worth backtracking for more than a certain percentage of the total distance; the route probably lies within a certain subset of the map, as described by an upper left and lower right, for example; look for roads that tend to be straight; and so on.

The fourth era is that of a special-purpose machine. It is composed of N labeled shower curtain rings interconnected to each other with kite string of a length proportional to the actual road distance between the cities. Once constructed, this computing mechanism can be employed by simply picking up the two rings that represent the two cities in question, by pulling, and by observing which strings become taut first. We have the optimum route generated by a machine. We call it the string-and-ring machine.

I tell this long story, not because I believe necessarily that there is a string-and-ring machine for architecture, but because I see a similar historical development. The first applications of computers to architecture were quite similarly characterized, as in era one, by exhaustive searching. The approach and attitude were to make the problem simple enough to examine all solutions in order to post the best. This approach has proved quite useless in all cases except the most belittling exercise and hence receives little further study.

The second era of computer-aided architecture has been the "partition paradigm": let the designer do what he is good at and let the machine do what it is good at, and so forth. Of course, computer graphics bolstered this approach and assisted in affording the requisite smooth interface. My own earlier work on URBAN5 can be considered exemplary of this approach, and it did not work. It did not work because no matter how many trinkets and how much paraphernalia the interface had, the machine still could not contribute to finding answers (and finding questions) because it did not understand! It could not handle missing information, context, and so on; and it was always at the mercy of the validity of its inputs (and me).

The third era is maybe where we are now. We are trying to understand just what the human does bring to the design process and, at the same time, who that human should be. What heuristics do we use, and how do we use them? Are some people innately better designers than others? If so, why? Questions like these characterize our present efforts. I believe that I can use "our" much more broadly than the polemics of this volume may suggest.

And maybe there is a string-and-ring machine for architecture.

Appendix 1

The Architecture Machine

As a Piece of Hardware

The following pages illustrate the growth of the Architecture Machine from 1968 through 1974. My purpose in recounting the story of its development so far is to clarify some myths and to reveal (through example) some startling details about computer hardware as it is today and might be tomorrow.

An Architecture Machine, as outlined in 1968 in the book, *The Architecture Machine*, is to be an inexpensive, dedicated computing system that will devote itself to the service of an individual designer and that will have access to "parent machines." The machine is to have formidable computing power, performing the bulk of the computing tasks locally. Arguments for such local computing power, in lieu of time-sharing, were based upon: (1) the need for high bandwidth interfaces; (2) the dependence upon "real time" (unsliced) to the microsecond, let's say; and (3) the emphasis on mutual interruptibility. Yet another reason, not enumerated in the book, is that minicomputers have become highly cost effective, and time-sharing is prohibitive for many applications.

The first implementation of this satellite computer called the Architecture Machine was realized in 1968 with an Interdata Model 3 computer with 8K bytes of core, a teletype, three storage tube displays, and a communication line with an IBM 360/67. The Interdata was selected to be the nucleus of our system because it was the only machine at the time to which it was easy to interface peripheral devices, which would be necessary to deal with the hardware aspects of experimentation in the domain of sensors and effectors. It also had the convenience of an IBM-like machine language, in which M.I.T. students tend to be well versed. And, it had a microprogramming facility that could lend itself to making special-purpose instructions for graphics, for example.

Anybody who has worked with a time-sharing system knows how the interactiveness and the immediacy of response stimulate involvement. In a similar but more exaggerated way, hands-on access to a minicomputer breeds deep involvement, which in turn expands visible output. This advantage, combined with the credibility of having such a device in the first place, led to a rapid growth of hardware through a multitude of small grants and donations, augmented by some military surplus equipment.

At first this growth was straightforward: additions to memory, faster input and output, and more peripheral gadgetry. By 1970 the system was a bigger and faster version of the initial configuration, with no major revisions of strategy for growth and the allocation of computing. As a rule of thumb, the local processor would tend to the peripherals (servicing interrupts and sampling data at fast rates, for example), perform small computing tasks, and communicate with the larger time-sharing system. In turn, it would be the large machine, in our case an IBM 360 model 67, that would: (1) store vast amounts of information, (2) act as a switching network for communicating with other human users or minicomputers, and (3) tackle the major computing tasks (it will be important to note that this third role for the remote machine usually disappears in our revised strategies for the allocation of computing).

1

2

3

4

5

6

1 June 1969. An 8K Interdata Model 3 with three storage tube displays.

2 September 1969. More memory, sound output, high speed paper tape reader.

3 November 1969. GROPE is added and SEEK is started.

4 January 1970. The Sylvania data tablet is added; general purpose interface is built.

5 March 1970. Second processor arrives with disk, card reader, and high-speed punch.

6 January 1971. Some neatening, a magnetic tape drive, more memory.

7 January 1972. Third processor.

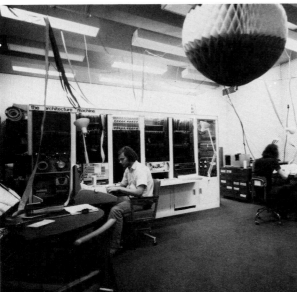

7

the architecture machine

3CCFC0   15   433D

8213D1 3 E 16 C1 C

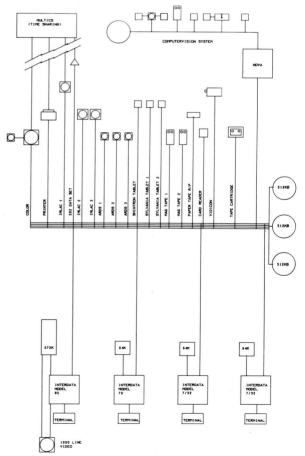

MULTICS
(TIME SHARING)

COMPUTERVISION SYSTEM

NOVA

COLOR
PRINTER
IMLAC 1
202 DATA SET
IMLAC 2
IMLAC 3
ARDS 1
ARDS 2
ARDS 3
SKIATRON TABLET
SYLVANIA TABLET 1
SYLVANIA TABLET 2
MAG TAPE 1
MAG TAPE 2
PAPER TAPE R/P
CARD READER
VIDICON
TAPE CARTRIDGE

512KB
512KB
512KB

272K

64K

64K

64K

INTERDATA
MODEL
85

INTERDATA
MODEL
70

INTERDATA
MODEL
7/32

INTERDATA
MODEL
7/32

TERMINAL

TERMINAL

TERMINAL

TERMINAL

1000 LINE
VIDEO

1 June 1969. An 8K Interdata Model 3 with three storage tube displays.

2 September 1969. More
memory, sound output, high
speed paper tape reader.

3 November 1969. GROPE
is added and SEEK is started.

4 January 1970. The Sylvania data tablet is added;
general purpose interface is
built.

5 March 1970. Second
processor arrives with disk,
card reader, and high-speed
punch.

6 January 1971. Some
neatening, a magnetic tape
drive, more memory.

7 January 1972. Third
processor.

6

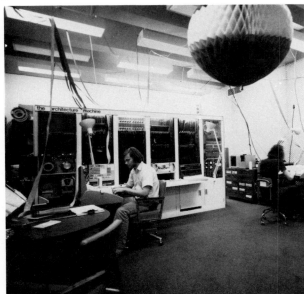

7

the architecture machine

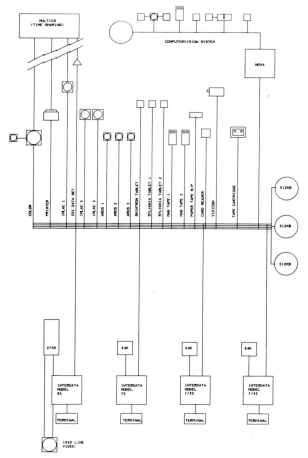

September 1974. At this writing the system is being redesigned from scratch and will be rebuilt over the next years. While the ad hoc expansion shown in the preceding illustrations has afforded excellent, cost-effective computing, moving from a small remote display facility to a large multiprocessor computing service has caused serious growing pains.

About the beginning of the academic year 1970-1971, a major change took place that caused serious revision of our original notions about hardware. The change was stimulated by our reaching a critical size as the result of two additions: a disk drive and a high-speed printer. On the surface, it would appear (as it did to us) that these peripherals would simply add more memory and faster output in the same spirit as previous additions. However, upon reflection, we realized that these two particular peripherals created a serious imbalance of usage and amortization in that the printer and the disk, for example, are each more expensive than the central processor. The first question is obvious: Can these new devices gain more usage by being shared among several processors? The next question to be answered is: Can all peripherals be shared among a family of processors?

The answer is surely *yes*. It was at this point that we developed the scheme of sharing the "bus" upon which all peripherals must hang. Notice that contrary to the typical time-sharing or batch-processing system where one large central processor shares several printers, disks, etc., our scheme is to share printer, disk, et al. among several processors. The strategy is extended to: scopes, modems, readers, punches, tape drives, vision apparatus, and general-purpose input/output media (see illustration). As a method of growth, once set up, this strategy allows for rapid expansions with minor additions. For example, following the printer and the disk, the addition of a single 16K processor ($6,500) doubled our throughput inasmuch as two people could partake in computing alongside a handsome set of peripherals, grabbing and releasing peripherals

1 The Sylvania tablet used horizontally.

2 The Sylvania tablet used vertically, aligned with the display. This position has the disadvantage of creating a double line when the two images do not register because of the viewer's angle of vision.

1

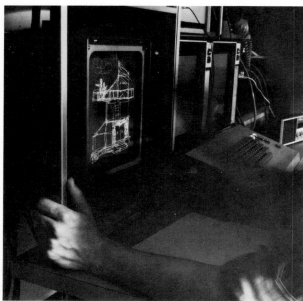

2

as they were needed and waiting or spooling if necessary.

Today, at this writing, there are eight processors. With the addition of special-purpose display processors, for color as well as dynamic graphics, the boundary between processor/memory and bank of peripherals becomes less categorical; communication is achieved quite often through ad hoc procedures. Nevertheless, it remains a community of hardware that has a very important feature: it is not hierarchical, that is, it does not have a central or i/o processor through which all information must pass. If a peripheral is critical to all operations, we make sure that we have at least two. In this manner, any part of the hardware can go down and the rest carries on.

Our experiences with the development of this particular configuration result in the following prediction: the future of general-purpose computing does not lie in time-sharing; the costs are simply too high and the limitations too restricting. Instead, I believe that the emergence of a very large population of small, fast, inexpensive computers will serve most of the community of computing needs. Time-sharing will be used only as a network switching device for intercommunication among minis or as a receptacle for large common data banks, accessed and updated from a variety of geographically separated points. Note that in both cases, the time-sharing system is being used, not by humans, but by other machines (which should cause a revision in time-sharing strategies).

About Its Graphics

Developments in "computer graphics," since its inception in the early sixties, can be characterized by a phenomenal growth in hardware and an amazingly small set of achievements in software. Offhand, one can attribute this to an inherent impracticality or to overblown promises. However, if we turn our attention to historical developments, we find concurrences and diversions that account for misplaced emphasis and for gratuitous programming. Remember the parallel but unrelated development of computer graphics and time-sharing.

Early graphics systems were of the refresh type (I am discounting plotters) that demanded an associated memory to store the instructions that controlled the electron beam's path of movement and intensity (often just on/off). It was the need for this memory (then expensive) and constant refreshing that made graphics unamenable to time-sharing. However, it was the same memory requirement that made the so-called "light pen" easy to implement (a simple photocell could tell the display process to stop as soon as it saw the electron beam pass, and a program could query the memory to report which line was in the process of being drawn at the instant). Unfortunately it was called "pen"; the French almost made the proper decision in calling it doigt—finger—but alas, it was called a plume lumineuse. Its generally fat, clumsy nature, along with the necessary gymnastics for tracking, diverted a great deal of effort into handling the light pen (for example, zooming to meet the coarseness of the light pen). Also, with memory so precious, pictures were kept simple, and drawing

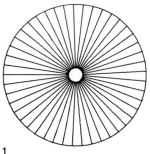

1

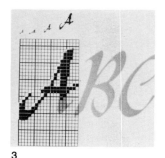

2

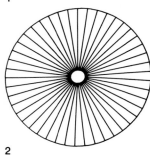

3

1 Vectors displayed on an experimental Xerox system. Note the "jaggies," especially pronounced as the lines approach 0, 90, 180, and 270 degrees. Photograph courtesy of Richard Shoup and Xerox Corporation.

2 Jaggies removed with the addition of graytone information. Photograph courtesy of Richard Shoup and Xerox Corporation.

3 A bit map of the letter *A* superimposed upon its vidicon image

4 One character set

5 Another character set. These characters are converted on the fly. The resolution of the television is high enough to remove the "presence" of horizontal lines. The text is as close to type quality as we have ever seen from on-line displays. Photographs courtesy of Alan Kay and Xerox Corporation.

The AGONY and The ECSTACY

A NOVEL OF MICHELANGELO

by Irving Stone

THE STUDIO

*before the mirror of the second- floor bedro
ng his lean cheeks with their high bone ridg
oad forehead. and ears too far back on the I
air curling forward in thatches. the amber c
de-set but heavy-lidded.
"J'm not well designed," thought the
t-year-old with serious concentration. "My
rule. with the forehead overweighing my mou
Someone should have used a plumb line."
He shifted his wiry body lightly so as not*

4

The AGONY
and The ECSTACY

A NOVEL OF MICHELANGELO

by Irving Stone

THE STUDIO

before the mirror of the second-floor bec
ng his lean cheeks with their high bone
oad forehead, and ears too far back on th
ir curling forward in thatches, the ambc
de-set but heavy-lidded.
"I'm not well designed," thought the
n-year-old with serious concentration. "I
rule, with the forehead overweighing my
Someone should have used a plumb line."
He shifted his wiry body lightly so as

5

was for the most part achieved with the insidious rubber-band line.

In the middle sixties, with time-sharing in mind, the storage tube was developed. Its outstanding property is that the image does not have to be refreshed; this means that it is able to support infinitely complex drawings. While the storage tube was being developed, minicomputers were surfacing as a major, inexpensive source of computing power, which, as you can imagine, was overlooked in the first storage tube display stations (as evidenced in their slow drawing rates and stepping functions, sensible only in the context of time-sharing).

At the same time, tablets were gaining acceptance, making an excellent tracking medium and a poor "finger." Once again, a tablet is unwelcome in the time-sharing environment (unless used as a point-by-point digitizer) because the stream of input demands too large a bandwidth and continuous servicing. However, if you take these three items—a tablet, a storage tube, and a minicomputer—you have an excellent and inexpensive graphics station, appropriate for a wide variety of applications. In particular, it is pertinent to sketching. Until quite recently, this has been the only graphics available on the Architecture Machine. It is the basis of HUNCH.

The particular tablet we employ has special features that make sketching suitably smooth. First, it is transparent, which allows it to be employed as a work surface upon which you rest sheets of paper or as a window set in front of the cathode-ray tube, registered with the displayed image. Second, it is an electromagnetic device whose stylus is an antenna, which affords the opportunity of collecting limited three-dimensional information (four levels of Z adjustable with a screwdriver) and the additional opportunity of drawing with your finger (if you ground yourself suitably). Third, it has a homemade, miniature load cell to register pressure. Fourth, it reports a constant two hundred points per second, which automatically bears information about speed and accelerations.

The storage tube has only two interesting features, beyond the opportunity not to refresh: (1) you can vary the focus by commands from the computer, which lends a control on the width of lines—variable, for example, as a function of pressure upon the pen; and (2) it offers the opportunity to refresh in the so-called write-thru mode, which allows the mixing of dynamic (and dim) images within a plethora of lines and points, for example, diagrammatic demarcations on a complex base map.

Until recently, the Architecture Machine was composed of three sketching stations of this sort. At present there are four additional displays of the refresh variety, one in color. They are used in conjunction with simple images or post-HUNCH data that require dynamic transformations. Because these sketching stations have to deal with dynamic images, one must struggle with the additional display processor, which worries about updating and maintaining the image thirty times per second (or thereabouts). Only lately have such displays become economically viable in that the cost of memories and processors has been dropping dramatically. At the same time, display technologies have been developing high-

1

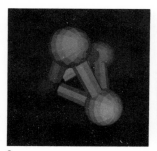

2

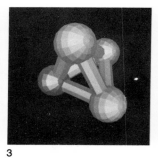

3

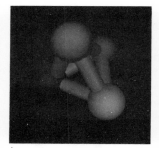

4

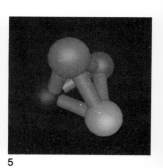

5

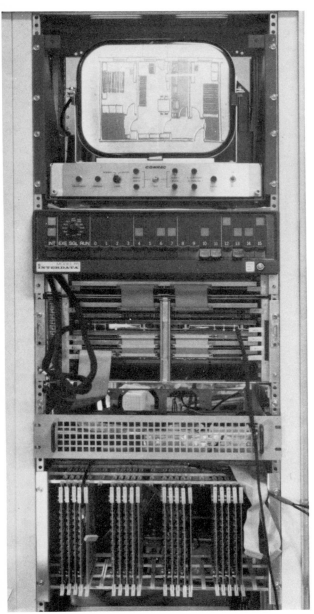

1 Two figures, one with and one without jaggies. They are displayed with splines similar to those described in Chapter 2. The illustrations were originally in color, as are the actual displays. The grid on the upper left-hand corner is a color "pallet" for inking a simulated brush to paint or fill areas. Photographs courtesy of Bob Flegal and Xerox Corporation.

2 Off-line raster scan; originals also in color. The shading technique is attributed to J. E. Warnock.

3 Warnock shading with highlights

4 Gouraud shading

5 Phong improved shading. These four photographs are the result of student and staff work at the University of Utah's Department of Computer Science. Courtesy of Ivan Sutherland and the University of Utah.

6 The Architecture Machine's raster scan display, driven by 272K bytes of 350 nanosecond MOS memory shared by the display processor (built by Jeffrey Entwisle) and an Interdata Model 85 with control store

A sample painting. Raster
scan with computer graphics,
on-line. The original figure
was in color. Courtesy of
Xerox Corporation.

resolution, fast-drawing capabilities to the point that the general consensus in the computer graphics community is that the life of storage tubes will be short.

The disappearance of the storage tube will take longer in applications, like sketching, that demand hundreds of vectors than in those uses that employ the storage tube merely as an inexpensive display medium for a modest number of lines and characters. In contexts like sketching we must anticipate other technologies, like plasma display or crystal-grown light-emitting diodes. One more immediate alternative is the raster scan display, which is generally considered to hold the future of computer graphics.

This alternative is presently under study by the Architecture Machine Group. It most closely approximates a system presently operational at the Xerox Research Center in Palo Alto, California. Briefly, the display is a thousand-line television (over double the resolution of your home set) with one million bits of semiconductor memory available to store the state of each raster. I mention this method of display (an extravagance in memory today but not tomorrow) because it has one important feature: this picture is memory. In previous experiments we have had to maintain a surrogate sheet of paper as a list map or disk or we had to attach a vision apparatus to look at the drawing. This technology holds an important future because such devices are not necessary; the program can query the display. Similarly, a combination "tablet-light pen" can draw directly into memory and serve the dual purpose of pointing and tracking. And finally, it will afford the hitherto unavailable mixing of computer graphics techniques with picture processing inasmuch as the drawing surface need no longer be a black or white "paper," but may be a photograph (for example) that has meaning to the user and some meaning to the machine. Some of this work is illustrated on the preceding pages.

As an Assemblage of Software

If one looks at the man-hours of computer programming spent at any of the centers for artificial intelligence (Stanford, MIT, or Edinburgh), one finds that most of the time has been allocated to the development of time-sharing systems, editors, compilers, and general software packages for usage by applications, that is, subsequent users. The applications are usually dwarfed by the systems programming. In exactly the same way, the Architecture Machine Group has been guilty of allocating similarly disproportionate amounts of time to making things tick for the use of others (in our case, mostly students in course work). It is always the case that one is not satisfied with one's original specifications once they are achieved and that we accordingly devote more and more time to refining, tuning, and redesigning the system's programs. It's a problem that never goes away.

Development of software on the Architecture Machine has fallen into two categories: specific experimentation and a general operating system. Note that the implementation of languages has not been undertaken, with the minor exception of S. K. Gregory (1972) and presently ongoing implementation of PL/1. Most development under research grant or contract has been implemented in machine language, and most student projects have been conducted in FORTRAN IV.

Previous chapters have described some specific experimentation like HUNCH and SQUINT. Other experimentation has been undertaken in conjunction with thesis work (Flanders, 1971; Lippman, 1971; Shaw, 1972; Entwisle, 1973; Lavin, 1973; Taggart, 1973) or with term projects concerned with matters outside the scope of this volume.

The operating system, on the other hand, merits some mention because it is responsible for driving the shared bus, for file sharing, and for making the "space-sharing" (versus time-sharing) as transparent as possible to the user. While minicomputers are very cheap, they are characteristically inappropriate for most general scientific computing demands because of the (present) lack of software, in particular, the lack of handsome operating systems.

The particular package developed for the Architecture Machine is called MAGIC. Its prime purpose is to manipulate and share files (that reside on disk or on tape) among many processors. Other purposes include controlling peripherals, managing storage, and calling forth the services of editors, compilers, assemblers, and so forth. It is a command language that has been fashioned (superficially) at the command level, after MIT's time-sharing system, MULTICS (Organick, 1972).

Each user can create an unlimited (except by the size of the storage medium) number of directories, all of which can contain files: source programs, object code load modules, data, or a variety of special-purpose "types" (like help, exec, or synonym files). Directories are appended to a user's "active chain of directories" by a command that specifies access (to allow or not allow others to employ the same directory at the same time, for example) and position on the chain (important because they are searched from top to bottom). In the following example, the command FORTRAN

HARRY causes the system to do four things: (1) search the chain of directories for the first occurrence of a program called FORTRAN. LOADMOD (which happens to be the compiler); (2) (as a result of the particular .LOADMOD) search the chain again, this time for a program called HARRY.FORTRAN; (3) execute the program, that is, compile HARRY; (4) create a new file or replace the old one called HARRY.TEXT.

The user can make his own programs behave in a manner similar to FORTRAN.LOADMOD. He can even make his own FORTRAN and override the system's by placing his directory above the system directory (on his chain). This feature is particularly important for building simple command-oriented systems or initiating a series of demonstrations.

MAGIC's other role is to assist in the management of core. Unlike larger machines, most minicomputers are machines with word lengths of 16 or 18 bits with subsequently small address spaces. As a consequence, virtual memory systems are not attractive methods for executing large programs, because you are limited by the largest "direct" address. Overlaying programs is more viable. For this reason the user must reckon with being somewhat explicit about where his programs are to sit in core (at this time, more explicit than we would like). The standard Architecture Machine processor is a 64K byte machine; the operating system takes about 10K including 2K for transient commands, drivers, and utilities. The remainder of core is available for the user to allocate to his programs or to the system (allowing it to be more core resident and hence run faster). Since the program usually exceeds the remaining 22K, the user has to take care in linking programs and accessing large arrays and tree structures that reside on disk.

The specifics of MAGIC are less important than the general spirit of making a small machine behave more and more like the operating systems to which we are accustomed on large machines. The experiences with MAGIC so far suggest that minicomputers are practicable general-purpose devices, more powerful and flexible than initially imagined. This further implies that some of the notions of one-man-one-machine suggested in *The Architecture Machine* are not so fanciful.

Appendix 2

Some Programming Techniques and Attitudes

Constraints and Criteria

The noun "criterion" does not have a verb. Regrettably, we refer to criteria as "constraining" this or that, using the verb derived from "constraint." While this may appear to be a picayune observation, I believe that it can account for some oversights (perhaps only semantic, but probably not) in distinguishing criteria from constraints. The difference is particularly important in techniques for generating design alternatives. It also implies an attitude toward problem specification inasmuch as just about any requirement can be phrased as either a constraint or a criterion. The choice has subtle but serious implications that go beyond the programming conveniences of choosing one format over another.

In brief, a criterion is a target and a constraint is a limit. In the comment "I wish to build the least expensive house with not less than 2000 square feet of net floor area," the problem is specified by a constraint—not less than 2000 net square feet—and a criterion—least expensive. Notice that the problem as stated is by definition solvable (through trial and error or empirically in *any* fiscal environment). If, on the other hand, both "constraining" features are turned into constraints: "I wish to have 2000 square feet of net floor area for less than $15,000," it may not be solvable (in the United States it is not). Or, if I make both requirements into criteria: "I wish to have the largest possible house for the least cost," I have no way to depart on the problem as stated; there are many solutions, and I must know what *you* mean. One way of looking at the distinction is to view a constraint as being a bound delimited by -*er*: greater than, cheaper than, less than, etc.;

and to view a criterion as a direction with -*est*: smallest, widest, cheapest, least, most, and so on. Any statement of an architecture problem is a mixture of criteria and constraints, not always as obviously signaled as in the previous example. Site boundaries can be viewed as constraints, whereas the capturing of a view or the buffering of the wind can be taken as criteria. It is important to recognize that as long as the constraints do not contradict themselves (often a matter of context) the problem is solvable. By the same token, if only criteria are specified, there exist an infinite number of possible (perhaps trivial) solutions.

As soon as there is more than one criterion, the issue becomes messy because it is necessary to relate criteria to each other (that is, weight them). This implies a common unit for comparison in testing (all too often the dollar). For example, if the original house example were revised: "I would like 2000 net square feet at the least possible cost with the most possible exposure to the south" it is necessary to relate southern exposure to cost and look, for example, at diminishing returns. Another route would be to examine the problem statement and achieve a rephrasing of it, making one of the criteria into a constraint, but ideally not making the problem insolvable. For example: "I would like 2000 net square feet with at least 500 square feet of wall with southern exposure at the least possible cost." This latter alternative is typically selected. I propose that it is precisely because of this practice of forever making criteria into constraints that automated space planning yields distorted and unproductive results. While it facilitates computer programming and while it conveniently removes context, the continual rephrasing of criteria into constraints disregards all circum-

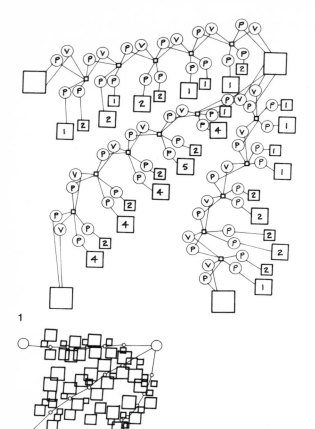

1

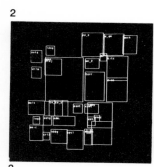

2

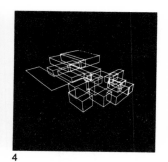

3   4

1 A "constraint pattern"
from IMAGE. Taken from T.
Johnson et al. (1970).

2 A sample output from the
constraint resolution procedure

3 More recent output from
IMAGE. Photograph courtesy
of Guy Weinzapfel.

4 A perspective glance.
Photograph courtesy of Guy
Weinzapfel.

stances where a good solution can be found fractionally beyond one (usually arbitrarily set) limit.

"Near to," "very near to," and "the nearest possible to" are goals fashioned as legitimate criteria. "Next to" is a constraint. The major difference is that the constraint format does not allow for any interpretation of proximity; it has made the interpretation! Grason's (1971) "locational constraints" and "length constraints" are exemplary of constraint reduction. His class of floor plans is reduced to: "1) Contiguity, space *A* is contiguous to space *B* on the North, South, East, West, or unspecified side; 2) Communication, there exists a door between them; 3) Physical dimensions, the length of the wall segment is specified in metric units." The reduction is necessary in order to have a well-behaved system.

An additional distinction (perhaps idiosyncratic) can be found in the adjectives *subjective* and *objective*. Constraints are certainly specified objectively (whether or not they can be tested). Does it follow that criteria ought to be viewed as subjective goals? I raise this possibility because of the general tendency in so-called "design methods research" to "objectify" everything. The emphasis is on finding a context-free way of designing or, at least, talking about. The intent is plausible in view of computer augmentation (with respect to existing machines), but, in the light of full participation or responsive architecture, it might be ill-suited to yield a quality of architecture equal to or better than what we already have.

A solution-generating system should be able to handle criteria in my terms rather than squelch them and have me enumerate that the bathroom must be adjacent to the bedroom, the dining room next to...,and so on. Unfortunately, from this point of view, a statement of criteria, as viewed in reference to me, can quickly degenerate into a motherhood statement.

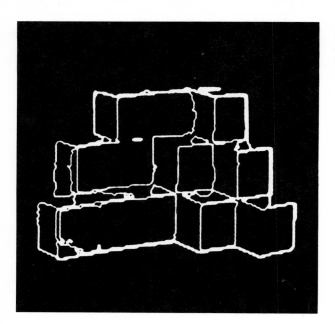

A display of the light
level contours derived from
vidisector input. Note the
abundance of missing lines.

Heuristic Techniques

Simon (1970) claims that: "When heuristic techniques are used for satisfying goals, the asymmetry between criteria and constraints disappears." This position is put forward in the important light of his distinction (which I believe is crucial) between optimizing and satisfying. Unfortunately, he does not go on to give cogent examples of heuristic techniques. What is a heuristic technique?

In literature and in conversation, the definition of a "heuristic program" has ranged from a trick or general principle for efficient and resourceful allocation of computing to any programming prowess deployed to handle a task we might generally think of as "interesting." It has fallen into being a catchall for any clever method of search or a buzzword with hairline and opaque distinctions. I should point out and admit, to add to the confusion, that the use of the term "heuristic" as a noun is grammatically wrong, but it assists the definition.

A heuristic is usually held synonymous with a "rule of thumb." It is a device that we have been taught explicitly or have learned empirically that permits us to make a selection from a large number of alternatives without looking at all of them or to make a decision without complete information. In short, it is a way of wisely (it is hoped) limiting the computations necessary to achieve a goal. It in no sense guarantees a good answer, the most apropos selection, or any kind of idealness.

As humans we use heuristics in our day-to-day lives, from hour to hour, and they work most of the time. For the most part we learn these heuristics from experiences in a particular context. For example, living in Boston, one recognizes that it is usually faster to take a taxi from one point to another, at almost any time of the day, than to use public transportation. In New York, however, at most times of the day and particularly in some sections, this would be the wrong rule of thumb; the goal to get from *A* to *B* fast would be poorly satisfied. At the same time, in Athens, between 1:30 P.M. and 2:00 P.M. it is impossible to find a cab; thus the heuristic—*to take a cab*—would fail miserably.

A heuristic is not a rule. At the same time, it is not the opposite of an algorithm (as is so often imagined). It has two salient characteristics: an action—*to develop evidence that*—and a qualification—*probably*. Both the action and the qualification are governed by experiences where, for example, at the daily problem-solving level, we often share heuristics, especially if we are from the same culture.

The adjacent illustration is taken from an experiment in machine vision; I find machine-vision problems particularly interesting because no set of rules can be established to work in all cases and because as humans we are not conscious of the assumptions and rules of thumb we constantly use to perceive. In the machine-vision experiment we use a device called a vidisector (one kind of computer eye) that has the salient feature of being almost blind and consequently needs very bright illumination.

A result of such intense lighting is that any two parallel planes that overlap will appear as a single surface (the highlights at the edge being

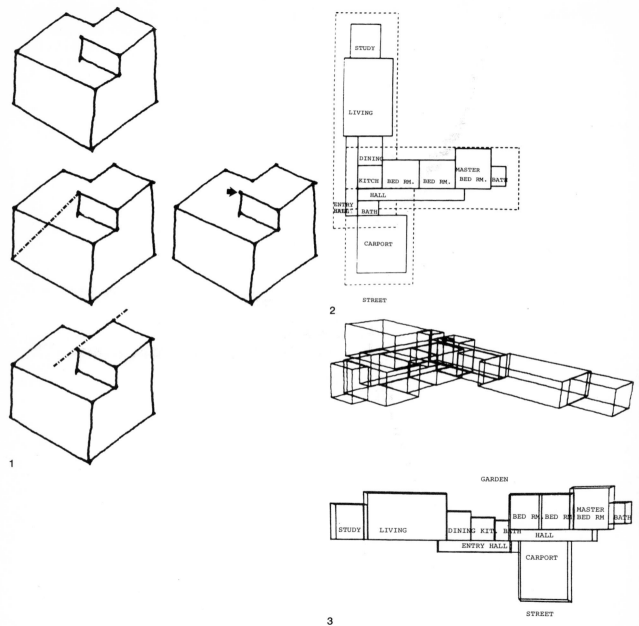

STUDY

LIVING

DINING

KITCH BED RM BED RM. MASTER BED RM. BATH

HALL

ENTRY HALL

BATH

CARPORT

STREET

2

GARDEN

STUDY LIVING DINING KIT BATH BED RM BED RM MASTER BED RM BATH

HALL

ENTRY HALL

CARPORT

HALL

STREET

1

3

1 Examples of a rule and two heuristics

2 Plan of Frank Lloyd Wright's Rosenbaum house, generated by computer. The program generates a large number of alternatives in Wrightian vernacular.

3 An alternative plan and perspective

indistinguishable by the vidisector). Hence we need a computer program to fill in the missing lines. Within the context of a broad geometry (let us say, restricted to arbitrary polyhedra) we could use the following sample strategy, a mixture of rules and heuristics: (1) *rule*: no two points can be connected such that the connecting (by definition, straight) line intersects another line. (2) *heuristic*: any point that is not on the silhouette and has only two incoming lines is *probably* incomplete; (3) *heuristic*: any added line will *probably* be the continuation of one of the existing line segments. The adjacent diagrams illustrate the one rule and two heuristics. On the following page you will find examples of cases where the two heuristics fail.

In architecture we frequently use heuristics in estimating costs and structures. Cost estimation programs (as opposed to cost accounting) are good examples of a use of heuristics as well-tuned rules of thumb that can be exercised at finer and finer grains as a design progresses. Notice that the heuristic is, in a sense, a fact as opposed to a precedure. The distinction is typical of an emerging overlap between "data" and "process." In the example of cost estimation, we can guess (a process) at an overall cost (a datum) of a high school in the Midwest on a per-square-foot basis. This estimate is subsequently refined if we specify that it is built of concrete, and so on, until we have the detailed specification from which to make an accurate accounting. The heuristics in this case are drawn from a consensus of experience and a well-tempered judgment. Their utmost importance results in the ability to proceed with *good* information without premature technical scrutiny. In this sense, a heuristic can be viewed as a low-resolution or fuzzy rule. Note that in this

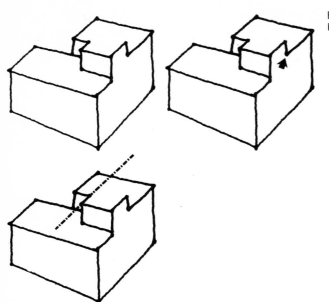

Examples of how the two
heuristics fail

example the problem to be solved is characterized not by a search for alternatives but by reasoned guesses.

In the early stages of design we employ other kinds of heuristics, with less consensus. Some of the most powerful, although not necessarily desirable, are: operational preconceptions, formal prejudices, and stylistic habits. These are heuristics, too! They are evidenced in the drawing of analogies, replicating of similar solutions, extrapolating of tendencies, or initializing of an overall form. I would emphasize that prejudice and preconception, two apparently iniquitous and corrupt behaviors, are powerful heuristics, and their use generates criticism that can be leveled at *both* the worst and the best architects. Prejudice and preconception are not necessarily used in bad faith; they often work well. One of Huck Rorick's theses (1972) is that famous architects have developed personal heuristics (he does not call them either prejudices or preconceptions) that appear to work with a high rate of success. It should be noted, however, that they seem to fail at an equally high rate when mimicked by others. I suggest that this failure when copying can be accounted for by the fact that one tends to recognize the "heuristics of form," rather than the "heuristics of method," which leads, for example, to many second-rate Wrights and LeCorbusiers.

About Random Numbers

Random numbers can be used effectively to simulate missing information and nonlinear events. At the same time, they can be very misleading by creating an illusion of learning (which is false), and they can be counterproductive by generating a fake picturesqueness. There exists a large body of literature on the topic of random numbers and stochastic processes. I will not attempt to synopsize the subject. In this section, I am interested in highlighting some of the strengths and weaknesses, the advantages and disadvantages, of using random numbers as integral parts of a computer-aided design system. (In the following appendix, I will enumerate some of the pedagogical benefits.)

The mini-theory of missing information described in the first chapter of this book and earlier in *The Architecture Machine* has been one of the incentives for pursuing machine intelligence and intimate participation. In more modest applications, particularly in the generation of candidate solutions, missing information must be accounted for (even if we do not happen to have an intelligent species of machines). In the absence of participation, probabilistic distributions can be used to appropriately reflect contingencies that may result from undeterminable (at some point in time) or unknown events. Based on samples of past experiences, statistical techniques can yield distributions (normal or Gaussian, for example) to represent parameters that are subject to fluctuations. One particular architectural application of these techniques can be found in Aguilar (1971).

More complicated distributions can be found in Windheim et al. (1972). These distributions are

181

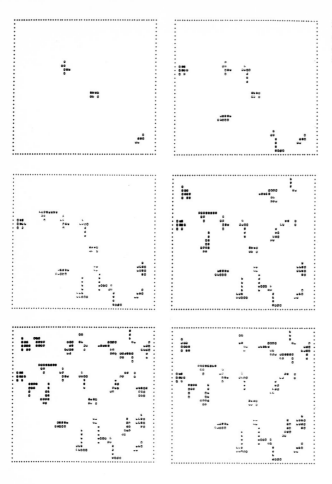

Schnarsky's complexity generator. Computer output courtesy of Anthony Schnarsky.

generally characterized by their use of irregular histograms that follow simple rules and that reflect a stage of growth or development at discrete intervals of time. The Windheim experiment (which I assisted) was conducted in the context of hospital design: "The application of computer aids to the design of hospitals is one of the oldest applications of computers to architectural problems and, at the same time, has been the most misleading. This is because of the nature of hospital design: it is characterized by many variables and a large number of functions...many chunks of known information.... This vastness of information leads to the erroneous premise that design of hospitals enjoys the availability of 'complete' information" (Windheim et al., 1972).

This particular experiment took the labeled elements of the hospital (dermatology, cardiology, and the like) and associated them essentially within the format of the typical adjacency matrix but with three differences (from every adjacency matrix system of which I am aware): (1) the weightings of adjacencies were probabilities; (2) the second half of the matrix, usually symmetrical, was employed for probabilities of sequence of selection; and (3) the matrix did not need to be complete; it could even start in the limiting absurd case of a *tabula rasa*. The doctors as well as the architects could make specific statements of "this is to that" or they could implicitly affect the probabilities through tentative statements that such-and-such is good or bad.

It was correctly cautioned, however, that "One might mistake this approach for simulated evolution or even artificial intelligence. But it is neither. The method exhibits improvement over time by disturbing a probabilistic distribution of random numbers. This affords the machine the possibility to converge upon tendencies and biases while also allowing for exceptional cases to occur. To some extent it is antagonistic, disobedient and contradictory. But it does guarantee a design environment free of complacency and it can lead to design alternatives ultimately attributable to neither the man nor the machine alone. In effect, it is an interim step to artificial intelligence."

This example dealt with 240 elements in a hospital and worked effectively as a consequence of being able always to work with smallest elements of the hospital. It is pointed out, however, that the same technique used with 60,000 labeled elements dispersed over a square mile would require four millennia of computation (on an IBM 360 model 50). The proposal for further development included embedding heuristics and cautious partitioning of local and global parts: "The issues which are purely localizable should be handled with a small perimeter of influences, while the more global characteristics should disperse large influences over many spatially separate elements" (Windheim et al., 1972).

As a final note to random numbers, I will use Schnarsky's (1971) "complexity generator" (found at the end of an interesting paper) as an example of a misleading application of stochastic techniques. The "complexity generator" employs five rules, some expressed as categorical truths, some stated in terms of distributions. The adjacent figures depict sample output (unfortunately too small to reveal the three different symbols that demarcate living, sleeping, and garage units). The note of caution is somewhat semantic. Such a system is a viable tool to simulate the growth of a

Gravel Stones, by George Nees. A random number generator causes the increasing swaying of the squares. Many critics look upon so-called computer art with well found suspicion. Frequently, this suspect nature results from a fickle use of random numbers, a hope for an aesthetic in chance. The illustrations are from *Computer Graphics—Computer Art* (H. W. Franke, London: Phaidon, 1971).

neighborhood or to preview a predisposed policy (like Schnarsky's first rule—zoning regulation—"no house may be within 2 units of another"). However, it is flagrantly wrong to view such a system as a way to generate or design complexity. Complexity is not designed, it evolves. It is too easy to deploy random numbers for the purpose of superimposing a shallow "complicatedness" or picturesquesness. I refer the reader to the October 1972 issue of *Architectural Design* on "Complexity" (edited by Roy Landau), and to my own brief contribution (in the following issue), "Meaning as a Basis for Complexity in Architecture."

Default Options

The reader versed in techniques for computer programming and particularly computer-aided design systems might have wondered, in earlier sections, what was the difference between an inference and a default option. In short, a default option is a variable assumed by a computer program to be of a certain value if the user of that program has not provided a different value. The difference between this kind of assumption making and the drawing of an inference is that inference making is achieved in the process of interaction (with a computer program, for example); it is not embedded by the computer programmer.

The distinction is not mild. Default options can be very powerful devices in assuring smooth interaction with many types of computer program. For example, when I say FORTRAN HARRY to the Architecture Machine's operating system, it draws upon the default options of: put the object code on a file on the disk, print a listing on the printer, and send an error message to the console. If I wanted another arrangement, I could have specified FORTRAN HARRY ... with directions of where to print and whether I want a map, etc. The default options allow for a level of underspecification and quick operation.

In the context of a design problem, default options become less commendable as they can lead to the proliferation of a singlemindedness or preconception of the worst kind. It is possible to argue that the issue is relieved if defaults are presented a priori to the designer or if the defaults are given probabilistic twists and variations. However, the problem is somewhat deeper and is important, because we certainly do not want to resort to the paradigm of total specificity, and yet we do not want to accept the biases of a priori assumption making.

Where does the ability to make inferences come from? In previous sections I have put forth the position that inferences come primarily through experience in conversing with a partner (models of models, etc.). The distinction of evolved assumption-making ability versus a built-in default, embedded by someone "who knows better," is important. But there still exists a class of assumptions that we all draw from abilities gained in interacting with the physical world itself. This is evidenced, for example, in our visual perception, where we do a great deal of this sort of assumption making, and we all do it in pretty much the same way.

This question brings us back to approaches one and two to artificial intelligence. I would like to see machines evolve the ability to make inferences about the world and about design. It is much easier, nevertheless, to build these assumptions in. We reap more rapid returns on our efforts. A caricature of the default option paradigm that has yielded very rapid returns can be found in a computer program originally developed for Skidmore, Owings and Merrill by Neil Harper (1968) and his colleagues, (Bruce Graham, 1969) and recently expanded by Skidmore, Owings and Merrill's San Francisco office and most recently documented by Vladimir Bazjanac (1973).

The original and older version of the Building Optimization Program (BOP) in fact can be run without a single input, defaulting, for example, to 500,000 gross square feet. The remaining 128

inputs are similarly defaultable to "reasonable" limits as a function of cost data derived from over two hundred high-rise buildings already designed by Skidmore, Owings and Merrill. The resulting output is grouped into summaries or full reports on: architectural features, geometrical features, cost and budget, and engineering aspects. Just consider the awesome selling characteristic of being able to generate from meager inputs a building specification that includes investment data on operating expenses and mortgage!

This particular program uses many default options, some implicit, on the basis of the design attitude of the senior partner, Bruce Graham. His particular "heuristic" is one of parallelepipedism of the most simple genre, into which activities (usually those of an office environment) are plugged. I submit that this level of default option is counterproductive to the development of architecture. While some will maintain that it is only a tool for departure, I propose that it carries an unavoidable propensity to repeat the most banal and machine-compatible schemes. And what is even worse is that the cost of developing the program was high and hence must be amortized over a large number of design tasks. The fact that the prejudice (heuristic) was computerized makes it more difficult to evolve as we are more reluctant to shed it.

Optimization

Optimizing is both an obvious application of computers and a comforting one. Even within the tiniest context it is reassuring to be able to look at results and believe with confidence that they represent "bestness." Applications of this genre can be found in the classic paper of Philip Steadman (1971): "The Automatic Generation of Minimum Standard House Plans."

I am reminded of John Eberhard's closing of the first (and perhaps last) Design Methods Group conference held at MIT in 1968. He was enumerating his anxieties about design methods: "The third anxiety I see is one of optimization. We must optimize even if we end up having to minimize, even if we have to eliminate all goals except one, even if we have to attack only small problems because we cannot optimize large problems." I, too, am disturbed by optimization because, if there is a best, it is in the mind of the user, and because even that "bestness" changes from day to day. Optimization not only demands contextlessness and a single goal (utility function), but it insinuates a class of "knowbetters" who are capable of fixing the rules and implementing the results.

Herbert Simon introduced the term "satisficing" (see also P. Roberts, 1970) in contrast to "optimizing." The spirit is to look for good solutions, not necessarily the best. This sounds much more appropriate to architectural problems because it gives us the opportunity to consider and to display a variety of solutions, each of which may stem from a very different interpretation of "good." And, most important, these variations in "goodness" come, not from variations in parameter weighting, but from context. Therefore, the purpose of "satisficing" is to include contextual variants. This is in contrast to Simon's purpose, which results from the numerical hopelessness of optimizing anything but the most trivial problem.

If we agree that the design process associated with architecture is indeed characterized by missing information, then it is surely futile to optimize partial information. If we do not agree with the proposition of missing information, then we must examine the possible avenues to pursue in the light of optimization's demanding a single goal or utility function and in the light of its being so unmanageable for anything except the simplest problem.

The standard approach is to suboptimize. In any situation, the known information will surely be too cumbersome, and the problems must be "decomposed" into subproblems, with subgoals, to be suboptimized. Then, when each is satisfied separately, we put the pieces back together to arrive at a "reasonable" whole. Note that, as is the case with what I have called the aggregate model, it is necessary to separate the problem, delicately minimizing both the size of subproblems and the interconnections among them. This sort of compartmentalization is reminiscent of and typified by the early works of Alexander (1964), which he himself has long since refuted.

In general there are two ways to subdivide a design problem. One can extract families of activities and uses and cluster them as units to be related with other similarly clustered units and to be optimally arranged within themselves. For example, one might decompose hospitals into inpatient and outpatient or smaller divisions, like

medical and surgical. The other alternative is to subdivide the problem into "features" that cluster around general issues, like acoustics and circulation, or smaller ones, like vehicular, pedestrian, and vertical travel. An analogy can be drawn with the simple problem of getting from New York to Boston in a *good* way. The problem can be subdivided into traveling from New York to New Haven, New Haven to Hartford, and Hartford to Boston; each subtrip can be optimized. (Notice that this puts a cramp on flying directly from New York to Boston—a typical outcome of this sort of decomposition.) The other approach is to break down the New York to Boston problem into factors like speed, cost, and comfort, and to optimize these individually (with the typical outcome of conflicting answers—for example, plane, bus, ambulance, respectively—which must be resolved by trade-offs).

The reader interested in techniques of optimization should consult the large body of literature concerned with operations research (a discipline of British origin). It is recommended, however, that the reader seriously scrutinize the philosophies of optimization; I believe they are extremely antagonistic to the nature of architecture.

Appendix 3

Aspects of Teaching and Research

On Teaching Computer Sciences to Architects

The student of architecture is inherently a tactile person. He is accustomed not only to working with his hands but also to physical and graphical manifestations; and he is accustomed to *playing* with these. Seymour Papert and his colleagues make a strong plea for elementary education to consider a more transparent line between play and learning, between the classroom and sports field, and for project-oriented versus problem-oriented studies. Interestingly, these are veteran attitudes in architectural education. They can be accounted for in response to the nature of architecture and to the ways of dealing with it. In Avery Johnson's scale, architecture, unlike mathematics, lies somewhere in the middle, with the referent closer in time and space than a sine or cosine. In short, students of architecture are not accustomed to dealing with symbolic notion.

The standard approach to introducing the technology of computers into an architectural curriculum is to employ an existing course called something like "Introduction to Information Processing" offered by another department and to make it a prerequisite. The result is that the student is forced to deal in an alien language of symbols, usually referring to topics in which he has little background or interest. The consequence: he gets turned off.

Recently, departments of architecture around the United States and Europe have been choosing to offer this introduction on their own. The purpose is not only to offer the introduction in a more palatable and less frustrating manner but also to bring the concepts and metaphors into more direct contact with other design activities. The goals are noble, but, from what I have seen, the general case is that an "internally" offered introduction to computer sciences usually results in a lukewarm entry with exercises and problems lightly camouflaged to look more relevant.

One major feature that distinguishes an electronic computer from a mechanical engine is that if you make an error (in programming) it still does something, and (as with the recounted LOGO experiment) you can use the unexpected behavior to help you find the bug. In the case of a steam engine, if an oversized piston is designed and installed, the machine will not budge. In a teaching environment, this property of always-doing-something affords the important opportunity to immerse the novice rapidly in a very direct, hands-on relationship with a computer. In our experiences in teaching summer sessions (two-week minicourses) to practicing architects, we found that only four hours of explanation are necessary in order to have somebody with no previous experience sit down in front of a computer terminal and compose a program in FORTRAN (we usually employ the simple problem of reversing an arbitrary string of characters: sretcarahc fo gnirts yrartibra na gnisrever fo melborp elpmis eht yolpme yllausu ew). The bulk of this four-hour period involves neither FORTRAN itself nor the particular time-sharing system. It is mostly devoted to understanding the concept of an algorithm.

It is hard to imagine that somebody might not understand the notion of an algorithm. It is much like bicycle riding and skiing, inasmuch as once you have learned how, it is difficult to explain.

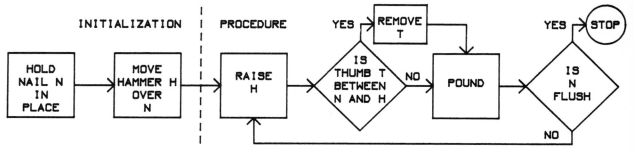

INITIALIZATION | PROCEDURE

HOLD NAIL N IN PLACE → MOVE HAMMER H OVER N → RAISE H → IS THUMB T BETWEEN N AND H — YES → REMOVE T — NO → POUND → IS N FLUSH — YES → STOP — NO

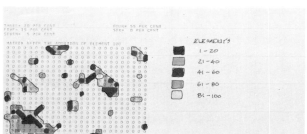

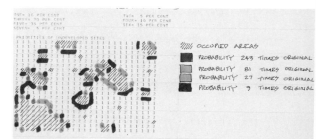

There are little tricks. The operators, the tests, and
the indicators of flow can be dressed in nonal-
gebraic terms, more comfortable to the student
(see adjacent examples). This model can be
expanded to illustrate subroutining and associated notions of recursion and re-entrancy. Along
these lines, I highly recommend the recent
introduction to FORTRAN programming by Oliver
Selfridge (1972).

The ploy of rapid immersion and immediate
hands-on experience yields a phenomenally fast
acquaintance and can be extrapolated to interactive graphics in half an hour. While the amount of
computer time "squandered" (in the eyes of a
computer scientist in the 1950s) is high, the
returns are rapid and, to say the least, exciting. In
a very real sense, in the proposed attitude of
playful and direct immersion, the problem
becomes one of turning students off so that they
can attend to other subjects. The reader should be
referred to "Twenty Things to Do with a Computer"
(Papert and Solomon, 1971); its spirit goes far
beyond its immediate target of introducing computers into elementary school education.

An example problem that I always use in class
is the simulation of the growth of a three-
dimensional community of hypothetical elements
that have an arbitrary but well-specified (by
the student) behavior within a three-
dimensional site of arbitrary but well-specified
(again, by the student) forces. The growth
is simulated through the use of a simple
three-dimensional histogram of probabilities. The
adjacent listing is a simple example. A four-hour
introduction to FORTRAN would include understanding the algorithm and its implementation. It

includes three simple rules about elements: (1) no two elements can occupy the same cell; (2) the presence of an element increases the probability of a surface-to-surface neighbor; (3) the presence of an element decreases the probability of a corner-to-corner neighbor. It also includes a simple statement of site (or physics): no elements can reside on the site unless directly supported from beneath.

The preceding illustrations show stages of growth at intervals. As cautioned in the previous appendix, the resulting complexity can be misleading if viewed as an end in itself. Note that the rules for generation extend only one unit in all directions and that the "influences" are rather trivial. With very little effort (most of it devoted to looking for site boundaries) the spheres of influence can be expanded and their rules can be embellished. This can be done to a point where the program (with modest interaction with humans) can exhibit an uncanny "authenticity" in simulating the growth of a neighborhood, the filling of a parking lot, or the emptying of a theater.

The important pedagogical point is not the faithful reconstruction of real-world events. It is simply the rapid return on a small investment of time and knowledge. I believe that this immediacy is crucial in an introduction to computer sciences.

As a final observation, I would like to bring to your attention aspects of computer programming that have a less specific manifestation, but still a crucial one. A computer is the only machine we can use to model human behavior. Its presence has quite drastically changed the behavioral and social sciences and is beginning, in some ways, to change the design disciplines. The computer is causing changes because of its ability to be used for modeling behaviors, of which "design" is just an example. In trying to build machines that can design, we have to do some looking at how we design. I am not proposing that we have to understand it at the level of synapses and neuron interactions, but we do have to understand causalities and responses in terms of *ourselves*. And as a consequence of this kind of introspection we learn a great deal about design itself. I am not talking so much about the design methodologist who seeks to understand "design" as a transfer and transformation of information and artifacts. I am speaking about the student who is interested in understanding himself and in ways of going about understanding design.

Attitudes toward Research

A special feature of computer-aided architecture is the inherent polarization of means and ends. Those aspects of architecture that we might recognize or feel to be the "real" (gutsy) design problems are beyond the scope of any existing machine. At the same time, those aspects that are presently manageable by computers are viewed, for the most part, as trivial design "services." The consequence is that the most pragmatic and applicable research is seen as kid's stuff, with little need for professional involvement by architects. At the same time, the far-reaching experimentation with cognitive and perceptual processes appears so distant from design that it too receives little attention from the architectural educator or practitioner.

There have been two main consequences of this polarity. First, the application of computers has suffered from the faddism that peaked in the late sixties, that promised to be a panacea for all, and that has not come through. Second, it has received most attention from the flunkouts of each discipline. Both of these conditions, however, are rapidly changing. In schools of architecture, at least, experiments in computer-aided design are receiving the careful attention of some of the most "talented" design students. Among other things, this leads me to believe there is room for optimism, inasmuch as this small discipline is finding substantive philosophical and technical bases, without making too much noise.

Research into computer-aided architecture has taken two forms: simulation and emulation (with some idiosyncratic qualifications). The simulation approach is epitomized by Sidney Gregory's (1971) second reason for pursuing design methods: "Design methodology, as I see it, attempts, through an understanding of the design process, first to design better, second to lay off the most readily comprehended and repetitive parts for machine computation, third to provide working techniques and strategies for designers in hitherto uncharted areas, fourth to externalize the activity of design for management and consumers."

The simulation approach to research is to be found most dramatically in the important works of Purcell (1972), Eastman (1970), and the earlier work of Krauss and Myer (1970). This approach is usually accompanied by careful observation and monitoring of human processes (in the case of Purcell, with time-lapse photography; Eastman, with observation; and Krauss and Myer, with retrospection) for the purpose of dissecting strategies and protocols, in a manner amenable to their future incorporation into computational models. The success of such research depends most critically on this machine compatibility. Many experiments have been fruitless in that the results of scrutinizing the process have led to a better understanding in human terms of how we design (which is a noble result) and not to suggestions of how we might transpose this behavior to a computer. The approach must nevertheless be pursued relentlessly for the purpose of understanding our own behavior, regardless of the growth of the design talent of machines. It must be recognized that this approach does suffer from the Heisenberg uncertainty principle. R. Buckminster Fuller (1969) writes of "Heisenberg's principle of indeterminism which recognized the experimental discovery that the act of measuring always that which is being measured turns experience into a continuous and never-repeatable evolutionary scenario. One picture of the scenario about the caterpillar phase does not communicate its transformation into the butterfly phase, etc."

The second route, which I have called emulation and into which I would place my own studies, does not look at "how" but at "what." It studies the loops and interfaces with machines, the inputs and outputs, the sensing and effecting, and internal (to the machine) structures of knowledge, for the purpose of developing machine processes (most surely quite different from those used by humans) that can yield results as favorable as or more favorable than those produced by humans. This approach suffers the risk of being superficial in only parroting formal behaviors but, at the same time, enjoys the benefits of reviewing the means and methods that we commonly take for granted and often apply gratuitously.

The pitfalls of this approach are epitomized in three experiments conducted within the Architecture Machine Group: LEARN (Negroponte, 1970a), MIMIC (undocumented), and The Frank Lloyd Writer (Rorick, 1972). They have in common the feature that they attend to formal characteristics and discharge stilted, reconstituted editions of those characteristics. Each of the experiments is exciting in terms of the computational methods for recognizing and describing features. At the same time, they are not rewarding as true "emulators" even though (particularly because) they yield surprisingly good results. Their common failing is that they give heed only to what are in fact results of deeper intentions, unrecognizable by the program. For example, it is not difficult to embed a Wrightian heuristic—long horizontal connections to the ground—but one should at least understand that this formal heuristic results from deeper

intentions, perhaps something like: attachment to earth.

Unfortunately, as soon as one entertains the notion of pursuing and capturing deeper intentions, one always finds indications of yet deeper ones. The recursive nature of intentions can be carried back to basic wants and instincts, which are not particularly productive at this time. I believe that machines must *want* to learn in order to be intelligent, but I do not see implications that such instinctive desires will arise in the near future.

Both approaches, simulation and emulation, have found application throughout the entire spectrum of computer-aided architecture, from problem specification to solution implementation. The two extremes of this spectrum have found the most pragmatic applicability (data collection, specification generation, and the like), and it is the center portion that captures the most attention in research. One is tempted to call this center portion Design and to take a stance somewhere between believing it is all magic and postulating that it is all deterministic, algorithmic, and understandable. Researchers take a position implicitly. They design and implement experiments (dramatically affected by available funds and hardware) that can be characterized by their interest in and commitment to interaction, puzzle solving, or recognition.

A conservative and widely accepted model for computer-aided architecture is to split the design process into well-defined regions of supposedly computable and noncomputable aspects. The goal is to capitalize upon the complementary capabilities of the man and the machine. This approach is epitomized in the important and thorough work of Aiko Hormann (1971): "Man is accredited with imaginative and innovative mental functions, which in turn depend on his capabilities for making plausible inferences in the face of incomplete information, for recognizing patterns and relationships and inventing categories, and for taking differing points of view and restructuring the original problem." A prerequisite to this approach is the "rich" interface between the two protagonists; as the one toils the other intuits. Given just an inkling of richness, dynamic graphics, for example, this approach can dramatically assist and augment the role of the human designer, as has been shown, in part, in URBAN5 (Negroponte and Groisser, 1967a and b) and more recently in the work of Kamnitzer and Hoffman (1970).

The puzzle-solving approach to research in computer-aided architecture is less conservative and less interested in estimating what can and what cannot be achieved by the computer. While the previous approach made the problem manageable by forming a partnership, this approach achieves manageability by bounding problems in small packages. Whether it is the design of a bathroom or the allocation of urban services, the pieces must be well labeled and have well-defined physical properties, such that their unification can be tested and evaluated by an unaided machine, using well-formed statements of criteria (and their trade-offs) and constraints. The payoff of this approach usually lies in the understanding of causalities, rather than the taking advantage of solutions. Experiments usually end up generating very limited solutions but very powerful and convincing observations of a "what if..." nature. The most advanced work in this area can be found in the wide-ranging experiments and publications of The Institute of Physical Planning at Carnegie-Mellon University (heavily influenced by two of the most distinguished computer scientists, Allan Newell and Herbert Simon).

The recognition approach strives quite specifically toward having a machine furnish that which the human was providing in the synergistic approach. As an attitude toward research, it is plagued with paradoxes and defeats that go hand-in-hand with the philosophies and consequences of an artificial intelligence. Critics of this "far left" attitude correctly point out that the results so far are in no measure equal to the research efforts expended. While it is grand to talk about the recognition of intentionalities, for example, one must realize continually that something like HUNCH only finds straight lines and curves and does some mapping into three dimensions; both maneuvers can be performed by a three-year-old child.

Bibliography

Ackoff, Russell L, and Fred E. Emery	Our Purposeful Systems	Chicago: Aldine Atherton	1972
Adelson, Marvin, and Samuel Aroni	Group Images of the Future	Los Angeles, Calif.: University of California, School of Architecture and Urban Planning	1972
Aguilar, Rodolfo J.	Architectural Optimization under Conditions of Uncertainty: Stochastic Models	University of Kentucky, Proceedings of the Kentucky Workshop on Computer Applications to Environmental Design, Michael Kennedy (editor), 174-178	1971
Alexander, Christopher	The Timeless Way of Building (in press)		
	What Was Design Methodology, Daddy?	Architectural Design	1971a December
	What Was Design Methodology, Daddy?	DMG Newsletter, 5, 3	1971b March
	Notes on the Synthesis of Form	Cambridge, Mass.: Harvard University Press	1964
Alexander, Christopher, Sara Ishikawa, and Murray Silverstein	A Pattern Language Which Generates Multi-Service Centers	Berkeley, Calif.: Center for Environmental Structure	1968
Alexander, Christopher, Sanford Hirshen, Sara Ishikawa, Christie Coffin, and Shlomo Angel	Houses Generated by Patterns	Berkeley, Calif.: Center for Environmental Structure	1969
Allen, Edward	The Responsive House	Cambridge, Mass.: M.I.T. Press	1974
	Continuous Construction— A Research Report	Cambridge, Mass.: M.I.T., Department of Architecture	1970 October
Amarel, S.	Representation of Problems and Goal Directed Procedures in Computers	Communications of the American Society for Cybernetics,/- 1, No. 2, 8-34	1969
Anderson, R. H., and W. L. Sibley	A New Approach to Programming Man Interfaces	Santa Monica, Calif.: The Rand Corporation, AD-742755	1972 March

Anderson, S.	Problem Solving and Problem Worrying	American Institute of Architecture Teachers Seminar, Bloomfield, Mich.: Cranbrook Academy	1966 June
Andrews, Harry C.	Introduction to Mathematical Techniques in Pattern Recognition	New York: Wiley-Interscience	1972
Anonsen, Sheldon Lee	Interactive Computer Graphics in Architecture	Computers and Automation, 19, No. 8, 27-30	1970 August
Apter, Michael J.	The Computer Simulation of Behavior	London: Hutchinson & Co.	1970
Arbils, Michael A.	The Metaphorical Brain	New York: Wiley-Interscience	1972
Arnoff, E. L., and S. S. Sengupta	The Traveling Salesman Problem	Progress in Operations Research, R.L. Ackoff (editor). New York: Wiley, 150–157	1961
Ashby, W. Ross	Setting Goals in Cybernetic Systems	Cybernetics, Artificial Intelligence, and Ecology, H. W. Robinson and D. E. Knight (editors). New York: Spartan Books, 33-44	1972
	Design for a Brain	London: Chapman and Hall, 2nd Edition	1960
Auger, B.	The Architect and the Computer	New York: Praeger	1972
Banerji, R. B.	Theory of Problem Solving: An Approach to Artificial Intelligence	New York: American Elsevier	1969
Banham, R.	Case for Computerized Design	Industrial Design, 17, 22-29	1970 March
Barachet, L. L.	Graphic Solution of the Traveling Salesman Problem	Operations Research, 5, 841-845	1957
Barney, G. O.	Understanding Urban Dynamics	Proceedings of the Fall Joint Computer Conference, 631-637	1971

Barralt-Torrijos, J., and L. Ciaraviglio — On the Combinatory Definability of Hardware — School of Information and Computer Science, Georgia Institute of Technology, NSR-GN655 — 1971 February

Bartlett, F. — Thinking — New York: Basic Books — 1958

Battro, A. M., and E. J. Ellis — L'Estimation Subjective de L'Espace Urbain — L'Année Psychologique, Paul Fraisse (editor). Presses Universitaires de France, 39-52 — 1972

Bazjanac, V. — BOP—An Experiment in Architectural Design — Building Research and Practice (in press)

Towards a New Breed of Simulation Models in Architectural Design — Proceedings of the Design Activity International Conference, 2-24 — 1973 August

Beardwood, J. J., H. Halton, and J. M. Hammersky — The Shortest Path through Many Points — Proceedings of the Cambridge Philosophical Society, 55, 299-327 — 1959

Beer, Stafford — The Liberty Machine — Cybernetics, Artificial Intelligence, and Ecology, H. W. Robinson and D. E. Knight (editors). New York: Spartan Books — 1972

Bellmore, M., and G. L. Nemhauser — The Traveling Salesman Problem: A Survey — Operations Research, 16, 538-558 — 1968

Benthall, Jonathan — Science and Technology in Art Today — London: Thames and Hudson — 1972

Bergstrom, Lennart Axel — An Approach to Computer Graphics in Planning — Stockholm: Statens Institut for Byggnadsforskning — 1971

Berlin, G. Lenis, and William W. Ray — Application of Aerial Photographs and Remote Sensing Imagery to Urban Research and Studies — Council of Planning Librarians, Exchange Bibliography, 119 — 1970 March

Bernholtz, Allen — LOKAT — Laboratory for Computer Graphics and Spatial Analysis, William Warntz (editor). Cambridge, Mass.: Harvard University, IV.4 — 1969 March

Bijl, A.	Application of CAAD Research in Practice—A System for House Design	London: The British Computer Society. University of York, International Conference on Computers in Architecture, 286-294	1972 September 20-22
Blasi, Cesare and Gabriella	Visualizzazioni con il Computer	Argomenti e Immagini di Design, 4, 43-51	1972 January-February
Bledsoe, W. W.	Man-Machine Facial Recognition	Palo Alto, Calif.: Panoramic Research Inc., Report PRI: 22	1966 August
Bobrow, Daniel G.	Natural Language Input	Semantic Information Processing for a Computer Problem-Solving System, Marvin Minsky (editor). Cambridge, Mass.: M.I.T. Press, 146-226	1968
Bock, Peter	Responsive Democracy: Just Pick Up a Phone and Vote!	6th Annual Urban Symposium, Papers on the Application of Computers to the Problems of Urban Society. New York: Association for Computing Machinery, 43-57	1971
Bonsteel, David L.	The Suzzcello Quad: A Computed Graphics Simulation of Sequential Experience	University of Washington Architecture/Development Series	1969
Botuta, H., and R. Dussud	Coute de Construction et Ordonnancement	Gamsau: Marseilles, 12	1972 January
Bradbury, Ray	The Martian Chronicles	New York: Bantam Books	1958
	The Illustrated Man	New York: Bantam Books	1951
Breeding, K. J.	PADEL: A Pattern Descriptive Language	Ohio State University AD 713594	1970 June
Brewer, Garry D.	Accommodating Increased Demands for Public Participation in Urban Renewal Decisionmaking	Santa Monica, Calif.: The Rand Corporation, P-4868	1972 July
Broadbent, Geoffrey	Design in Architecture	New York: Wiley	1973

Brodey, W. M.	Soft Architecture—The Design of Intelligent Environments	Landscape, 17, No. 1, 8-12	1967
Brodey, W. M., and N. Lindgren	Human Enhancement: Beyond the Machine Age	Institute of Electrical and Electronics Engineers Spectrum, 5, No. 2, 79-93	1968 February
	Human Enhancement Through Evolutionary Technology	Institute of Electrical and Engineers Spectrum, 4, No. 9, 87-97	1967 September
Brunner, Ronald D., and Garry D. Brewer	Policy and the Study of the Future: Given Complexity, Trends or Processes?	Santa Monica, Calif.: The Rand Corporation, P-4912	1972 August
Buchanan, Bruce G.	Review of Hubert Dreyfus' What Computers Can't Do: A Critique of Artificial Reason	Stanford University Artificial Intelligence Project, Memo AIM-181, Computer Science Department Report No. CS-72-325	1972 November
Bunselmeier, Erich	Computerized Location—Allocation	Yale University, School of Architecture	1973
Butas, L. F.	A Directionally Oriented Shortest Path Algorithm	Transportation Research, 2, 253-268	1968
Camarero, E. G.	A Mathematical Model for the Automatic Generation of Behaviours	London: The British Computer Society. University of York, International Conference on Computers in Architecture, 72-79	1972 September 20-22
Campion, D.	Computer-Aided Preparation, Retrieval from and Updating of Architectural Schedules	London: The British Computer Society. University of York, International Conference on Computers in Architecture, 295-302	1972 September 20-22
Carbonell, Jaime R.	On Man-Computer Interaction: A Model and Some Related Issues	Institute of Electrical and Electronics Engineers, Transactions, SSC-5, 1, 16-26	1969 January
Casalaina, V., and H. Rittel	Morphologies of Floor Plans	Paper for the Conference on Computer-Aided Building Design	1967

203

Charniak, Eugene	Toward a Model of Children's Story Comprehension	Cambridge, Mass.: M.I.T., Thesis for Ph.D. in Electrical Engineering	1972
Chomsky, Noam	Language and Mind	New York: Harcourt, Brace & World	1968
Churchman, C. West	The Design of Inquiring Systems	New York: Basic Books	1971
Clowes, M. B.	Foreword:Picture Language Machines, S. Kaneff (editor).	London and New York: Academic Press, ix	1970
Cohen, J.	Human Robots in Myth and Science	London: G. Allen	1966
Coles, L. Stephen	Talking with a Robot in English	Washington, D. C.: Proceedings of the International Joint Conference on Artificial Intelligence, 587-596	1969 May 7-9
Coleman, J. R.	A Computer Program Package for User-Participation in Housing Design	Proceedings for the Design Activity International Conference, 3-6	1973 August
Coons, S. A.	An Outline of the Requirements for Computer-Aided Design Systems	Cambridge, Mass.: M.I.T., Electronic Systems Laboratory Technical Memorandum 169	1963 March
Cooper, L.	Heuristic Methods for Location-Allocation Problems	SIAM Review, 6, 37-53	1964
Courtieux, G.	Recents Developpements dans les Applications des Ordinateurs a la Construction Civile, a l'Architecture et a l'Urbanisme	Techniques & Architecture, 33, No. 4, 44-48	1971 May
	Vous n'y Pouvez Rien, Petite Histoire de l'Architecte et du Robot	Architecture d'Aujourd'hui, 145, 9-13	1969 September
Croes, G. A.	A Method for Solving Traveling Salesman Problems	Operations Research, 6, 791-814	1958

Cross, Nigel	Impact of Computers on the Architectural Design Process	The Architects' Journal, 623	1972 March 22
Cross, Nigel (editor)	Design Participation	London: Academy Editions	1972
Dacey, M. F.	Selection of an Initial Solution for the Traveling Salesman Problem	Operations Research, 8, 133-134	1960
Dale, Ella, and Donald Michie	Machine Intelligence 2	New York: American Elsevier	1968
Dantzig, G. B.	On the Shortest Route through a Network	Management Science, 6, 187-190	1960
Dantzig, G. B., D. R. Fulkerson, and S. M. Johnson	On a Linear Programming Combinatorial Approach to the Traveling Salesman Problem	Operations Research, 7, 58-66	1959
	Solution of a Large Scale Traveling Salesman Problem	Operations Research, 2, 393-410	1954
Davidoff, Paul	Advocacy and Pluralism in Planning	Journal of the American Institute of Planners, 31, 331-338	1965 November
Davies, Ross	Computer Graphic Techniques in Planning	Planning Outlook, 8, 29-34	1970 Spring
Diephus, A. R. J.	Computers Come to the Aid of Logic Designers	Electronics, 44, 50-54	1971 March 29
Dietz, Albert G. H., and Laurence S. Cutler (editors)	Industrialized Building Systems for Housing	Cambridge, Mass.: M.I.T. Press	1971
Dodson, E. N.	Cost Effectiveness in Experimental, Low-Cost Housing Programs	5th Annual Urban Symposium, Papers on the Application of Computers to the Problems of Urban Society. New York: Association for Computing Machinery, 158-169	1970
Draper, Dianne	Public Participation in Environmental Decision-Making	Waterloo, Canada: University of Waterloo, Geography Department	1973
Dreyfus, Hubert L.	What Computers Can't Do	New York: Harper & Row	1972

Dreyfus, S. E.	An Appraisal of Some Shortest-Path Algorithms	Operations Research, 17, 395-412	1969
Duda, Richard O., and Peter E. Hart	Pattern Classification and Scene Analysis	New York: Wiley-Interscience	1973
	Use of the Hough Transformation to Detect Lines and Curves in Pictures	Communications of the ACM, 15, No. 1, 11-15	1972 January
Eastman, Charles M.	Requirements for Man-Machine Collaboration in Design	Environmental Design Research, Wolfgang F. E. Preiser (editor). Proceedings of the Fourth International EDRA Conference. Stroudsburg, Pennsylvania: Dowden, Hutchinson and Ross, Inc.	1973 April
	Adaptive-Conditional Architecture	Design Participation, Nigel Cross (editor). London: Academy Editions, 51-57	1972a
	Requirements for Men-Machine Collaboration in Design	Pittsburgh: Carnegie-Mellon University, Institute of Physical Planning, Research Report No. 35	1972b November
	General Space Planner: A System of Computer-Aided Architectural Design: User Documentation	Environmental Design: Research and Practice, William J. Mitchell (editor). Proceedings of the EDRA 3/ar 8 Conference, University of California at Los Angeles, 23.1	1972c January
	Automated Space Planning and a Theory of Design: A Review	Pittsburgh: Carnegie-Mellon University, Institute of Physical Planning, Research Report No. 29	1972d January
	Heuristic Algorithms for Automated Space Planning	Second International Joint Conference on Artificial Intelligence. London: Proceedings of The British Computer Society, 27-40	1971a
	Adaptive Conditional Architecture	Pittsburgh: Carnegie-Mellon University, Institute of Physical Planning, Research Report No. 24	1971b November

	GSP: A System for Computer Assisted Space Planning	Pittsburgh: Carnegie-Mellon University Institute of Physical Planning, Research Report No. 23	1971c June
	On the Analysis of Intuitive Design Processes	Emerging Methods in Environmental Design and Planning, Gary T. Moore (editor). Cambridge, Mass.: M.I.T. Press, 21-27	1970
	Cognitive Processes and Ill-Defined Problems: A Case Study from Design	Washington, D. C.: Proceedings of the International Joint Conference on Artificial Intelligence, 669-690	1969 May 7-9
Eastman, C., and Schwartz, M.	Methods for Treating Variable Shaped Objects in Computer Aided Design	Proceedings of the Design Activity International Conference, 2-8	1973 August
Ellis, T. O., J. F. Heafner, and W. L. Sibley	The Grail Project: An Experiment in Man-Machine Communications	Santa Monica, Calif.: The Rand Corporation, Memorandum No. RM-5999-ARPA	1969 September
Elms, David G.	A Comprehensive Computer-Aided Building Design System	Cambridge, Mass.: M.I.T., Department of Civil Engineering, Structures Publication No. 343	1972 June
Encarnacao, J. L.	A Survey of and New Solutions for the Hidden-Line Problem	Interactive Computer Graphics Symposium, Delft, The Netherlands	1970 October
Entwisle, Jeffrey	Visual Perception and Analysis of Musical Scores	Cambridge, Mass.: M.I.T., Thesis for B.S. in Department of Humanities	1973 January
Ernst, G. W., and A. Newell	GPS, A Study in Generality and Problem Solving	New York: Academic Press	1969
Ershov, A. P.	Aesthetics and the Human Factor in Programming	Communications of the ACM, 15, No. 7, 501-505	1972 July
Evans, Thomas G.	A Program for the Solution of Geometric-Analogy Intelligence Test Questions	Semantic Information Processing, Marvin Minsky (editor). Cambridge, Mass.: M.I.T. Press, 271-353	1968

	A Program for the Solution of Geometric-Analogy Intelligence Test Questions	Cambridge, Mass.: M.I.T., Ph.D. Thesis in Mathematics	1963
Faiman, M., and S. Neivergelt (editors)	Pertinent Concepts in Computer Graphics	Urbana: University of Illinois Press	1969
Feigenbaum, E. A., and J. Feldman (editors)	Computers and Thought	New York: McGraw-Hill	1963
Feldman, J. A., G. M. Feldman, G. Falk, G. Grape, J. Pearlman, I. Sobel, and J. M. Tenenbaum	The Stanford Hand-Eye Project	Washington, D. C.: Proceedings of the International Joint Conference on Artificial Intelligence, 521-526	1969 May
Finrow, Jerry, and Robert Heilman	Toward a User Based Automated Architectural Design System: Theory, System Operation and Future Development	DMG-DRS Journal, 7, No. 2, 124	1973 April-June
Flanders, Stephen	The Design of Evolution	Cambridge, Mass.: M.I.T., Thesis for B.Arch. in Department of Architecture	1971
Fleisher, Aaron, and Chuck Libby	The Thinking Eye	Cambridge, Mass.: M.I.T., Proposal Submitted to The Cambridge Project	1972
Flood, M. M.	The Traveling Salesman Problem	Operations Research, 4, 61-75	1956
Fogel, L. J., A. J. Owens, and M. J. Walsh	Artificial Intelligence by Simulated Evolution	New York: Wiley	1966
Forrester, Jay W.	World Dynamics	Cambridge, Mass.: Wright-Allen	1971a
	Testimony for the Hearings Before the Ad Hoc Subcommittee on Urban Growth of the Committee on Banking and Currency, House of Representatives, Ninety-First Congress, Second Session on Industrial Location Policy	Washington, D. C.: U. S. Government Printing Office, 208-209	1971b

	Systems Analysis as a Tool for Urban Planning	For the Symposium: The Engineer and the City. Washington, D. C.: National Academy of Engineering	1969a October 22-23
	Urban Dynamics	Cambridge, Mass.: M.I.T. Press	1969b
	Industrial Dynamics	Cambridge, Mass.: M.I.T. Press	1961
Fox, Jerome (editor)	Computers and Automata	New York: Wiley	1972
Franke, H. W.	Computer und Visuelle Gestaltung	Elektronische Datanverarbeitung, 12, 66-74	1970 February
Freeman, P., and A. Newell	A Model for Functional Reasoning in Design	Second International Joint Conference on Artificial Intelligence, London: Proceedings of The British Computer Society, 621-633	1971
Freire, Paulo	Pedagogy of the Oppressed	New York: Herder and Herder	1971
Friedman, Yona	Realisable Utopias (in press)		
	Society=Environment	Brussels: C.E.A.	1972a
	Information Processes for Participatory Design	Design Participation, Nigel Cross (editor). London: Academy Editions, 45-50	1972b
	Flatwriter: Voice by Computer	Progressive Architecture, 52, 98-101	1971 March
Frost, Martin	Reading the Associated Press News	Stanford University: Artificial Intelligence Memo No. 1511	1973
Fu, K. S.	A Critical Review of Learning Control Research	Pattern Recognition and Machine Learning, K. S. Fu (editor). Nagoya, Japan: Proceedings, Japan-U.S. Seminar on the Learning Process in Control Systems, 288-296	1971

Fu, K. S. (editor)	Pattern Recognition and Machine Learning	Nagoya, Japan: Proceedings, Japan-U.S. Seminar on the Learning Process in Control Systems	1971
Fullenwider, Donald R., and Charles E. Reeder	Implementation of a "Space Planning" System in a Small-Scale Architecture Office	DMG-DRS Journal, 7, No. 2, 124	1973 April-June
Fuller, R. Buckminster	Operating Manual for Spaceship Earth	Carbondale: Southern Illinois University Press	1969
Furman, T. T. (editor)	The Use of Computers in Engineering Design	New York: Van Nostrand Reinhold	1972
Galimberti, R., and U. Montanari	An Algorithm for Hidden Line Elimination	Communications of the ACM, 12	1969 April
Garvin, P. J. (editor)	Cognition: A Multiple View	Rochelle Park, N. J.: Spartan Books	1970
Gaunt, S.	A Non-Computer Method Using Search for Resolving the Traveling Salesman Problem	Journal of the Canadian Operational Research Society, 14, 210-232	1968
Gavin, James M.	The Social Impact of Information Systems	Computers and Automation, 18, 8, 16-18	1969 July
Gero, John S.	Computers and Design in a Constrained Environment	Sydney, Australia: University of Sydney, Department of Architectural Science, Computer Report CR11	1970
Gibson, J. J.	The Senses Considered as Perceptual Systems	Boston: Houghton Mifflin	1966
	The Perception of the Visual World	Boston: Houghton Mifflin	1951
Giloi, W., R. Gnatz, and W. Handler	Gesellschaft für Informatik	Berlin: Symposium on Computer Graphics	1971 October 19-21
Gingerich, Jeffrey Z.	Computer Graphics Building Definition System	DMG-DRS Journal, 7, No. 2, 124	1973 April-June

Glenn, J. W., and M. H. Hitchcock	With a Speech Pattern Classifier, Computer Listens to Its Master's Voice	Electronics, 44, 84-89	1971 May 10
Gold, E. M.	Universal Goal Seekers	Information and Control, 18, 396-403	1971 June
Goldstein, R. C.	The Substantive Use of Computers for Intellectual Activities	Cambridge, Mass.: M.I.T., AD-721618	1971 April
Gomory, R. E.	The Traveling Salesman Problem	Proceedings of the IBM Scientific Computing Symposium on Combinatorial Problems. White Plains, New York: IBM Data Processing Division, 19-121	1966
Gonzales, R. H.	Solution to the Traveling Salesman Problem by Dynamic Programming on the Hypercube	Cambridge, Mass.: M.I.T., Operations Research Center, Technical Report No. 18	1962
Goodman, Robert	After the Planners	New York: Simon & Schuster	1971
Gordon, Richard, and Gabor T. Herman	Reconstruction of Pictures from Their Projections	Communications of the ACM, 14, No. 12, 759-768	1971 December
Graham, Bruce	Computer Graphics in Architectural Practice	Computer Graphics in Architecture and Design, M. Milne (editor). New Haven: Yale School of Design, 24-30	1969
Grason, J.	An Approach to Computerized Space Planning Using Graph Theory	Proceedings of SHARE-ACM-IEEE, Design Automation Workshop, 170-179	1971
Gregory, R. L.	Concepts and Mechanisms of Perception	London: Gerald Duckworth and Company (in press)	
		Machine Intelligence 6, B. Meltzer and D. Mitchie (editors). New York: American Elsevier	1970

	Social Implications of Intelligent Machines	Machine Intelligence 6, B. Meltzer and D. Mitchie (editors). New York: American Elsevier	1970
Gregory, S. A.	Design Task Patterns— Morphological Analysis or Combinative Methods and Other Possibilities in Practice and Theory	Proceedings of the Design Activity International Conference, 1-7	1973 August
	The State of the Art	DMG Newsletter, Design Methods Group, 5, No. 6/7, 3	1971 June-July
Gregory, Steven K.	The Use of Minicomputers in Planning	Cambridge, Mass.: M.I.T., Thesis for M.S. in the Department of Urban Studies	1972 May
Gunderson, Keith	Mentality and Machines	New York: Anchor Books, Doubleday	1971
Guzman, A.	Decomposition of a Visual Scene into Three-Dimensional Bodies	Automatic Interpretation and Classification of Images, A. Grasselli (editor). New York: Academic Press	1969
	Some Aspects of Pattern Recognition by Computer	Cambridge, Mass.: M.I.T., AD-656041	1967 February
Hamilton, Blair	Pneumatic Structures, Cybernetics and Ecology: Toward Ecostructures for Habitation of People and Other Lively Systems	Cambridge, Mass.: M.I.T., Department of Architecture, Paper presented at Edward Allen's Shirt Sleeve Session	1972 May
Handler, A. Benjamin	Systems Approach to Architecture	New York: American Elsevier	1970
Hardgrave, W. W., and G. L. Nemhauser	On the Relation between the Traveling Salesman Problem and the Longest Path Problem	Operations Research, 10, 647-657	1962
Harmon, L. D.	Automatic Recognition of Print and Script	Proceedings of the IEEE, 60, 10, 1165-1176	1972 October
	Line Drawing Pattern Recognizer	Electronics, 39-43	1960 September

Harper, G. N. (editor)	Computer Applications in Architecture and Engineering	New York: McGraw-Hill	1968
Harris, S. A.	Style in Architecture	Computer Studies in the Humanities and Verbal Behavior, 2, 204-212 ·	1969 December
Hart, P. E., and R. O. Duda	Survey of Artificial Intelligence	Stanford Research Institute AD-718318	1971 January
Hayes-Roth, Frederick	The Meaning and Mechanics of Intelligence	Cambridge, Mass.: M.I.T., Industrial Liaison Program	1971 July
Hebert, Budd H.	Stochastic Programming: A Selected Bibliography	Council of Planning Librarians, Exchange Bibliography, 132	1970 June
Heller, I.	On the Traveling Salesman's Problem	Proceedings of the Second Symposium in Linear Programming, A. H. Antosiewicz (editor). Washington, D.C.: National Bureau of Standards and Directorate of Management Analysis, DCS/Comptroller, USAF, Vol. 2, 643-665	1955
Hershberger, Robert G.	Toward a Set of Semantic Scales to Measure the Meaning of Architectural Environments	Environmental Design: Research and Practice, William J. Mitchell (editor). Proceedings of the EDRA 3/ar 8 Conference, University of California at Los Angeles, 6.4	1972 January
Hoffman, A. J., and H. M. Markowitz	A Note on Shortest Path, Assignment and Transportation Problems	Naval Research Logistics Quarterly, 10, 375-380	1963
Hormann, Aiko M.	Machine-Aided Evaluation of Alternative Designs	Environmental Design: Research and Practice, William J. Mitchell (editor). Proceedings of the EDRA 3/ar 8 Conference, University of California at Los Angeles, 22.2	1972 January

	A Man-Machine Synergistic Approach to Planning and Creative Problem Solving	International Journal of Man-Machine Studies, 3, 167-184, 241-267	1971
Horn, Berthold K. P.	Shape from Shading	Cambridge, Mass.: M.I.T., Ph.D. Thesis in Electrical Engineering	1972
	Shape from Shading: A Method for Obtaining the Shape of a Smooth Opaque Object from One View	Cambridge, Mass.: M.I.T., Artificial Intelligence Laboratory, Project MAC, TR-79	1970 November
Hu, T. C.	A Decomposition Algorithm for Shortest Paths in a Network	Operations Research, 16, 91-102	1968
Hu, T. C., and W. T. Torres	Shortcut in the Decomposition Algorithm for Shortest Paths in a Network	IBM Journal of Research and Development, 13, 387-390	1969
Iberall, A. S., and W. S. McCulloch	The Organizing Principle of Complex Living Systems	Transactions of the American Society of Mechanical Engineers, Journal of Basic Engineering, 293	1969 July
Ingersoll, J.	Computer House: A House to Match Our Age	House Beautiful, 113, 20, 45-55	1971 February
Isaac, A. M., and E. Turban	Some Comments on the Traveling Salesman Problem	Operations Research, 17, 543-546	1969
Jaki, Stanley L.	Brain, Mind and Computers	New York: Herder and Herder	1969
Jencks, C.	Toward the Year 2000	A. A. Quarterly, 1, 56-60	1971
Johnson, Avery R.	The Three Little Pigs Revisited	Collaborative Design in Community Development, Eleven Views, Peter Batchelor and Jacob Pearce (editors). Raleigh, North Carolina: North Carolina State University, Student Publication of the School of Design, 20, No. 2, 173-186	1971

	Dialogue and the Exploration of Context: Properties of an Adequate Interface	Washington, D. C.: The American Society for Cybernetics, The Fourth Annual International Symposium, 3	1970 October
Johnson, Timothy	Sketchpad III: A Computer Program for Drawing in Three Dimensions	American Federation of Information Processing Proceedings, Spring Joint Computer Conference, 23, 347-353	1963
Johnson, Timothy, Guy Weinzapfel, John Perkins, Doris C. Ju, Tova Solo, and David Morris	IMAGE: An Interactive Graphics-Based Computer System for Multi-constrained Spatial Synthesis	Cambridge, Mass.: M.I.T., Department of Architecture	1970 September
Jones, J. Christopher	State of the Art	DMG Newsletter, 5, No. 10, 2	1971 October
	Design Methods	London: Wiley-Interscience	1970
Kamnitzer, Peter	Urban Problems	Computers and the Problems of Society, Harold Sackman and Harold Borko (editors). Monvale, N. J.: AFIPS Press, 263-338	1972
	Computer Aid to Design	Architectural Design, 39, 507-508	1969 September
Kamnitzer, P., and A. Hoffman	INTUVAL: An Interactive Computer Graphic Aid for Design and Decision Making in Urban Planning	EDRA Two, Proceedings of the 2nd Annual Environmental Design Research Association Conference, Pittsburgh, Penna., John Archea and Charles Eastman (editors), 383-390	1970 October
Kaneff, S. (editor)	Picture Language Machines	London and New York: Academic Press	1970
Karg, L. L., and G. L. Thompson	A Heuristic Approach to Solving the Traveling Salesman Problems	Management Science, 10, 225-248	1964

Kaufman-Diamond, Sharon	On Evaluation of Man-Computer Problem Working Systems	Environmental Design: Research and Practice, William J. Mitchell (editor). Proceedings of the EDRA 3/ar 8 Conference, University of California at Los Angeles, 22.4	1972 January
Kelly, M. D.	Visual Identification of People By Computer	Stanford University AD 713252	1970 August
Kennedy, Michael (editor)	Proceedings of the Kentucky Workshop on Computer Applications to Environmental Design	Lexington, Ky.: College of Architecture of the University of Kentucky	1971
Kilmer, W. C., W. S. McCulloch, and J. Blum	A Model of the Vertebrate Central Command System	International Journal of Man-Machine Studies, 1, No. 3, 279-310	1969
Kling, Robert Elliot	Reasoning by Analogy with Applications to Heuristic Problem Solving: A Case Study	Stanford University Artificial Intelligence Projects, Memo AIM-147, Computer Science Department Report No. CS216	1971
Kmetzo, L.	Building Automation	Progressive Architecture, 51, 110	1970 October
Kracht, James, and William A. Howard	Applications of Remote Sensing, Aerial Photography, and Instrumented Imagery Interpretation to Urban Area Studies	Council of Planning Librarians, Exchange Bibliography, 166	1970 December
Krakauer, Lawrence J.	Computer Analysis of Visual Properties of Curved Objects	Cambridge, Mass.: M. I. T., Project MAC, TR-82	1971 May
Krampen, M.	Type Psychology and Representative Citizen Participation in Planning Projects	Proceedings of the Design Activity International Conference, 3-10	1973 August
Krauss, Richard, and John R. Myer	Design: A Case History	Emerging Methods in Environmental Design and Planning, Gary T. Moore (editor). Cambridge, Mass.: M.I.T. Press	1970

Krawczyk, Robert, and Elliot Dudnik	Space Plan: A User-Oriented Package for the Evaluation of and the Generation of Spatial Inter-Relationships	DMG-DRS Journal, 7, No. 2, 124	1973 April-June
Kreitzer, Norman H., and William J. Fitzgerald	A Video Display System for Image Processing by Computer	IEEE Transactions on Computers, C-22, 129-134	1973 February
Kubert, B., J. Szabo, and S. Giulieri	The Perspective Representation of Functions of Two Variables	Journal of the ACM, 15, 2	1968 April
LaVine, Glenn	Computer Aided Solution of Functional Relationships for Architectural Design	Urbana, Illinois: University of Illinois, Coordinated Science Laboratory, Report R-492	1970 October
Lafue, G., and S. Charalambides	PAVLOV: A Program Based on a Learning Method as an Aid to Architectural Design	Proceedings of the Design Activity International Conference, 2-22	1973 August
Lambert, F.	The Traveling Salesman Problem	Paris: Cahier du Centre d'Etudes de Recherche Operationelle, 2, 180-191	1960
Lapied, F.	Informatica e Architettura	Architettura 16, 756-759	1971 March
Lavin, Mark	Recognition of People through Low-Order Features	Cambridge, Mass.: M.I.T., Thesis for B.S. and M.S. in Department of Electrical Engineering	1973
Lee, K., and C. D. Stewart	ARK 2—An Implementable Computer-Aided Design System	London: The British Computer Society. University of York, International Conference on Computers in Architecture, 261-266	1972 September
Lee, T. M. P.	Report on 1971 Conference on Computer Vision	SIGART Newsletter, New York: Communications of the ACM, No. 34, 19-26	1972 June
	Three-Dimensional Curves and Surfaces for Rapid Computer Display	Detroit, Michigan: Management Information Services	1970

Levin, P. H.	The Use of Graphs to Decide the Optimum Layout of Buildings	The Architect's Information Library, 140, No. 15, 809-815	1964 October 7
Liggett, Robin Segerblom	Floor Plan Layout by Implicit Enumeration	Environmental Design: Research and Practice, William J. Mitchell (editor). Proceedings of the EDRA 3/ar 8 Conference, University of California at Los Angeles, 23.4	1972 January
Lippman, Andrew	MAG Tape Interfaces for the Interdata	Cambridge, Mass.: M.I.T., Thesis for B.S. in Department of Electrical Engineering	1971
Little, J. D. C., K. G. Murty, D. W. Sweeney, and C. Karel	An Algorithm for the Traveling Salesman Problem	Operations Research, 11, 972-989	1963
Loefgren, L.	The Relative Explanation of Systems	Trends in General System Theory, J. G. Klir (editor). New York: Wiley	1972
	An Axiomatic Explanation of Complete Self Reproduction	Bulletin of Mathematical Biophysics, 30, No. 31, 415-425	1968
Loutrel, P.	A Solution to the Hidden-Line Problem for Computer-Drawn Polyhedra	IEEE Transaction on Computers, 19, 3	1970 March
McCarthy, John	A Display Terminal System for the Computer Science Department	Stanford University: Artificial Intelligence Memo No. 1436	1973a February
	Monopolies in Home Computer Services	Stanford University: Artificial Intelligence Memo No. 1428	1973b February
	Research Aimed at Home Computer Terminal Systems	Stanford University: Artificial Intelligence Laboratory Proposal to The National Science Foundation	1973c February
McCulloch, W. S.	Embodiments of Mind	Cambridge, Mass.: M.I.T. Press	1965

Markus, Thomas	A Doughnut Model of the Environment and its Design	Design Participation, Nigel Cross (editor). London: Academy Editions, 84-91	1972
Martin, James, and Adrian R. D. Norman	The Computerized Society	Englewood Cliffs, N. J.: Prentice-Hall	1970
Martin, Thomas E.	Methods for Problem Solving in Environmental Design: An Assessment of the Current State of Design Methodology	College of Fellows Scholarship 1970, Royal Institute of Canada	1971 June 15
Masakazu, Ejiri, Takeshi Uno, Hauro Yoda, Tatsuo Goto, and Kiyoo Takeyasu	An Intelligent Robot with Cognition and Decision-Making Ability	Second International Joint Conference on Artificial Intelligence, London: Proceedings of The British Computer Society, 350-358	1971
Maturana, Humberto R.	Biology of Cognition	Urbana, Ill.: University of Illinois, Department of Electrical Engineering, Biological Computer Laboratory, Report No. 9.0	1970a November
	Neurophysiology of Cognition	Cognition: A Multiple View, P. J. Garvin (editor). Rochelle Park, N. J.: Spartan Books	1970b
Maver, Thomas	Simulation and Solution Teams in Architectural Design	Design Participation, Nigel Cross (editor). London: Academy Editions, 79-83	1972
Maxwell, P. C.	The Perception and Description of Line Drawings by Computer	Computer Graphics and Image Processing, 1, No. 1, 31-46	1972 April
May, Judith V.	Citizen Participation: A Review of the Literature	Council of Planning Librarians, Exchange Bibliography, 210-211	1971 August
Meadow, Charles T.	Man-Machine Communication	New York: Wiley	1970
Mehring, H. E. (editor)	Interactive Graphics in Data Processing	IBM Systems Journal, 7, 3-4	1968
Meisel, William S.	Computer-Oriented Approaches to Pattern Recognition	New York: Academic Press	1972

Meltzer, Bernard, and Donald Mitchie	Machine Intelligence 6	New York: American Elsevier	1971
	Machine Intelligence 5	New York: American Elsevier	1970
	Machine Intelligence 4	New York: American Elsevier	1969
Mesthene, Emmanuel G.	Technology and Humanist Values	Computers and the Humanities, 4, No. 1, 1-10	1969 September
Millar, P. H.	On Defining the Intelligence of Behaviour and Machines	Second International Joint Conference on Artificial Intelligence, London: Proceedings of The British Computer Society, 279-286	1971
Miller, Arthur R.	The Dossier Society—Cybernetics and Surveillence	The Assult on Privacy, MBA, 5, 30-32	1971 March
Miller, C. E., A. W. Tucker, and R. A. Zemlin	Integer Programming Formulation of Traveling Salesman Problems	Journal of the Association of Computing Machinery, 7, 326-329	1960
Miller, Irvin M.	Computer Graphics for Decision Making	Harvard Business Review, 47, 121-132	1969 November-December
Miller, W. R.	Computer-Aided Space Planning	Proceedings of SHARE-ACM-IEEE, Design Automation Workshop, 28-34	1970
Mills, G.	A Heuristic Approach to Some Shortest-Route Problems	Journal of the Canadian Operational Research Society, 6, 20-25	1968
	A Decomposition Algorithm for the Shortest-Route Problem	Operations Research, 14, 279-291	1966
Milne, M.	From Pencil Points to Computer Graphics	Progressive Architecture, 51, 168-177	1970 June
Minsky, Marvin (editor)	Semantic Information Processing	Cambridge, Mass.: The M.I.T. Press	1968
Minsky, Marvin, and Seymour Papert	Artificial Intelligence	Cambridge, Mass.: M.I.T., Artificial Intelligence Memo No. 252	1972 January

	Perceptrons	Cambridge, Mass.: M.I.T. Press	1969
Minty, G. J.	A Comment on the Shortest Route Problem	Operations Research 5, 724	1957
Mitchell, William J.	Experiments with Participation-oriented Computer Systems	Design Participation, Nigel Cross (editor). London: Academy Editions, 73-78	1972a
	Simple Form Generation Procedures	London: University of York, International Conference on Computers in Architecture, 144-156	1972b September
	Computer-Aided Spatial Synthesis	5th Annual Urban Symposium, Papers on the Application of Computers to the Problems of Urban Society. New York: Association for Computing Machinery, 101-121	1970
Mitchell, William J., and Robert Dillon	A Polyomino Assembly Procedure for Architectural Floor Planning	Environmental Design: Research and Practice, William J. Mitchell (editor). Proceedings of the EDRA 3/ar 8 Conference, University of California at Los Angeles, 23.5	1972 January
Mitchie, Donald	Heuristic Search	Computer Journal, 14, 96-102	1971 February
	Machine Intelligence 3	New York: American Elsevier	1968
Mohr, Malte	A Computer Model of the Design Process that Uses the Concept of an Apartment Floor Plan to Solve Layout Problems	Cambridge, Mass.: M.I.T., Master's Thesis in Civil Engineering	1972a
	A Computer Model of the Design Process that Uses a Concept of an Apartment Floorplan to Solve Layout Problems	Environmental Design: Research and Practice, William J. Mitchell (editor). Proceedings of the EDRA 3/ar 8 Conference, University of California at Los Angeles, 23.6	1972b January

Mor, M., and T. Lamdan	A New Approach to Automatic Scanning of Contour Maps	Communications of the ACM, 15, 809-812	1972 September
Moran, Thomas P.	The Cognitive Structure of Spatial Knowledge	Pittsburgh, Pennsylvania: Carnegie-Mellon University, Department of Computer Science	1973 January
	Architecture: Computers in Design	Architectural Record, 149, 129-134	1971 March
Morton, G., and A. H. Land	A Contribution to the Traveling Salesman Problem	Journal of the Royal Statistical Society, Series B, 17, 185-194	1955
Murray, Richard D. (editor)	Computer Handling of Graphical Information	Washington D.C.: Society of Photographic Science and Engineers	1970
Nakamura, K., and M. Oda	Heuristics and Learning Control	Pattern Recognition and Machine Learning, K. S. Fu (editor). Nagoya, Japan: Proceedings, Japan-U.S. Seminar on the Learning Process in Control Systems	1971
Narasimhan, R.	Picture Languages	Picture Language Machines, S. Kaneff (editor). New York: Academic Press	1970
Negroponte, Nicholas	Recent Advances in Sketch Recognition	Proceedings of the National Computer Conference, New York, New York	1973 June 4-6
	Meaning as the Basis for Complexity in Architecture	Architectural Design, 42, 11, 679-681	1972a November
	Mijloace Electronice in Proiectarea de Arhitectura si Urbanism, translated by Mircea Enache	Romania: Arhitectura, 20, Nos. 3-4, 127-131	1972b
	Aspects of Living in an Architecture Machine	Design Participation, Nigel Cross (editor). London: Academy Editions, 63-67	1972c

HUNCH—An Experiment in Sketch Recognition	Environmental Design: Research and Practice, Proceedings of the EDRA 3/ar 8 Conference, Los Angeles	1972d January
HUNCH—An Experiment in Sketch Recognition	Berlin: Gesellschaft für Informatik	1971a October
The Architecture Machine	Werk	1971b August
The Architecture Machine	Architecture and Urbanism	1971c January-August
The Semantics of Architecture Machines	Techniques & Architecture	1971d May
The Architecture Machine— A Mini in Teaching and Research	Institute for Electrical and Electronics Engineers Digest	1971e March
The Architecture Machine	Cambridge, Mass.: M.I.T. Press	1970a
URBAN5—A Machine that Discusses Urban Design	Emerging Methods in Environmental Design and Planning, Gary T. Moore (editor). Cambridge, Mass.: The M.I.T. Press	1970b
The Semantics of Architecture Machines	Architectural Forum	1970c October
The Semantics of Architecture Machines	Architectural Design (G.B.)	1970d September
URBAN5: An Experimental Urban Design Partner	Computer Graphics in Architecture and Design, M. Milne (editor). New Haven: Yale School of Art and Architecture	1969a
Architecture Machine	Architectural Design, 39, 510	1969b September
Toward a Humanism Through Machines	Architectural Design, 39, 511-512. Reprinted from Technology Review, 71, No. 6, April 1969, Copyright 1969	1969c September
Towards a Humanism Through Machines	Technology Review, 71, No. 6, 2-11	1969d April

	Humanism Through Machines	The Canadian Architect, 14, No. 4, 29-34	1969e April
	Toward a Theory of Architecture Machines	American Institute of Architects Journal, 51, No. 3, 71-74	1969f March
Negroponte, Nicholas, and Leon B. Groisser	Semantica delle Macchine per l'Architettura	Parametro, 10, 44-50	1972
	URBAN5: A Machine that Discusses Urban Design	Emerging Methods in Environmental Design and Planning, Gary T. Moore (editor). Cambridge, Mass.: M. I. T. Press	1970
	Environmental Humanism Through Robots	Proceedings of the First Annual Environmental Design Research Association Conference, H. Sanoff and S. Cohn (editors). Raleigh: Design Research Laboratory, North Carolina State University	1969a
	Machine Vision of Models of the Physical Environment	Cambridge, Mass.: M. I. T., Department of Architecture, Proposal to The National Science Foundation	1969b
	URBAN5	Ekistics, 24, No. 142, 289-291	1967a September
	URBAN5: An On-Line Urban Design Partner	IBM Report, 320-2012. Cambridge, Mass.	1967b June
Negroponte, Nicholas, Leon B. Groisser, and James Taggart	HUNCH: An Experiment in Sketch Recognition	Environmental Design: Research and Practice, William J. Mitchell (editor). Proceedings of the EDRA 3/ar 8 Conference, University of California at Los Angeles, 22.1	1972 January
Nestor, Robert	Mies Machine: A Synthetic Reconstruction of the Style of Mies van der Rohe	Berkeley, Calif: for Architecture 230, Mr. Rittel, University of California	1968 March
Newell, Allen, and Herbert Simon	Human Problem Solving	Englewood Cliffs, N. J.: Prentice-Hall	1972

Newman, William M.	Graphics Systems for Computer-Aided Design	Environmental Design: Research and Practice, William J. Mitchell (editor). Proceedings of the EDRA 3/ar 8 Conference, University of California at Los Angeles, 22.6	1972 January
	Display Procedures	Communications of the ACM, 14, No. 10, 651-660	1971 October
Newman, William M., and Robert F. Sproull	Principles of Interactive Computer Graphics	New York: McGraw-Hill	1973
Nicholson, T. A. J.	A Boundary Method for Planar Traveling Salesman Problems	Operations Research Quarterly, 19, 445-452	1968
	Finding the Shortest Route between Two Points in a Network	The Computer Journal, 9, 275-280	1966
Nilsson, Nils	Problem Solving Methods in Artificial Intelligence	New York: McGraw-Hill	1971
Noble, J., and J. Turner	Evaluating Housing Layouts by Computer	Architect's Journal, 315-318	1971 February 10
Noll, A. Michael	The Effects of Artistic Training on Aesthetic Preferences for Pseudo-Random Computer-Generated Patterns	Granville, Ohio: The Psychological Record, Denison University, 22, 449-462	1972a
	Man-Machine Tactile Communication	SID Journal	1972b July/August
	Man-Machine Tactile Communication	Polytechnic Institute of Brooklyn: Dissertation for the Degree of Doctor of Philosophy in Electrical Engineering	1971 June
Obrero, Banco	Description of Two Applications to a Mosaic Composition Technique as Employed in the Random Organization of Architectural Layouts	London: The British Computer Society. University of York, International Conference on Computers in Architecture	1972 September
Oestreicher, H., and D. R. Moore (editors)	Cybernetic Problems in Bionics	New York: Gordon and Breach	1968

Olsten, C. J.	A Summary of Architectural Involvement with Computers	Proceedings of SHARE-ACM-IEEE, Design Automation Workshop, 50-55	1971
Organick, Elliott	The Multics System: An Examination of Its Structure	Cambridge, Mass.: M.I.T. Press	1972
Papert, Seymour	Teaching Children Thinking	Teaching Mathematics, No. 58	1972 Spring
	A Computer Laboratory for Elementary Schools	LOGO Memo No. 1. Cambridge, Mass.: Artificial Intelligence Laboratory, M.I.T.	1971a October
	Teaching Children Thinking	LOGO Memo No. 2. Cambridge, Mass.: Artificial Intelligence Laboratory, M.I.T.	1971b October
	Teaching Children to be Mathematicians vs. Teaching About Mathematics	LOGO Memo No. 4. Cambridge, Mass.: Artificial Intelligence Laboratory, M.I.T.	1971c July
Papert, Seymour, and Cynthia Solomon	Twenty Things to do With a Computer	LOGO Memo No. 3. Cambridge, Mass.: Artificial Intelligence Laboratory, M.I.T.	1971
Parker, Dorn B.	The Antisocial Use of Computers	Computers and Automation, 21, No. 8, 22-36	1972 August
Parslow, R. D.	Linking Man and Computer	Design, 263, 64-65	1970 November
Parslow, R. D., and R. Elliot Green (editors)	Advanced Computer Graphics	London: Plenum Press	1971
Parslow, R. D., R. W. Prowse, and R. Elliot Green (editors)	Computer Graphics	London: Plenum Press	1969
Pask, Gordon	Learning Strategies, Memories, and Individuals	Cybernetics, Artificial Intelligence, and Ecology, H. W. Robinson and D. E. Knight (editors). New York: Spartan Books, 42-63	1972a

CASTLE: The Embodiment of a Theory of Learning, Memory and Belief	ASC Conference (invited paper)	1972b December
Interaction between Individuals, Its Stability and Style	Mathematical Biosciences, 11, 59-84	1971 June
Learning Strategies, Memories and Individuals	Cybernetics, Artificial Intelligence and Ecology (Proceedings of the Fourth Annual Conference of the ASC), H. Robinson and E. Kyle (editors). Rochelle Park, N. J.: Spartan Books	1970a
The Meaning of Cybernetics in the Behavioural Sciences	Progress of Cybernetics, 1, 15-45, J. Rose (editor). New York: Gordon and Breach. Reprinted in Cybernetica, No. 3, 140-159, 1970, and No. 4, 240-250, 1970. Reprinted in Artoga Communications, 146-148, 1971	1970b
The Computer-Simulated Development of Populations of Automata	Mathematical Biosciences, 4, 101-127	1969a
Architectural Relevance of Cybernetics	Architectural Design, 39: 494-496	1969b September
Early Work on Learning and Teaching Systems	Survey of Cybernetics, J. Rose (editor), 163-186. Iliffe Books Ltd.	1969c
A Cybernetic Model for Some Types of Learning and Mentation	Cybernetic Problems in Bionics, H. C. Oestreicher and D. R. Moore (editors), 531-585. New York: Gordon and Breach	1968
A Cybernetic Experimental Method and Its Underlying Philosophy	International Journal of Man-Machine Studies, 3, No. 4, 279-337	1966

	Comments on the Organization of Men, Machines and Concepts	Education for Information Science, L. B. Heilprin, B. E. Markussan, and F. L. Goodman (editors), 133-154. Rochelle Park, N. J.: Spartan Books	1965
	The Use of Analogy and Parable in Cybernetics with Emphasis Upon Analogies for Learning and Creativity	Dialectica, 17, 167-202	1963
	A Proposed Evolutionary Model	Principles of Self-Organization, H. Von Foerster (editor), 229-254. New York: Pergamon Press	1962
	An Approach to Cybernetics	London: Hutchinson, reprinted 1968	1961
	The Growth Process in the Cybernetic Machine	Proceedings of the Second Congress of the International Association of Cybernetics, Namur, 1958, 765-794. Paris: Gauthier-Villars	1960
	Physical Analogues to the Growth of a Concept	Mechanisation of Thought Processes, A. Uttley (editor), 877-922. London: H.M.S.O.	1959
Pask, Gordon and R. J. Feldman	Tests for a Simple Learning and Perceiving Artifact	Cybernetica, 2, No. 2, 75-90	1966
Pask, Gordon and B. N. Lewis	The Use of a Null Point Method to Study the Acquisition of Simple and Complex Transformation Skills	British Journal of Mathematical and Statistical Psychology, 21, Part 1, 61-84	1968 May
Pask, Gordon and B. C. E. Scott	Learning and Teaching Strategies in a Transformation Skill	British Journal of Mathematical and Statistical Psychology, 24	1971
Pavageau, F.	Current Computer Applications in the Architectural Field in France	London: University of York, International Conference on Computers in Architecture, 346-353	1972 September
Peart, R., P. Randolph, and T. Bartlett	The Shortest Route Problem	Computer Journal, 8, 19-21	1960

Pereira, L.	Interactive Dimensional Layout Schemes from Adjacency Graphs	Proceedings of the Design Activity International Conference, 2-19	1973 August
Playner, J. S., and J. C. Mangin	Approximation d'un Relief Naturel	Marseilles: Gamsau, 10	1972 January
Pollack, M., and W. Wiebenson	Solutions of the Shortest Route Problem: A Review	Operations Research, 8, 224-230	1960
Poore, J., J. Barralt-Torrijos, and L. Ciaraviglio	On the Combinatory Definability of Software	School of Information and Computer Science. Georgia Institute of Technology, NSR-GN-655	1971 March
Preiser, Wolfgang F. E. (editor)	Environmental Design Research	Proceedings of the Fourth International EDRA Conference. Stroudsburg, Pennsylvania: Dowden, Hutchinson and Ross, Inc.	1973 April
Purcell, P. A., and J. Wood	Analysis for Computer-Aided Architectural Design	London: The British Computer Society. University of York, International Conference on Computers in Architecture, 191-209	1972 September
Pylyshyn, Zenon W.	Perspectives on the Computer Revolution	Englewood Cliffs, N.J.: Prentice-Hall	1970
Quinlan, J. R.	A Task-Independent Experience-Gathering Scheme for a Problem Solver	Washington, D. C.: Proceedings of the International Joint Conference on Artificial Intelligence, 193-198	1969 May 7-9
Quintrand, Paul	Considérations Générales sur Informatique et Architecture	Techniques & Architecture, Série 33e, No. 4, 66-68 (Special)	1971 May
Raman, P. G.	Form, Models and Design Synthesis	Proceedings of the Design Activity International Conference, 1-15	1973 August
Raymond, T. C.	Algorithm for the Traveling Salesman Problem	IBM Journal of Research and Development, 13, 400-407	1969

Reisenfeld, Richard	Applications of B-spline Approximation to Geometric Problems of Computer-Aided Design	Syracuse University, Computer Science Department, Ph.D. Thesis	1973
Ricci, A.	An Algorithm for the Removal of Hidden Lines in 3D Scenes	Comitato Nazionale Energia Nucleare Centro di Calcolo, (Doc.Ceo(70)14), Bologna, Via Mazzini 2	1970 November
Ricci, K.	Memory as Meaning: The Cybernetic Role of Tradition in Architecture	Progressive Architecture, 51, 90-95	1970 August
Rittel, Horst	Democratic Decision Making	Summer Session, '71, Architectural Design, 4, 233-234	1972 April
Roberts, L. G.	Machine Perception of Three-Dimensional Solids	Optical and Electro-Optical Information Processing, J. T. Tippett et al. (editors). Cambridge, Mass.: M.I.T. Press, 159-197	1965
Roberts, Paul O., Jr.	The Treatment of Multiple Goals in Systems Models	Emerging Methods in Environmental Design and Planning, Gary T. Moore (editor). Cambridge, Mass.: M.I.T. Press, 190-192	1970
Roberts, S. M., and B. Flores	An Engineering Approach to the Traveling Salesman Problem	Management Science, 13, 269-288	1966
Robinson, H. W., and D. E. Knight (editors)	Cybernetics, Artificial Intelligence and Ecology	New York: Spartan Books	1972
Rorick, Huck	An Evolutionary Architect Wright (manuscript in preparation)	Journal of Architectural Education, 26, Nos. 1 and 2, 4-7	1971 Winter/Spring
Rose, J. (editor)	Progress in Cybernetics, Vol. 1	New York: Gordon and Breach	1970
Rothkopf, M.	The Traveling Salesman Problem: On the Reduction of Certain Large Problems to Smaller Ones	Operations Research, 14, 532-533	1966
Rubinger, M.	State of the Art: A Reply to Christopher Alexander	DMG Newsletter, 5, Nos. 8/9, 4	1971 August-September

Rudofsky, Bernard	Architecture without Architects	New York: Museum of Modern Art	1964
Rusch, Charles W.	On Responsive Environments	DMG-DSR Journal, Design Research and Methods, 6, 1, 14-16	1972 January-March
Russel, R.	Playing for Fun: Computers in Future Life	Architectural Design, 40, 220-223	1970 May
Sackman, Harold, and Harold Borko (editors)	Computers and the Problems of Society	Monvale, N. J.: AFIPS Press	1972
Safdie, Moshe	Beyond Habitat	Cambridge, Mass.: M.I.T. Press	1970
Sammet, J. E.	Challange to Artificial Intelligence: Programming Problems to be Solved	Second International Joint Conference on Artificial Intelligence, London: Proceedings of The British Computer Society, 59-65	1971
Sanoff, Henry, and Man Sawhney	Residential Livability: A Study of User Attitudes Toward Their Residential Environment	Environmental Design: Research and Practice, William J. Mitchell (editor). Proceedings of the EDRA 3/ar 8 Conference, University of California at Los Angeles, 13.8	1972 January
Say, D. L.	High Resolution Shadow Mask	SID Journal, 5-8	1972 November-December
Schnarsky, A. J.	Some Computer Aided Approaches to Housing	Proceedings of SHARE-ACM-IEEE, Design Automation Workshop, 57-67	1971
Schulitz, Helmut C.	Structure for Change and Growth	Los Angeles, Calif.: University of California, School of Architecture and Urban Planning	1971 March
Schumacker, B.	URBAN COGO—A Geographic-Band Land Information System	Proceedings of the Fall Joint Computer Conference, 619-630	1971
Scott, Allen J.	Combinatorial Programming, Spatial Analysis and Planning	London: Methuen, 44-45	1971

Seick, S. D.	How Publishers Can Benefit from the New Minicomputers	Publishers Weekly, 200, 24-26	1971 August 9
Selfridge, Oliver	A Primer for Fortran IV: On-line	Cambridge, Mass.: M.I.T. Press	1972
Selfridge, Oliver, and U. Neisser	Pattern Recognition by Machine	Computers and Thought, E. A. Feigenbaum and J. Feldman (editors). New York: McGraw-Hill, 237-250	1963
Shaw, Wade David	Textural Input for Graphic Display	Cambridge, Mass.: M.I.T., Thesis for M.S. in the Department of Electrical Engineering	1972 February
Shubik, Martin, and Garry D. Brewer	Models, Simulations, and Games—A Survey	Santa Monica, Calif.: The Rand Corporation, A Report Prepared for Advanced Research Projects Agency	1972 May
	Methodological Advances in Political Gaming: The One-Person Computer Interactive, Quasi-Rigid Rule Game	Santa Monica, Calif.: The Rand Corporation, P-4733	1971a November
	Systems Simulation and Gaming as an Approach to Understanding Organizations	Santa Monica, Calif.: The Rand Corporation, P-4664	1971b June
Siders, R. A., et al.	Computer Graphics	New York: American Management Association	1966
Silbar, Margaret L.	In Quest of a Humanlike Robot	Analog Magazine	1971 November
Simon. Herbert A.	Representation and Meaning; Experiments with Information Processing Systems	Englewood Cliffs, N. J.: Prentice-Hall	1972

	Style in Design	EDRA Two, John Archea and Charles Eastman (editors). Proceedings of the 2nd Annual Environmental Design Research Association Conference, Pittsburgh, Pennsylvania, 6	1970 October
	The Sciences of the Artificial	Cambridge, Mass.: M.I.T. Press, 26, 75	1969
	Thinking by Computers	Mind and Cosmos, E. G. Colodny (editor). Pittsburgh, Pa.: Pittsburgh University Press	1966
	Models of Man	New York: Wiley	1957
Simon, Herbert A., and Laurent Silclossy	Representation and Meaning: Experiments with Information Processing Systems	Englewood Cliffs, N. J.: Prentice-Hall	1972
Slagle, James R.	Artificial Intelligence: The Heuristic Programming Approach	New York: McGraw-Hill	1971
Slagle, James R., and Carl D. Farrell	Experiments in Automatic Learning for a Multipurpose Heuristic Program	Communications of the Association for Computing Machinery, 14, No. 2, 91-99	1971 February
Sloman, Aaron	Interactions between Philosophy and Artificial Intelligence: The Role of Intuition and Non-Logical Reasoning in Intelligence	Second Internatonal Joint Conference on Artificial Intelligence, London: Proceedings of The British Computer Society, 270-278	1971
Sperandio, M., and H. Botta	Doctab	Marseilles: Gamsau, 11	1972 January
Spillers, William R.	On the Use of Examples in Adaptive Systems	Cybernetics, Artificial Intelligence and Ecology, H. W. Robinson and D. E. Knight (editors). New York: Spartan Books, 217-223	1972

	An Algorithm for Space Allocation	5th Annual Urban Symposium, Papers on the Application of Computers to the Problems of Urban Society. New York: Association for Computing Machinery, 142-157	1970
	Artificial Intelligence and Structural Design	Journal of the Structural Division Proceedings of the American Society of Civil Engineers, 92 ST6, 491-497	1966 December
Srinastava, S. S., et al.	Generalized Traveling Salesman Problem through *n* Sets of Modes	Journal of the Canadian Operational Research Society, 7, 97-101	1969
Stauber, J.	Life With Computers	Atlas, 19, 22-23	1970 June
Stea, David, and J. M. Blaut	Studies of Geographic Learning	Los Angeles, Calif.: University of California, School of Architecture and Urban Planning	1971
	Notes Toward a Developmental Theory of Spatial Learning	Los Angeles, Calif.: University of California, School of Architecture and Urban Planning	1970
Steadman, Philip	Minimal Floor Plan Generation	Cambridge University, Center for Land Use and Built-Form Studies	1971
Stringer, Peter	A Rationale for Participation	Design Participation, Nigel Cross (editor). London: Academy Editions, 26-29	1972
Sutherland, Ivan	A Head Mounted Three Dimensional Display	American Federation of Information Processing Proceedings, Fall Joint Computer Conference, 33, 757-766	1968 May
	SKETCHPAD—A Man-Machine Graphical Communication System	AFIPS Conference Proceedings, Spring Joint Computer Conference, 23, 329-346	1963

Taggart, James	Reading a Sketch by HUNCH	Cambridge, Mass.: M.I.T., Thesis for M.S. in the Department of Electrical Engineering	1973 May
	Senior Independent Research Project	Cambridge, Mass.: M.I.T., Department of Architecture	1970
Talbot, P. A., J. W. Carr, R. R. Coulter, and R. C. Hwang	Animator: An On-Line Two-Dimensional Film Animation System	Communication of the ACM, 251-259	1971 April
Tange, Kenzo, Nicholas Negroponte, Richard Buckminster Fuller, and Yona Friedman	La Ville Totale	Revue de l'Amenagement du Territoire 2000, 8F, No. 24, 5-7	1973
Taylor, F. E.	The Essence of C.A.D.	Data Processing, 12, 138-142	1970 March-April
Teague, Lavette C., Jr.	Network Models of Configurations of Rectangular Parallelepipeds	Emerging Methods in Environmental Design and Planning, Gary T. Moore (editor). Cambridge, Mass.: M.I.T. Press	1970
Teague, Lavette C. Jr., and Charles F. Davis, III	Information Systems for Architectural Programming	Environmental Design: Research and Practice, William J. Mitchell (editor). Proceedings of the EDRA 3/ar 8 Conference, University of California at Los Angeles, 19.3	1972 January
Tou, Julius T., and Rafael C. Gonzales	Automatic Recognition of Hand-Written Characters via Feature Extraction and Multi-Level Decision	International Journal of Computer Information Sciences, 1, No. 1, 43-65	1972 March
Traviss, Irene, and Judith Burbank (editors)	Implications of Computer Technology	Cambridge, Mass.: Harvard University Press, Research Review No. 7	1971
Turing, A. M.	Intelligent Machinery	Machine Intelligence, Vol. 5. B. Maltzer and D. Mitchie (editors). Edinburgh: Edinburgh University Press	1969

	Computing Machinery and Intelligence	Computers and Thought, E. A. Feigenbaum and J. F. Feldmann (editors). New York: McGraw-Hill	1963
	Computing Machinery and Intelligence	Mind, 59, 433-460	1950
Uhr, Leonard, and Manfred Kochen	MIKROKOSMS and Robots	Washington, D. C.: Proceedings of the International Joint Conference on Artificial Intelligence, 541-555	1969 May 7-9
Uttley, A. M. (editor)	The Mechanisation of Thought Processes, Vols. 1 and 2	London: Her Majesty's Stationery Office	1959
van Emden, M. H.	Hierarchical Decomposition of Complexity	Machine Intelligence 5, B. Meltzer and D. Mitchie (editors). New York: American Elsevier, 361-380	1970
van Zye, F. D. W.	Some Relationships Between Technology, Cybernetics, and Social Systems	Sydney: Architectural Science Review, 19-23	1971 March
Verblunsky, S.	On the Shortest Path through a Number of Points	Proceedings of the American Mathematical Society, 2, 904-913	1951
Vincendon, Daniel	Les Machines Vivantes	Paris: Albin Michel	1972
Vinklers, B.	Art and Information; Software at the Jewish Museum	Arts, 45, 46-49	1970 September
Von Foerster, H.	Direct Access Intelligence Systems	Illinois University, AD-748287	1972 October
	Notes and Thoughts	Cognition: A Multiple View, P. J. Garvin (editor). Rochelle Park, N. J.: Spartan Books	1970a
	Molecular Ethology	Molecular Mechanisms in Memory and Learning, G. Ungar (editor). Plenum Press	1970b

Von Foerster, H., J. D. White, I. J. Peterson, and J. W. Russel (editors)	Purposive Systems	Rochelle Park, N. J.: Spartan Books	1968
Von Foerster, H., and G. W. Zopf (editors)	Principles of Self-Organization	New York: Pergamon	1962
Von Neumann, J.	Theory of Self-Reproducing Automata, A. W. Burkes (editor)	Urbana, Ill.: University of Illinois Press	1966
Waltz, David L.	Generating Semantic Descriptions from Drawings of Scenes with Shadows	Cambridge, Mass.: M.I.T. Artificial Intelligence Laboratory, AI TR-271	1972 November
Ward, Wesley S., Donald P. Grant, and Arthur J. Chapman	A PL/I Program for Architectural and Space Allocation	5th Annual Urban Symposium, Papers on the Application of Computers to the Problems of Urban Society. New York: Association for Computing Machinery, 122-141	1970
Warner, Malcolm, and Michael Stone	The Data Bank Society: Organizations, Computers and Social Freedom	London: Allen and Unwin	1970
Watanabe, Satosi (editor)	Frontiers of Pattern Recognition	New York: Academic Press	1972
Webber, Melvin M.	Design Participation	DMG-DRS Journal, 7, 1, 60-64	1973 January-March
Weinzapfel, G.	It Might Work, but Will It Help?	Proceedings of the Design Activity International Conference, 1–16	1973 August
Weizenbaum, Joe	On the Impact of the Computer on Society	Science Magazine, 176, 4035, 609–614	1972 May
Wellesley-Miller, Sean	Self-organizing Environments'	Design Participation, Nigel Cross (editor). London: Academy Editors, 58–62	1972a
	Control Aspects of Pneumatic Structures	Proceedings of the International Symposium on Pneumatic Structures, Delft, The Netherlands	1972b

| White, Anthony G. | Urban Futures: Science Fiction and the City | Portland, Oregon: City-County Charter Commission | 1973 |

| Whitehead, B., and M. Z. Eldars | An Approach to the Optimum Layout of Single-Story Buildings | Architectural Journal (Ba4), 1371-1380 | 1964 June 17 |

| Whiting, P. D., and J. A. Hillier | A Method for Finding the Shortest Route through a Road Network | Operational Research Quarterly, 11, 37-40 | 1960 |

| Wiggins, Lyna L. | Semantic Differential | DMG-DRS Journal, 7, No. 1, 1-10 | 1973 January-March |

| Wilton, John | An Architect's Look at Cost Control in Building Design with Particular Reference to the Uses of Computers | Bartlett School of Architecture, MSc Thesis | 1970 June |

| Windheim, Lee Stephen, Nicholas Negroponte, and Stephen Flanders | Computer-Aided Hospital Design | Environmental Design: Research and Practice, William J. Mitchell (editor). Proceedings of the EDRA 3/ar 8 Conference, University of California at Los Angeles, 23.8 | 1972 January |

| Winograd, Terry | Understanding Natural Language | New York: Academic Press | 1972 |

| | Procedures as a Representation for Data in a Computer Program for Understanding Natural Language | Cambridge, Mass.: M.I.T., Project MAC, MAC TR-84 | 1971 February |

| Winston, Patrick H. | Learning Structural Description from Examples | Cambridge, Mass.: M.I.T., Thesis for Ph. D. in the Department of Electrical Engineering, Artificial Intelligence Laboratory (MAC-TR-76) AD-713-988 (AI TR-231) | 1970 September |

| Wood, Peter | The Use of Computers in Town Planning | Long Range Planning, 3, 59-64 | 1971 April |

| Wootton, J. | A Traveling Salesman Algorithm | Metra, 8, 535-542 | 1969 |

Yessios, Christos I.	Site Planning with SIPLAN	Proceedings of the Design Activity International Conference, 2-9	1973 August
	Modeling the Site Planning of Homogeneous Uses	Pittsburgh, Pa.: Carnegie-Mellon University, Institute of Physical Planning. Research Report No. 30	1972a April
	FOSPLAN: A Formal Space Planning Language	Environmental Design: Research and Practice, William J. Mitchell (editor). Proceedings of the EDRA 3/ar Conference, University of California at Los Angeles, 23.9	1972b January
Zatorski, R. J.	Picture/Language Interaction in Artificial Intelligence	Australian Computer Journal, 2, No. 4, 173-179	1970 November
Zobrak, M. J., and T. W. Szg	A Method of Recognition of Hand Drawn Line Patterns	Proceedings of the First Annual Princeton Conference on Information Sciences and Systems, 240-244	1967 November

NA
2728
N44

Negroponte,
Nicholas.

Soft architecture
machines